A Little History of
BRITISH GARDENING

IN TENUI LABOR.

By the same author

The Macmillan Dictionary of Women's Biography

George Eliot

Elizabeth Gaskell: A Habit of Stories

The Vintage Book of Ghosts

Henry Fielding
(Writers and their Works Series)

Cultural Babbage: Time, Technology and Invention
(ed. with Francis Spufford)

Hogarth: A Life and a World

Dr Johnson and the Club
(National Portrait Gallery)

The Lunar Men: The Friends Who Made the Future

Nature's Engraver: A Life of Thomas Bewick

Words & Pictures: Writers, Artists and a Peculiarly British Tradition

A Gambling Man: Charles II and the Restoration

The Pinecone: The Story of Sarah Losh

In These Times: Living in Britain Through Napoleon's Wars, 1793–1815

A Little History of
BRITISH GARDENING

JENNY UGLOW

Chatto & Windus
LONDON

1 3 5 7 9 10 8 6 4 2

Chatto & Windus, an imprint of Vintage,
20 Vauxhall Bridge Road,
London SW1V 2SA

Chatto & Windus is part of the Penguin Random House group of companies
whose addresses can be found at global.penguinrandomhouse.com.

First published by Chatto & Windus in 2004
This edition, with new material, first published by Chatto & Windus in 2017

penguin.co.uk/vintage

A CIP catalogue record for this book is available from the British Library

ISBN 9781784740313

Typeset in 11.5/15 pt Fournier MT
Jouve (UK), Milton Keynes
Printed and bound in India by Replika Press Pvt. Ltd.

For Alison and Penny

CONTENTS

IV FRUIT

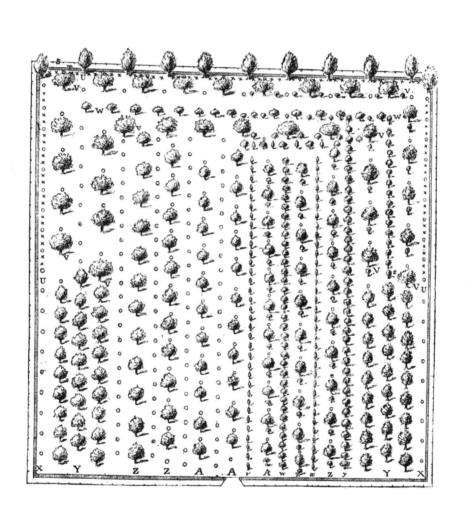

Foreword

It is lovely to revisit this book, which I so enjoyed writing ten years ago. It is March, and I'm doing that anxious pacing up and down that all gardeners do, waiting for things to come up, wondering what has survived the frost and what has mysteriously disappeared. It's strange to remember the lushness of late summer, when rose-bay willowherb took over the bank by the stream, when the flowerbeds were overflowing with colour, and the main worry was if the rabbits, or the slugs, would eat all the remaining lettuces.

Gardeners work with and against nature. We are constantly interfering, arranging, delighting in success, groaning at failure, and we are always looking forward – to the tips of bulbs appearing in winter soil, to buds opening, peas climbing, strawberries ripening. I confess that my own plot has changed little in the last 10 years except in tune with the rhythm of our lives – filling the pond with pebbles to stop toddlers falling in, planting more strawberries for grandchildren and helping them sow easy, wildly coloured flowers: marigolds and nasturtiums, and dahlias from seed. I love the old, familiar shapes, but it's exciting, too, to make something different, so this year it's a new raised bed for vegetables.

When I look back at the past, I see that digging and delving for sustenance has always been tough, but for those who loved gardens, escapism and dreams of Eden were also part of the lure. Gardens are like a gate into history, but still with a link to the present. Medieval and Renaissance gardens, with their high trellises, scented herbs and tinkling fountains, were like our modern 'outdoor rooms', places for sensual enjoyment, music and play; Elizabethan housewives took just as much pleasure in their herbs as we do; and while rich people changed whole landscapes, poorer folk also grew special plants, tended allotments, filled their window boxes. As the story moves forward over the centuries and more and more people are able to enjoy gardening, so the idea of the perfect design, or the desirable plant, alters and changes, like a signature of the times.

I learn something every time I read about gardeners of the past, great and small, or visit historic gardens – walking down alleys, breathing in the scent of roses, admiring the vegetables in their neat rows, marvelling at the climbers straggling over old walls. I know how much work is needed to make that beauty. And just as something always 'needs' doing in a garden, like staking or dead-heading, so I've done some weeding and tidying of this text – adding new books to the 'Further Reading', inserting new gardens into the list of places to visit, and writing a short postscript, to see if I can work out what aspects of British gardening in the early twenty-first century have flowered, or changed, or intrigued us or made us argue. And just as we look at our gardens in the spring, to see what will come up, so I'm left wondering just what changes will come next.

January 2017

274

は POLAKII

ERZAITAN

Introduction
'Mrs Woodcock's irises'

IT IS A MISTY NOVEMBER morning. Each blade of grass gleams and leans, heavy with moisture, and the air is so still that leaves from the oak tree at the end of my garden fall straight down, twirling and landing like a whisper. Across the road the young lime trees with their conical shape are bare at the top, their lower branches still clad in skirts of pale yellow-green. Behind them, towering over the mock-Tudor semis, a copper beech burns orange and brown. It is the end of the year when gardens are fading. The shabby annuals are pulled up, the geraniums taken in, the bulbs are planted: sturdy souls are dividing their perennials. On vegetable patches and allotments cabbages are swelling, Brussels sprouts budding, waiting for the first frost. Smoke from illicit bonfires curls through the streets.

Because I want to write about the history of gardens, as I walk to the shop I lean over every wall and wonder. Did the Romans grow broccoli? When did that prunus reach our shores? What genius first noticed that dung made things grow? Which tools hung in an Elizabethan shed? Do many people, like myself, know their plants better by the person who gave them to them – 'Mrs Woodcock's yellow irises' – than by their proper Latin names?

I am writing this book out of curiosity and pleasure, and because a friend asked me some intriguing questions about who had gardens in earlier times and what they grew in them. My aim is modest: a quest to uncover the gardens, plots and people of Britain in the past. I hope to find glimpses of the gardens of both rich and poor, and to see how they changed in response to new conditions – the coming of the monasteries or the rise of empire, the journeys of plant hunters and the building of bungalows.

The British Isles have an amazingly varied, complicated geology and since the old truism that the answer lies in the soil is undoubtedly true, gardens in one area are very different from those in another. Climatic conditions vary, too, from the gulf-stream-warmed western coats to the frosty moors of the Pennines. The climate has changed often: in the 'sub-Atlantic' period, from around 500 BC, it was wet and cool, but between AD 1000 and 1300, the south was hotter and vines could be grown here. Then, from the mid-sixteenth to the mid-nineteenth century the weather was colder, a 'mini Ice Age', while today we are moving into warmer times again. In addition, over centuries tastes change, new plants arrive. So although we all probably have a vague idea of 'an English garden', this is a fluid term – I suspect that I will find no such thing as a true native garden, any more than Defoe could find his 'true-born Englishman'.

Gardens are always unfinished, telling a long tale of immigration and connection and transformation. Even a small backyard or a window box, conceals stories of conquest, empire, aspirations and ideas: you can see this in miniature in the recently created period gardens at the Geffrye Museum, in east London, which show how town gardening changed from the sixteenth century to today. Yet every garden is also the personal creation of those who work in it. Gardening is hard work, as a Victorian apprentice up before dawn in January to sweep the gravel paths of the great could certainly tell you. And it can bring fears as well as pleasure, frets as well as promise: in the middle of the eighteenth century a stout doctor, Erasmus Darwin, was stomping around his garden in his boots and greatcoat, writing the name of every plant in a scuffed brown notebook and mapping his small kingdom 'near the sundial', 'behind the shed', 'between the house and the river' and writing anxious notes like 'lost', or, even more poignant, 'lost?'. Men and women before and after him know what it feels like to breathe deeply when spring comes, smelling the warm earth but wondering what the frost has done.

Gardens are an intimate clock of the seasons. I sometimes imagine a time lapse sequence, sitting in a garden chair, while plants rise and fall, flowers open, the leaves bud and open and darken and fall; fruit swells and ripens and vanishes back to the bare branch. It happens almost imperceptibly, but you only have to be away for a weekend to be amazed at the change. The novel *August* by Gerard Woodward has a vivid encapsulation of this, as his north London family return from holiday in Wales:

> The return to Fernlight Avenue after three weeks' absence in midsummer was always to a garden of dizzying voluptuousness. Entering the kitchen they were taken aback by the thickening of greenery beyond the windows. The lawn would be a yard high with hay, the trees would be scraping the windows and would have unloaded their fruit on the ground ... The roses would have bloomed and fallen, leaving puddles of pink petals on the grass, and the lower end of the garden, where it narrowed to an avenue between soft fruits, would be impenetrable, the black-berries and raspberries having closed the gap between themselves.

Although we set out to control nature, whether we plan sweeping landscapes or small roof gardens, year in year out it still takes us by surprise. The garden is merely a boundary between us and the wild, a tamed sphere that always wants to revert to wilderness. It is sexy and fecund, prone to chaos and pests, but controlled (we hope) into beauty and order. The word 'garden' itself comes from *ghordos*, an ancient Indo-European word for 'enclosure', and the same root is in 'yard' and 'orchard'. Garden historians remind us, too, that the ancient Persian word for 'enclosure' was *pairidaeza* – which applied both to the hunting parks of kings and to walled gardens for produce and ornamental plants. This became *pardes* in the Old Testament, *paradeisos* in Greek and our 'park' in English. But of course it is also 'paradise', the Garden of Eden and the fields of heaven, free from the ravages of death and of time. There have always been two main types of garden, although often mixed together. One is the useful plot of vegetables and herbs and fruit for the household, at one remove from farming. The other is the pleasure garden, which may be a sensual haven of flowers and trees and scent, or a tended green landscape. Beyond them lies the park, the tamed landscape, and mingled with them all, perhaps, is the idea of the garden as the sacred grove, the haunt of gods.

So, to begin at the beginning. Or at least in the prehistory of British gardening, when the last great Ice Age retreated. There were a few areas, perhaps, where the ice had held back, like the western coast of Ireland where old species from a warmer world such as the strawberry tree clung on during the frozen era, but elsewhere all that was left after the glaciers was a tundra-like desert of lichen and moss. Into this world men and women came from Europe across the land bridge – and plants came too, borne by the wind, carried by animals and birds, moving northwards as the climate warmed over millennia: birches and willows, oak and elm and Scots pine. Around 5000 BC Britain became an island, but as wanderers crossed the narrow straits they also brought their plants with them – and we have been introducing new species ever since.

As Timothy Mowl wrote recently, much of the history of gardens has been written from an academic or literary perspective, seizing on a poem or a painting for evidence rather than ransacking record offices and then undertaking a 'walking history', searching and exploring Britain's hidden gardens. I have delved a little and walked a lot, but I still follow the trail of poets and painters and writers and I have deliberately included famous gardens like Hatfield, Stowe, Stourhead, Chatsworth, because so many of us visit them and they really do stand as landmarks of change. This is a long history but a shortish book, so birth and death dates have been placed, by and large, in the index. I am following in the footsteps of garden historians from the Victorians to today and we each, inevitably, echo each other – nipping quotations and examples, as avid garden visitors pinch irresistible cuttings. I hope I have acknowledged my many debts, but some odd gleanings may well have got transplanted without my thinking and if so, I apologise. And if the map I draw is familiar to experts, I hope that for many others – like myself – the changing landscape of the garden will be new.

I
SEED

I
———

Did the Romans have rakes?

WELL, YES – AND THEY grew turnips. When the Roman legions came, bringing their roads and amphitheatres, town plans and temples, baths and underfloor heating, they also brought their gardening lore. They created our first plant-filled spaces intended purely for enjoyment, adapting the patterns of the Mediterranean to the cold climate, just as they had in Germany and Gaul.

In 54 BC Julius Caesar described the land as thickly studded with homesteads. Tribes of Belgae, immigrants from the Continent two generations before, grew wheat and tended cattle in the valleys while the native British, the older Celtic peoples, lived on the uplands, 'on milk and meat and wear skins'. Caesar saw no true gardens, nothing but clearings amid dense forests and swampy treacherous marshes.

Yet even the earliest nomadic peoples had cultivated the land, clearing the forests of birch, ash, hazel and holly with stone axes, grubbing up trees with scapula made from the shoulder-blades of oxen, tilling the earth with stone hoes and wooden digging-sticks. More settled ways of life began around 2000 BC and by 1200 BC the ancient wildwood had already diminished. Some long-lived settlements like Fengate and Flag Fen near Peterborough in Cambridgeshire, which lasted for nearly 2000 years, show Neolithic, Bronze Age and later Iron Age field patterns, a long record of tilling and toil. In winter the families stayed on the dry fen edge and in spring, when water levels fell, they moved out with their sheep and a few cows to the open fen pastures: among the treasures found here are beautiful bronze shears in a special wooden case. Were they gardeners?

When the Celtic tribes, spreading slowly west from the Danube, arrived around 700 BC they brought their own tradition of agriculture, tending flocks and using shallow ploughs, storing the grain in great underground granaries. Tall, blond, blue-eyed, the Celts lived in well-organised tribes, their ranks descending from the high-ranking nobles and warriors and the priestly Druids to the virtual slaves who worked the soil. They loved bright colours, gold and jewels, and they knew the power of plants: in Welsh myth the legendary Doctors of Myddvai were the sons of Nelferch, a fairy woman who came out of a lake in the Black Mountains and instructed them in the healing arts of herbs.

The great hill forts, like Danebury or Maiden Castle, with round dwellings and grain storage pits clustered within the mighty earth walls, tell a long tale of tribal conflict. But there were lowland settlements, too, where a palisade or ditch encircled round houses of timber and thatch, or stone and turf, and webs of ditches marked out fields, with larger areas for cattle and cereals: the Celts became such skilled farmers that they were renowned for producing two crops in a year. Bones show that families kept sheep, cattle and pigs, and excavations turn up iron sickles and stone querns for grinding corn, while evidence from pollen reveals the plants they used: nuts and fruit, like crab apples, wild pears and strawberries and sloes; celery, carrots, beet, leafy brassicas and asparagus, black bindweed and the spinach-like Good King Henry and Fat Hen with its rich seeds.

This is farming and gathering more than gardening, but it does seem that they kept small plots closer to home, protected from animals by a sprouting hazel hedge, or belt of hawthorn set by striking winter hardwood cuttings. Some vegetables go back to the Iron Age, like the broad bean, the beet and the tall, celery-like alexanders (still grown in Victorian kitchen gardens), now more often found in roadside verges. The Britons also grew peas and the tubers of onion-couch, and herbs like mint and coriander and even the opium poppy, brought by traders from the East. They had dome-like wickerwork beehives, covered with dung or clay. And they had sacred 'gardens', too, groves where they worshipped their gods at a tree or spring – often marked by later Roman temples.

At the start of the first millennium Britain was far from isolated. The tribes exported their surplus grain and metals to the Continent, and took in refugees from Roman-dominated lands, who brought new knowledge of tools and farming techniques. But within the first decade of Roman conquest the landscape changed. The old upland tracks were replaced by a new web of roads; garrisons were housed in forts and old soldiers were granted settlements or 'colonia'. When Agricola became governor in AD 78 he started to build towns, which pulled in the rural communities through their markets. Many farmers profited from the Roman stay and British tribal leaders became local princes.

The Romans brought the legacy of the ancient cultures of the Mediterranean and Middle East. Before 3000 BC the Sumerian tribes were irrigating the swampy land between the Tigris and Euphrates, and in Egypt the first gardeners were protecting their produce from the desert winds with high palisades. Lotus, daisies, roses, lilies, olives and date palms all appear in ancient architecture or jewellery, and the first garden picture, from an Egyptian tomb around 1475 BC, shows a funeral ceremony, with lotus flowering on a deep blue pool, fringed with date and sycamore. The rectangular lines, easier for irrigation, dictated the formal shape of gardens for generations. This is the small, enclosed courtyard garden. But in Assyria, as the centuries passed the kings also laid out great hunting grounds, and made the beautiful parks of Nineveh and the seventh-century hanging gardens of Babylon, while to the east the Persians created their own intimate garden, their 'paradise'.

After Alexander the Great marched through Persia in 330 BC, the Greeks took to horticulture: Aristotle's students raised plants from seeds; Persian-style pleasure gardens were built; scholars made the first classification of plants and their medicinal uses. Later, in Rome, many such herbals were written and the most famous, the *De Materia Medica* of Dioscorides, remained a standard work for many centuries. Rome also had its agricultural authorities like Cato, Varro and Columella, a farmer from Gadez (Cadiz) in Spain who composed a down-to-earth manual, even providing a monthly calendar of tasks and writing a wonderfully energetic, plant-packed hymn to his own small garden, rejoicing in the good crumbly soil and bewailing 'the bramble-bush to legs unkind'.

By the time the Romans were building their first towns in Britain, gardening was fashionable. Rome was full of plant hunters, outdoing each other in seeking exotic species from distant parts of the empire, or hunting down new forms of the ever popular rose. The city had nursery gardens and workshops to provide statuary and pots, and most houses, like those at Pompeii, had an inner courtyard garden with shrubs, pools, fountains and formal planting, and sometimes with statuary or stone dining couches and frescoes evoking the life of the country outside. The poets of the day celebrated the joys of retreating to the country life and wealthy landowners laid out lavish estates, practising 'rural simplicity' in luxurious style. In his letters, Pliny the Younger (whose uncle was also a great horticulturalist) described his two country houses, one by the sea and one in the Tuscan hills, surrounded by wild-flower meadows and woods. At the seaside he had a court for ball games, walkways edged with box and rosemary, a banqueting house and a large kitchen garden. In the hills there were beds of acanthus, a sunlit yard full of roses, a courtyard with a fountain and box alleys trimmed into curious shapes. Pliny's 'garden rooms' were always offset by outward-looking views, and the style he evokes would inspire the

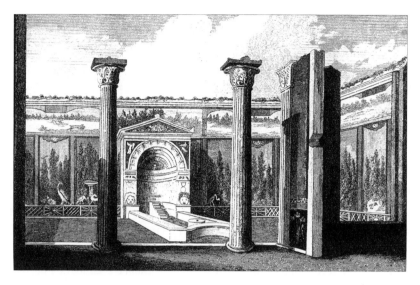

Pompeian peristyle garden, from W. Gell, *Pompeiana*, 1832.

grand Renaissance gardens of Europe and the British landscape gardens of the eighteenth century.

Roman gardeners were also skilled plantsmen, knowledgeable about techniques of grafting and layering, and the use of manure. For vegetables they laid out raised beds, three to six feet wide, separated by narrow paths for easy weeding. They were experts at forcing: when the Emperor Tiberius developed a passion for cucumbers his gardeners kept a perpetual crop ready by raising them in wheeled basketwork beds full of dung, brought into the sun even on cool days with their heat intensified by thin sheets of mica – like portable cold frames. They knew about pesticides, applying tar and bitumen, ammonia and lime, and amurca – a poisonous by-product of olive oil making. They fumigated their orchards with smoke from a sulphurous mixture brewed in copper cauldrons, and attacked mildew, gnats and cankers with smoke pellets made of dried dung and vinegar. This was the expertise that they brought to Britain.

Gardening flourished first here in the countryside, around the luxurious rural villas of the late first century. One of the greatest was at Fishbourne, near Chichester in Sussex. This is often linked with the British Cogidubnus, the king of the Artrebates, an educated ally of Rome, but all we know for sure is that it was an army depot until, in the AD 60s, a large house was built with mosaic floors, marble veneers and richly painted walls. There was a bath suite to the south, close to the sea, and a garden with colonnades, their columns topped with richly carved capitals.

Fishbourne was discovered by pure luck in 1961, when a workman digging a trench for a water main hacked through some tiles. Soon the mosaic floors were found and then the first traces of the formal garden, shown by differences in the soil, where the gardeners had filled trenches with loam to offset the acid and gravel. The large courtyard with its pool was enclosed like a cloister by colonnaded walkways, and divided by an avenue forty feet long, leading to the great audience chamber. The two halves, probably with grassy lawns, were marked out by topiary, with alternate square and semicircular niches, maybe for statues or urns or decorative shrubs. Gravel paths ran around the sides, between the small hedges (almost certainly of box, which the Romans loved), and beneath them ran a water pipe, feeding fountains and filling ornamental marble basins. The visitor, crunching across the gravel, would look back at a range of fruit trees, symmetrically planted in a framework of supporting timber, and behind them a mass of climbing plants. (One outside wall was even frescoed with roses and leaves, like the houses at Pompeii.)

Gardeners who knew about landscape design must have come here to work, bringing familiar elements like the great court and the intimate peristyle gardens, the clipped box and the fountains, the orchard and kitchen garden, the landscaped park with its distant views. At Fishbourne, as at Pliny's seaside villa, the view stretched down to the fields and the sea. The cost of levelling the land and bringing in trained men must have been huge, and all this would need a well-regulated, skilled workforce: perhaps Romans or freedmen from the northern provinces, directing local British labourers or slaves. The estate was run by an agent, with specialists in charge of the vegetables (the *olitor*), the trees (*aborator*), the clipped hedges and shrubs (*topiarius*). Each area had its own workers, both men and women, with their own tools: pruning hooks and special knives, wooden spades with metal 'shoes' to give a good cutting blade; rakes with four or six teeth, hurdles and baskets and watering pots, hoes and shears and sickles. Boys would be out at first light raking the gravel, scything the grass to keep its velvet sheen, trimming the topiary – then vanishing, retreating to the work of the kitchen garden and remaining invisible when the family and guests emerged, leaving the garden as if nature alone had created the spectacle just for their delight. A pattern, in fact, very like that of a Victorian country house.

And what did they grow? After a long cold period at the start of the first millennium BC, the climate was mild and many Mediterranean species flourished here. Tacitus (who was married to the daughter of the governor, Agricola) reported that the weather was unpleasant, 'with frequent rain and mist' but no severe cold, and that the soil was fertile and suitable for 'all crops except the vine, olive and other plants requiring warmer climes'. The juniper and box for the decorative edges established themselves quickly. In the beds behind them there might be lilies, acanthus and rosemary, native violets and periwinkles, new flowers like the crocus and pansy, and different species of roses. The Romans brought new trees like the sweet chestnut, eating its nuts raw or roasted and grinding them for flour. They also introduced walnuts and almonds, apricots and quince, plums and figs, mulberries and medlars. The sweet cherry, or bird cherry, ancestor of the varieties we eat straight from the tree, was already here – it grows all over Europe – but the Romans brought the sour cherry, the origin of the cooking varieties, originally discovered on the southern shores of the Black Sea: it was growing here by AD 46, three years after the invasion. Locally made pots with perforated bases have been found, which would allow trees to be raised in big nurseries in the area and planted when needed.

Vineyards were established and in AD 270 restrictions on British wine production were lifted by imperial edict: Emperor Probus allegedly came to England to plant the first vine himself, supposedly at The Vyne, in Hampshire. And the Romans brought leeks, onions, turnips, radishes, cucumbers, lettuce and kale, artichokes and asparagus, and herbs like dill, marjoram, parsley and mustard; Maggie Campbell-Culver tells us that dill was used to make a mild soothing drink (our name comes from the Anglo-Saxon *dillan*, 'to lull'). And with the legions came the white lily, later 'the Madonna Lily', originally from western Asia, and the perfumed *Rosa gallica*, which grew wild across Europe to Persia and beyond, and had long been cultivated in the gardens of Greece and Rome.

Fishbourne was exotic in the British landscape. But in the long era of Roman rule nearly 1000 villas small and large were built. Their rich owners might be Roman officials but were most likely to be British merchants, traders and councillors who had done well out of the occupation, or even wealthy incomers from Gaul, moving to a more peaceful land. Chedworth, in a slumbering fold of the Cotswolds, had a courtyard garden with colonnades, a spring flowing quietly into a deep pool and an elegant

Reconstruction of Chedworth, from the *Illustrated London News*.

fountain house. Other villas nearby included Great Witcombe, standing proud on a terraced hillside near Gloucester, the huge courtyard complex of North Leigh and the palace of Woodchester, near Stroud. These were equalled by Bignor in Sussex, Lullingstone in Kent and Latimer in Buckinghamshire, which was a long low house with different garden areas, including formal gardens and rows of beds for planting vegetables or orchard trees.

As these villas are excavated, they reveal traces of the gardens their owners enjoyed. Some had fish ponds, like the large rectangular ponds placed between the two wings at Eccles in Kent, so that they could be seen from the rooms and corridors, or the pool set in the ornamental garden which fronted the villa at Darenth in the same county. There were formal flower beds and pergolas covered with vines, trailing plants or roses. Even at the smaller Frocester Court, in Gloucestershire, a drive approached the villa, flanked by grass edges with rectangular flower beds. In the bedding plots found both in front and behind the house – identified by the darker soil, where manure was mixed in, and the marks of spade cuts in the subsoil – hairpins suggest that women worked here. In some places the garden colonnades were partly closed, acknowledging the colder British climate, but despite the chilly weather a summer dining couch – a mark of real optimism – has been found at the villa of Rockbourne in Hampshire.

Fishbourne was abandoned after a fire around 270 and a hundred years later many other villas lay desolate. The end was near. After a long period of attack by Picts and Scots as well as Saxons, in 410 BC the Emperor Honorius recalled his troops. Romano-British institutions clung on, but slowly the towns declined and the villas crumbled. Some were taken over by new Germanic settlers, others were gradually dismantled, their stones used for other buildings, their neatly tended gardens succumbing to the creeping march of nettles and saplings, their pools the haunt of frogs and wading birds. The great Roman legacy disappeared, to be discovered again in centuries to come.

2

Aelfric's list

THERE IS A SMALL cul-de-sac on the Isle of Dogs in London, running down to the Thames. Behind low walls every front garden is astoundingly neat, a mass of colour in summer with geraniums, petunias and lobelia: every garden except one, where rubbish bins and broken bikes replace shrubs and fuchsias: people tut-tut loudly as they pass. Anglo-Saxon gardening is a bit like this. Historians scurry past it, averting their gaze, noting tersely 'there was no gardening in Anglo-Saxon England' and moving straight on to the monasteries and the Normans. But can this really be so? Could Britain have lost the love of gardening for half a millennium or more?

Certainly there is no evidence of trowel-wielding Angles or Jutes. There was a word for garden – *wyrttun* – but gardens go unmentioned in wills, charters and land grants: the poetry we know best is of battles and blood and monsters, of seascapes, and drinking round the fire in the lord's hall. But these people had different cultural priorities: a heroic literature does not necessarily mean that outside the hall no one was cultivating a specially loved patch. Some Saxons had arrived even before the Romans withdrew at the start of the fifth century and they began to settle in earnest about AD 450. By then many towns and villas were already decaying. As for the gardens, it took no time for the brambles to annihilate the geometric plans and smother the imported plants. Some garden plants colonised the wild, like fennel, ground-elder and wormwood, brought by the Romans to cure wind, gout and worms. The sweet and sour cherry and the plums were too hardy to die out altogether, and went on blossoming and fruiting in odd gardens all through Saxon times. Among the vegetables and herbs, dill, fennel, lettuce, kale, radish and beet are old Roman survivals. Fruit trees like the fig, the almond and the peach, and glamorous vegetables like the artichoke may also have endured, or they may have vanished in these dark centuries and been reintroduced in the Middle Ages – we cannot be sure. As the Saxons gradually settled the land, odd British enclaves hung on. One was the little kingdom of Elmet in south Yorkshire, whose last king was Cedric. This was not conquered until 627 and could have remained an oasis of Roman gardening. As the historian John Harvey notes, it may not be a coincidence that this area is famous for its fine-flavoured 'winesour' plums, raised from suckers rather than by grafting. 'May we legitimately ask', Harvey wonders, if this variety 'is a survival, through fifteen centuries of storm and stress, from the royal orchards of the Romano-British ancestors of King Cedric?'

The Anglo-Saxons recognised some plants and trees as incomers, like the walnut, whose name comes from *wealh*, 'far away, foreign'. And we can make a guess at the Roman gardening survivors from a curious document, a Colloquy, or dialogue for teaching Latin, which the teacher Aelfric of Eynsham compiled and which was written down by his student, Aelfric Bata, in 995. He gives a long list of garden plants and, although this was primarily a vocabulary exercise so we have to tread with care, he chose words which were used in daily life. From his 200 names of plants and trees, we can guess which ones had lasted since the Romans because their Anglo-

Saxon name is very similar to the Latin – this was what the plant was called when the Saxons first encountered it. Here are a few examples:

Latin	*Anglo-Saxon*	*English*
Ruta	Rude	Rue
Feniculum	Finul	Fennel
Petrosilenum	Petersilie	Parsley
Ficus	Fic beam	Fig
Persica	Persoc Treow	Peach
Pirus	Pirige	Pear
Lilium	Lilige	Lily
Papaver	Popig	Poppy
Rosa	Ro-se	Rose
Vinea	Win Treow	Vine

These plants and their names with the old Roman echoes are with us today.

The settlers from the north Germanic tribes were farmers and warriors, not organised citizens. They used the sea and the rivers for their main routes, letting weeds grow through the paving stones of the roads built by the legions. They built in wood, not stone, and instead of moving into the Roman towns or villas they tended to build alongside them, ignoring the old gardens. Small farming communities remained, and some centres like Canterbury show continual occupation, but elsewhere the towns were deserted, perhaps even ploughed over, before the Saxons moved back to them again.

Romano-British culture crumbled: pottery and glass making ceased; the stopping of the coinage brought the end of trade. Many Britons fell into servitude – the Anglo-Saxon for Briton is the same as that for 'slave' – and others drifted away towards the western fringes. By the middle of the sixth century the separate Saxon kingdoms were firmly established: Kent, Sussex, Wessex; Essex and East Anglia, Northumbria and Mercia.

The restless, battling mode of life did not encourage the development of fine gardens. But slowly, under the sway of the Christian Church, came the first impulse towards a revival. In the fifth century British missionaries who had been trained in France, like St Patrick and St Ninian, converted the Irish and preached to the Picts. The Celtic bishops roamed widely, with no fixed diocese, and the monks lived austerely in small communities or hermitages, often on windswept islands, surviving off the few fields near their cells, where they had livestock, grain and vegetables. A second, different, wave came later, after Gregory the Great sent St Augustine to England in 597, and this time the stress was on organisation, with settled bishoprics and larger monasteries. The synod of Whitby in 664, where the two branches settled their differences, ushered in a veritable Saxon renaissance.

As the Saxon rulers were converted, so cathedrals and abbeys were built and monasteries established. One of the monks' first duties was to clear the land: when Bede wrote the lives of the abbots of Wearmouth, he told how even the abbots had to put their hand to the plough and help to forge the 'instruments of husbandry upon an anvil'. Writing from his monastery at Jarrow in the early eighth century, Bede noted that Britain was rich in grain and trees, and that in some places vines still flourished. Monastic farms and lands were always in better order than those of laymen, and in their gardens they grew mulberries, apples, pears and nuts.

Saxon monasteries were rich: their churches had silver bowls and fine carvings, and their libraries held precious illuminated manuscripts. Ironically, however, all the anecdotes about horticultural Anglo-Saxon monks concern their lives abroad. There is St Teilo, Bishop of Llandaff, for example, who planted a forest of fruit trees in Brittany in the mid-sixth century. Or the Irish nobleman, St Fiacre, who founded a monastery at Breuil in France in the mid-seventh century, where he cleared the woods and created such a miraculous garden that he became the patron saint of gardeners in France. Or Bede's contemporary, the Devon-born St Boniface, who travelled as a missionary in northern Europe and was asked to send home '*segmentum*', perhaps cuttings of medicinal plants; or Alcuin, in the next generation, master of the cathedral school at York, who ended his life as abbot of St Martin at Tours, where he decorated his cell with white lilies and red roses.

English monastic learning was so valued that when Charlemagne was crowned emperor in 800 he sent for Alcuin to establish the court school. Alcuin dispatched plants to Benedict of Aniane, near Montpellier in the south of France, the abbot who probably drew up the emperor's famous decree, the *Capitulare de Villis*. This laid down that every city should have a garden planted with all the 'herbs' (over seventy species of flowers and vegetables as well as herbs) and also sixteen kinds of fruit and nut trees. This list is one clue to the breadth of contemporary knowledge. Another is an early ninth-century plan for an idealised monastery, preserved through the ages at the abbey of St Gall in Switzerland.

The St Gall plan shows the whole community, from the fields for livestock to the stables and kilns, the cellars and baths and barns, the school and the guest house. The different gardens cover about three acres. In the north-east corner, next to the physician's house and near to the infirmary, is the walled physic garden where the 'Infirmarer' raised his herbs. Rather alarmingly, but sensibly, nearby is the monks' cemetery, laid out as an ornamental orchard and nuttery, with thirteen kinds of tree from medlars and mulberries to chestnuts and walnuts. South of the graveyard, alongside the poultry yard and within easy wheelbarrow distance of the refectory, is a large square garden for vegetables. The eighteen vegetable beds, arranged in two neat rows, are marked with separate names, which include favourites like onions, garlic, leeks and shallots, and 'eating herbs': parsley, chervil, coriander and dill. The paths were wide enough for a monk to kneel and the raised beds, edged with boards, were narrow enough to reach the centre without treading on the soil. The plan even has a gardener's house with a shed for his tools.

The Benedictine abbeys in England needed substantial gardens to feed the community, and for herbs to heal the sick among the brethren and

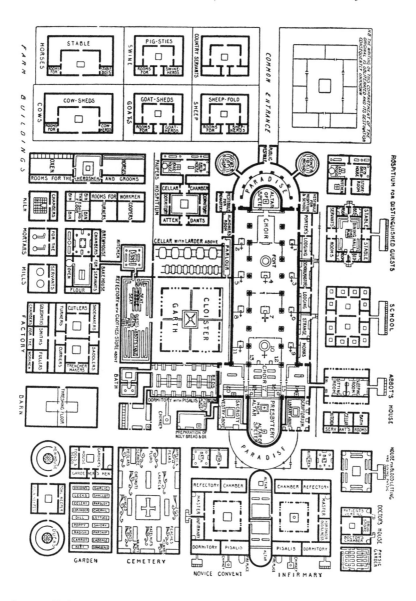

The St Gall plan (815–20) for an ideal monastery, redrawn by the Revd R. Willis.

in the neighbourhood. There are no British records for this time – everything we know about monastic gardens here comes from after the conquest – but the culture of the abbeys was similar to that on the Continent and, if we want to imagine a monk's gardening life, we can turn to Walafrid Strabo, who lived on Lake Constance and who wrote a lyrical hymn to gardens around AD 840, in his poem *Hortulus*, 'The Little Garden'. In his verse he hacks away at nettles, raises tender plants from seeds and cuttings, and mixes in some sound advice on manure and weeds. We can almost see him, tucking up his robes to keep them out of the mud, revelling in the scent and beauty (and medical usefulness) of the flag-iris and sage, the lily and rose.

To help our imaginations, we can visit reconstructions, like 'Bede's World' in Jarrow in Northumberland, which has an Anglo-Saxon farm and a courtyard garden, and a herb garden with raised beds containing Anglo-Saxon medicinal, aromatic and culinary herbs. An extra bonus is a small textile production area where they grow dye plants – woad, weld and madder – and fibrous plants for weaving, like nettles and flax.

And what of the laymen? The court was not interested. The kings and queens and their entourage spent much of the year travelling, staying on one noble estate after another, or moving between seasonal centres, like the seventh-century 'palace' of the Northumbrian kings discovered at Yeavering. Beneath the king came the nobles, the *ealdormen*, then the *ceorls* and below them the *serfs*. The *ceorls* worked the land in kinship groups, holding strips of arable or meadow land within great common fields. Most would also have a croft with a herb bed for medicine and seasoning, and for the inevitable kale or colewort (this was so much a part of the Anglo-Saxon diet that February was actually named 'Sproutkele'). In this patch they also kept bees to give honey for sweetening and to make mead.

The Saxon courts of the eighth century, like that of King Offa in Mercia, were impressed by the continental Carolingian renaissance, as we can see from the outpouring of decorated works, jewellery, bowls, carved caskets, and from poems like *Beowulf,* written down two centuries later. Yet in a Britain dogged by Viking raids there was never a long enough age of peace for the art of gardening to flourish, until Alfred managed to check the invaders. His dynasty brought stability and slowly more settled patterns of life developed. The great officials of the court, the *ealdormen,* held large tracts of land and their halls and courtyards were fenced.

In this climate a new rank of landowners emerged, the *thegns* (or thanes). Some thanes' landholdings were only a few acres, but others were vast, like those of Wulfric Spott, who founded the monastery at Burton-on-Trent in 1004 and who owned seventy-two estates spread across the Midlands. Over the years these men built fortified manor houses, enclosed in walls that allowed a garden to flourish, with a small parish church and cemetery next door. Such dwellings have been excavated at Portchester Castle in Hampshire, at Raunds in Northamptonshire and at Goltho in Lincolnshire, where an ordinary farmhouse was extended into a substantial settlement arranged around a courtyard. By now there were set parishes with well-defined boundaries and the land was gradually reordered into plots with single owners, a boost to production. Farming and gardening were helped by a shift in climate to longer, warmer summers and shorter, milder winters.

Perhaps the garden historians are right to ignore this warlike era. Yet, to return to Aelfric's list at the end of the tenth century, this does translate a common term for garden, *amoenus locus,* as a *luffendliche stede,* a lovely place. There are different kinds of gardens: *wyrttun* implies an orchard garden, while *lectun* is a 'vegetable enclosure', or 'leek enclosure'. Aelfric also distinguishes between woods and groves and copses, and speaks of 'sprouts' and seedlings and pruning. He and his contemporaries undoubtedly valued plants more for use than beauty. Even decorative flowers had their role: peony for pain relief; the root of Christmas roses (*Helleborus niger*) for mania and melancholy; the periwinkle for love and fertility ('something borrowed, something blue'). Many Anglo-Saxon plant names derive from the plant's practical value, like the foaming meadowsweet, which was not named for the scent it brought to the pastures and meadows but was *medowyrt*, the plant that flavoured mead; or the teasel (from *taesan*, to tease), which was used for raising the nap on newly woven cloth. Other common plants had magical powers, like the nettle, *netele*, for warding off sorcery. Still more combined magical and medical virtue, like the yarrow, *gearwe*, which was pounded with grease and used to salve wounds, or the foxglove, *foxes glofa*, which gives us digitalis and was used from earliest times as a vomit or purge.

In the next phase of history the monks would develop the use of these herbs and many of the pagan native names would be Christianised – the foxglove becoming 'Virgin's fingers' – or were given classical names. And just as the wild plant magic was tamed, so true gardens would be created, vegetables and orchards, pleasure gardens and bowers. But the Anglo-Saxons had their own feeling for nature. They revered the passing of the seasons, the blossoming and fruiting, the harvest and the false death of winter. And perhaps we should leave these non-gardeners, half Christian, half pagan, with a charm of their own for unfruitful land, the '*acerbot* charm', holding a promise for better times ahead:

> Take by night, before it dawns, four turfs from the four corners of the plot, and make a note of where they belonged. Then take oil and honey and yeast, and milk from each beast that is on the land, and a portion of each type of tree that is growing on the land, apart from the harder woods, and a portion of each nameable plant, excepting buckbean only, and then apply holy water and let it drip thrice on the underside of the turf and say then these words: grow, and multiply, and fill the earth.

3

Monastic lore

AFTER A HARD DAY's digging or pruning or grafting, a monk, it seems, could get clay on his feet and clippings on his coat just like any other mortal: the list of duties of the gardener at Westminster in the thirteenth century makes a special point of asking him to take off his cape and his boots before going into the church. But the monk in charge of the garden was a respected figure and in the festive run-up to Christmas an appropriate antiphon, 'O radix Jesse' ('O tree of Jesse') was sung in his honour: he led the singing and took a day off work, and his fellow monks laid on a special feast for him.

Since earliest times the blend of prayer and work was the basis of monastic life. When St Benedict founded Europe's first great monastery at Monte Cassino in AD 530 he decreed in his rule that gardening was a worthy, virtuous and godly occupation; one chapter of the rule even discusses the importance of caring for the gardener's tools. Everything the community needed had to be provided by the monks themselves, so that they could live without depending on outsiders. The vegetable garden was central, since Benedictines were vegetarian, while the later order of Cistercians (founded in Burgundy in 1098) even ruled out eating fish and eggs.

If I were a crow, flying across the British Isles in the tenth century, I would see forests and fields, iron forges and salt pans, small towns and settlements – occasionally I could circle over a deep park, or swoop down and feed on an orchard of ripe fruit, or pull worms from the newly turned earth in a small allotment. But by the twelfth century I would swoop over a different landscape of towns and castles, manor houses and villages, all with their flowers and fruit, herbs and vegetables. And the richest pickings of all would come from the monasteries.

The Normans changed the map of the countryside almost as fast, although not as drastically, as the Romans. The first step William the Conqueror took after his arrival was to build castles, bringing his own building materials from across the Channel. With the stones from Caen, so legend has it, came the first clove pinks, still found in their wild form around Norman ruins. To bring in the taxes William then undertook the 'Great Inquisition' of landholdings, the Domesday Book, completed by 1086, where many of our villages were formally named for the first time.

The Norman kings built new abbeys and monasteries to impose their power and encouraged new orders under their patronage. To the Benedictine monasteries were added those of the Augustinian canons. Next came the Cistercians, strict reformers who cleared the land in wild, remote areas and built soaring abbeys like Tintern, Beaulieu, and Rievaulx and Fountains in Yorkshire, where gardens and orchards ran down to the river. Two of the new orders were linked to the Crusades: the Hospitallers – the Knights of the Order of St John of Jerusalem – and the Knights Templar; the latter were said to have brought back the Oriental plane, like the one planted at their priory of Ribston in Yorkshire, and the windflower, *anemone coronaris*, 'the Blood Drops of Christ', which grew in great drifts in Palestine. Gardening was central to all the orders, but particularly to the most austere of all, the Carthusians, established here in 1173. Each Charterhouse had thirteen monks, in memory of Christ and his disciples, and each monk lived separately in his cell, meditating, praying and working, receiving his meals through a hatch in the wall. From the ruins of the fourteenth-century Mount Grace in Yorkshire we can still see how the cells were arranged around a cloister with a garden behind each one, about sixty feet by forty, a private territory for each monk to fill with fruit and trees and herbs, or to neglect, just as he wished.

These were all male communities, but new convents were built too, and double monasteries for monks and nuns. Today we know the abbeys only as gardenless ruins, serene and silent, but in the twelfth century they were bustling places, linked to a great continental web which shared a common allegiance, and wrote and spoke a common language, Latin. Monks exchanged and bought seeds across the Continent, carrying them carefully over land and sea in leather bags and airtight wooden boxes. Monasteries even sent fruit trees to sister houses in distant countries; one of the hard old English cooking pears, the Warden, was sent from Burgundy to grow in the Cistercian orchards of Warden in Bedfordshire.

The basic garden arrangement was adapted to meet local needs. At Canterbury, for instance, there was no room for many buildings on the south side of the church and we can see the altered layout from a plan made in 1165 when Abbot Gervase wanted a new drainage system. There are two courtyards to the north, one with coloured drawings of flowers labelled *herbarium*, which seems to have arcades on three sides and trellises on the fourth, and rows of plants within. To the west is the fish pond and outside the city wall are an orchard, a vineyard and a field (*pomarium*, *vinea* and *campus*). Most cathedrals and abbeys had a wide spread of 'gardens without', parks, and fish ponds stocked with the protein-rich carp.

Each institution had a body of officials with particular duties. The names change from place to place but the monk in charge of the gardens was often called the *hortulanus* or *gardinarius*: he had a special group of monks to help him, as well as hired labour. In some places he was subordinate to the cellarer, who was responsible for supplying all the provisions, including hay for the floor, rushes, mint and herbs for strewing (the best-known cellarer's garden is Covent Garden, which belonged to Westminster Abbey). In the 'great garden' grew all the brassicas and roots including parsnips, turnips and the long-rooted 'navews'. Almost everything went into the cooking pots to make the daily broth, spiced with salt and vinegar and mustard – the stronger the taste the better. The brewery plot produced yarrow and tansy to flavour the weak ale. In some places the kitcheners had their own plot – the first 'kitchen gardeners', a term found in the late fourteenth century in the Bishop of Stepney's account roll. All monasteries had large orchards and many still had vineyards, as 'Vine Street' in Westminster reminds us. At Ely in 1419 the gardener was called 'Adam Vynour' and that year he sold thirty gallons of 'verjuice'. And at the priory in West Tarring in Sussex, Thomas à Becket is credited with planting an Italian fig tree which he brought back from a pilgrimage to Rome: there is still a fig orchard here, a dense grove within the old flint walls.

Sometimes the plot was walled, but in many places it was fenced, as at Ely, where four cartloads of thorns were brought in to fence the garden. At the great Cistercian abbey at Beaulieu in Hampshire, which housed about 200 monks and employed double that number of labourers, there were an infirmary garden, a vegetable plot, an orchard, and a dozen other small gardens attached to different buildings and workshops, like the brewery, the gatehouse, the parchment maker. The kitchen gardener (or 'curtilage-keeper') there in the 1260s was Brother John: he had five under-gardeners and paid extra workmen to plant his beans and leeks. In 1268 he made a profit, selling the extra seeds and leeks and onions, bushels of beans, rye and oats and hemp, and making well over ten times as much as he paid his workmen. As well as vegetables he produced vats of cider, gallons of honey for sweetening and pounds of wax for candles.

The driest of the lists bring a vanished world to life. Brother John's accounts show him buying gravel for his paths, mending his manure carts, buying forks and spades, buckets and sieves and garden gloves. Other records paint the same vivid picture: the cleaning of fish ponds and the building of walls, the purchase of sieves and hoes and trowels. Accounts from Norwich (which include pay for a mole catcher and for men to get the moss out of the cloister green – a headache even then) tell us that in 1340 Brother Peter de Donewitch whitewashed his gates and fences, and give us the cost of flans and pancakes at rogations, and 'boots of the gardener with repairs'. There was clearly a well-kept garden shed, where the axes and saws for wood-chopping were stored, the scythes and vegetable knives, the string and trugs, buckets and pails and the spare locks for his newly painted gates. Sixty years later, at Ely, Adam Vynour was also fretting over the care of the garden tools: 'There remain two iron spades ("vange ferree"), 1 rake ("tribul"), 4 hoes ("howes"), and 1 lamp ("lucerna"), 1 "shave", 1 axe ("bolex"), 1 box for candles, 1 box for spices, the latter broken.'

Tools were important and expensive. They even merited a treatise in the 1190s by Alexander Neckam (or Neckham), *De Utensibilis*, who gives a very up-to-date list, including the wheelbarrow, or *cenevectoriam*, which had only appeared in Britain in this century, perhaps introduced by Crusaders who had seen them in the Middle East. The first ones look very wobbly, with a wheel in the middle and some uncertainty as to where the handles should be – front or back. As well as this modern convenience, Neckam thought that the peasant should have broad-bladed long knives, a spade and a shovel, a seed box, a billhook for brambles, two baskets and a trap 'to deal with the armies of mice', and (less realistically) 'a snare or a trap to catch wolves'.

Neckam's peasant would labour in the monastery garden, as well as working his own croft. Bigger monasteries had a couple of paid gardeners on the staff, provided with board and lodging and a salary, and with clothing for their job, thick gloves and boots and leggings. Day labourers from the local village grubbed out trees, weeded and dug, picked the fruit and scythed the grass and cleared the ditches. And for the first time we begin to see them: small men hacking at vines in the borders of illuminated manuscripts, and the epitome of all gardeners in Christendom, Adam delving with his spade, while his mattock hangs on a branch behind him, in the stained-glass windows of Canterbury.

If the Carthusians were the most removed from the world, the Dominican and Franciscan friars were the closest to it: they lived and preached near the towns, and most of their gardens and orchards are now buried under city streets (as at Clerkenwell, the 'Clerk's Well'). The town hospitals, too, were often staffed by monks and nuns. Like the monasteries, these were built round a courtyard, where nurses could find a moment's peace and convalescents could totter in the fresh air: the twelfth-century garden at the infirmary of the Augustinian priory of St Eadburg at Bicester was called 'The Trimles', from 'trimble' (lovely word), meaning to walk unsteadily.

Every garden in the late Middle Ages grew healing plants and mallow and marigold, valerian and comfrey, camomile and wormwood often spread and ran to seed between the rows of the vegetables. Hospital gardens were especially renowned for their powerful herbs and many were run by women, who were expert herbalists. They dried and pounded the herbs, seeds and roots into pastes to make potions, and gathered leaves and flowers to make perfumes and to infuse in baths for the sick; they made purgatives, ointments for skin and eyes, cordials and sedatives, stimulants and cough medicines. The gardener at St Giles's Hospital in Norwich sold the surplus, including powerful drugs such as henbane, an unusual garden plant, since poisonous herbs like henbane, nightshade and aconite were more often gathered in the wild. The healers of the late Middle Ages even used herbal and alcohol-based remedies as anaesthetics during surgery: recipes exist for 'dwale', for example, a lethal-sounding mix of henbane, hemlock and opium and natural laxatives, which would certainly knock you out. Archaeologists excavating infirmary waste at the lonely priory of Soutra near Edinburgh (which cared for the sick from the invading armies of Edward I and II, as well as the local people) have found evidence of these drugs, as well as of copious bloodletting, and they still warn people not to touch the soil for fear of lingering medieval infections.

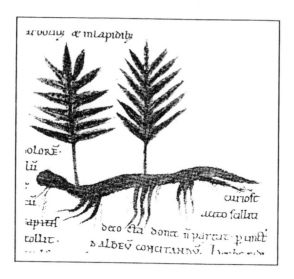

Polypody fern (*Polypodium*), from the Bury St Edmunds herbal of Pseudo–Apuleius, c. 1120.

The basis of medical-herbal knowledge was still Dioscorides's *De Materia Medica* but later Latin versions of this were often combined with a fifth-century herbarium, by Apuleius. This was the basis for the earliest English herbal, written around 1050. Such books were precious and beautifully decorated: around 1120 the monks of the Benedictine abbey at Bury St Edmunds were tenderly painting illustrations to a new manuscript of Apuleius, some drawn directly from plants picked nearby. There were English writers, too, like the Archdeacon of Huntingdon, who wrote an eight-book work on plants, perfumes and gems in the mid-twelfth century. But the greatest was the already mentioned Alexander Neckam, the Augustinian abbot of Cirencester, foster-brother to Richard I and a teacher at the universities of Paris and Oxford. In his *De Naturis Rerum* he listed many garden plants and fruits, including newcomers like the aromatic, bee-attracting hyssop. His main list was very clear:

> The garden should be adorned with roses and lilies, turnsole, violets, and mandrake; there you should have parsley and cost, and fennel, and southernwood and coriander, sage, savory, hyssop, mint, rue, dittany, smallage, pellitory, lettuce, garden cress, peonies. There should also be planted beds with onions, leeks, garlick, pumpkins, and shallots; cucumber, poppy, daffodil and acanthus ought to be in a good garden. There should also be pottage herbs, such as beets, herb mercury, orach, sorrel and mallows.

One favourite of cottage gardens appears in his book, *calendula*, the glowing orange pot marigold – useful for a host of things from flavouring soup to turning butter gold, with leaves that make a soothing ointment for stings. Neckam also noted exotics like the pomegranate, date palm, lemon and orange, and although these sound unlikely, in the warmer climate of the time it's just possible that keen gardeners may have raised them as tender pot plants, set outside in summer and brought inside in winter.

Not all the monastery gardens were for produce. There were other more mystical spaces, like the quiet court of the large central cloister. The word 'claustrum' means enclosed and could refer to the whole enclosed community as well as to the courtyard. The cloister was the communal heart, with the dormitory, the chapter house and the refectory opening off it, and monks could work in the window recesses here when the sun shone, looking out on to the garden. Like a Roman garden (or an Islamic paradise, where formal gardens were divided by four channels of water, representing the four rivers of Eden), the courtyard was often divided by paths into squares of grass or gravel, sometimes with flowers and blossom trees, and a fountain in the centre, or a yew tree for shade. The first use of our word 'lawn' – from the French *laund*, an open space among woods – comes from the thirteenth century, applied to the smooth green of the cloisters, a place of peace and contemplation.

The blend of protection and sensuality that haunts the enclosed garden is heard in a story which all garden historians have repeated since Alicia Amherst unearthed it a hundred years ago. This tells how William Rufus went to the convent at Romsey where the twelve-year-old Matilda (who later married his brother Henry) was staying. As soon as the abbess – her aunt Christina – heard the knights at the gate she feared for Matilda's safety and veiled her as a nun, so that when the king entered the cloister 'as if to look at the roses and other flowering plants', he let her pass by with the other silent nuns 'and quietly took his leave'. The 'garden enclosed' is one of the most beautiful and ambivalent of Christian symbols, implying both the fruitful cycle of nature and the pleasure of the senses, echoing back to the Song of Solomon, now sanctified and cut off from the world.

At the hospital in Norwich the sisters had an ornamental garden, a 'great garden' for fruit and vegetables, a pond, a piggery and a kitchen garden and meadow, and a separate flowery 'paradyse'. A 'Paradise' can be seen at each end of the church in the St Gall plan. The old Persian term for enclosure had been used in Christianity for the porticoes to Byzantine churches, where gardens were planted, but the Normans may also have seen Islamic 'paradises' in Sicily. The church paradises were sheltered areas where the Sacrist grew flowers for festivals – in a scented bower conjuring up notions of Eden, of the Virgin's bower and the heaven to come.

I wish there were medieval monastic gardens for us to visit, to wander from the cloister to the orchard, the infirmary to the fish ponds, the paradise to the rows of kale and leeks. But even if we cannot visit them we know that the monks and nuns enjoyed their gardens. At Winchester the clerk of works had a private garden called 'La Joye'. And in 1108, on the day that he died, the ailing archbishop of York walked in his garden to breathe the air and the scent of the flowers.

4

Pleasure . . .

THE IMAGE THAT SPRINGS to mind of a garden in the early Middle Ages, the twelfth and thirteenth centuries, is of a small courtyard enclosed by a wall or a trellis, where courtiers relax and take the air. Perhaps they are playing chess, or reading, while the birds sing in cages hung from the branches. This courtly garden is seen in many miniatures and in religious paintings it appears as the garden of the Virgin. But where did it come from and how does it fit with the reality in Britain?

The first thing to be said is that there were different kinds of gardens; the formal orchard with its blossom and fruit, its shady alleys and arbours, its grassy walks studded with flowers, was valued just as much as the enclosed bower, and so was the 'little park', not for hunting, but for walking, planted with ornamental trees, the home of animals and birds. We know most about royal gardens, but for a long time after the Conquest the Norman kings had no settled palaces; they travelled from castle to castle, moving on when affairs called them elsewhere. In time their stern castles and wild hunting lodges became domesticated. At Woodstock, for example, the old meeting place of Saxon kings in the heart of the forest, Henry I made a walled park in 1110 which became an exotic menagerie, with lions and leopards, lynxes and camels, and even a porcupine.

The early castles were simple motte and bailey structures, with orchards outside their walls – the orchard at Carlisle was destroyed by the Scots in a siege in 1173, but was soon replanted, and at the end of this century the royal gardener was granted all the apples that were left after the 'shaking down of trees', a right which he kept by custom for many years. The Carlisle garden could still be seen, curving round the sandstone walls, 600 years later. Sometimes the spreading estates were very beautiful, as we learn from Gerald of Wales, who praised his home castle of Manorbier in Pembroke, first for its strong defensive position, high on a hill overlooking the port, and next for its deep fish pond, its beautiful orchard, its graceful wood of hazel springing between the rocks.

Gardens outside the castle could be hazardous places in times of war, but as the precincts were extended with outer curtain walls, it became possible to create flowering havens inside them, a retreat in stressful times. The Plantagenets – that powerful, fascinating, red-haired clan, prone to wild rages yet alight with charm – had connections that brought to England new ideas on gardens from Europe and from the East. Royal marriages linked them to Burgundy and Provence, the Low Countries and Castile. The wives of Henry II and Henry III, Eleanor of Aquitaine and Eleanor of Provence, came with a retinue of servants, including gardeners who knew the lush horticulture of the south. Eleanor of Provence had a herb garden laid out at Windsor below her chamber, so that she could look at it from her new expensive glazed windows. She hired a permanent gardener, and between the royal chambers and the new chapel a courtyard was laid with grass, enclosed in a low fence of wooden palings. Over the years more gardens were made here, both within and without the walls, with orchards and vineyards, lawns and fountains.

Across Europe there was a growing sense of delight simply in being in a garden. In the early twelfth century William of Malmesbury wrote of how 'the flowers of the plants, breathing sweetly, give life' and talked of the smooth stems of the fruit trees, stretching up to the stars. Gardening was not only for the courtiers and barons in their castles, but for the townsmen too. Medieval towns were quite spread out, with pools and streams, patches of grass and orchards and gardens of all sizes. This was true even in London, especially in Holborn, an affluent suburb outside the city walls where many wealthy merchants and court officials lived in fine manor houses, often with bigger gardens and outbuildings than their country equivalents. The street names reflected this – Saffron Hill, Pear Tree Court – and when Alexander Neckam arrived in the city as a young clerk in 1178, dazed by the ringing of church bells and the cries of the street sellers, he found Holborn full of pleasing gardens and trees. Two years later William FitzStephen wrote, 'Everywhere without the houses of the suburbs, the citizens have gardens and orchards planted with trees, large, beautiful, and one joining to another.'

Around 1260 an elaborate definition of a 'pleasure garden' was written by the Dominican Albertus Magnus – probably copied from a lost section of an encyclopaedia written about twenty years before by the Englishman Bartholomew de Glanville. This summed up how ideas had crystallised over the past hundred years. Pleasure gardens, wrote Albertus, were mainly for the delight of two senses, sight and smell. The first requirement was a fine lawn, with beds of fragrant flowers and herbs, and raised turf benches to sit on beneath the shade of fruit trees or a vine-covered pergola. Best of all were the gardens with a fountain in the middle, tinkling into a stone basin. The lawn must be created with great care:

> For the sight is in no way so pleasantly refreshed as by fine
> and close grass kept short . . . so it behoves the man who
> would prepare the sight for a pleasure garden, first to clear
> it well from the roots of the weeds, which can scarcely be

done unless the roots are first dug out and the site levelled, and the whole well flooded with boiling water so that the remaining roots and seeds cannot germinate.

Then it must be covered with 'rich turves of flourishing grass, the turves beaten down with broad wooden mallets and stamped down well with the feet until they are hardly able to be seen'. Soon the grass would grow close and rich, like a green cloth. (The idea of the level, velvety lawn as an essential element of British gardens was taking hold: the lawn at Westminster was being carefully rolled in 1259 and within twenty years bowls was being played in England.)

A game of bowls, from an English manuscript, c. 1280.

For the best effect in the pleasure garden or orchard, the grass was studded with small flowers like violets, daisies and periwinkles to create a flowery mead such as Adam and Eve walked on in Eden. Artists painted flower-studded lawns, weavers wove them into tapestries, poets like Boccaccio and Chaucer, in the *Romaunt of the Rose*, exclaimed at their delights :

> Ful gay was al the ground, and quaint,
> And powdred, as men had it peint,
> With many a fressh and sundry flowr,
> That casten up ful good savour.

Whether they had a lawn, or were divided geometrically into rectangular beds, separated by sand or gravel paths, pleasure gardens were usually square or rectangular. Fragrance came from scented herbs, including rue, which would keep 'noxious vermin' away, and the ladies' skirts brushed against low hedges of box, or lavender or wild catmint. More scented flowers grew in the beds: clove pinks and wallflowers, periwinkles, forget-me-nots and violets. Behind them grew hollyhocks and peonies, lilies and marguerites, and the blue columbine. The garden shrubs included juniper and bay, and the scents were intensified on the summer evenings because the whole plot was sheltered by a wall or a trellis, or by hedges, with honeysuckle and other climbers intertwined. In the hot months young trees were set outside in large ornamental earthenware pots and wooden tubs.

British gardens contained all these plants. Still more would arrive in the fourteenth century, including two forms of lychnis, *Lychnis coronaria*, the rose-campion, from Greece and southern Europe, and *Lychnis challedonica*, sometimes called the Jerusalem Cross or Maltese Cross, which came from Asia Minor – the Latin name refers to the classical name for the district opposite Istanbul and old herbals describe it as 'Flower of Constantinople'. The first lupins arrived, the bushy varieties that grow wild in the Mediterranean lands, with their scented sprays of yellow or purple, and the biennial clary, among the first of many salvias, with tall flower spikes of cream, and pink and blue.

In the garden hedges grew the old wild native rose, the sweet briar or eglantine. But the roses most often chosen were the *Rosa alba*, known as the Great White Rose, thought to have originated in southern France: this was the emblem of Eleanor of Provence and her son Edward I made it part of the design of his Seal of State, while the red *Gallica* was the emblem of his brother Edmund. Later these two roses would become the badges of the house of York and Lancaster. The flag-iris also had royal associations. It was the emblem of the French kings, borne by Louis VII when he went on the Crusades – thus fleur de Louis, or fleur-de-lis – and was taken into the English arms when Edward III claimed the French throne in 1339.

The pleasure garden was a secret, sexy, private space. The turf benches were sometimes roofed and more shade was provided by 'sweet trees', with scented flowers. Half a century after Albertus the Italian Pietro Crescenzi recommended creating elaborate shelters in noble gardens from trees with interlinked branches or even 'a palace with rooms and towers'. I don't know if this was every achieved in Britain, but it is at this point that the word 'herber', a general word for a garden, becomes confusingly entwined with 'arbour', from *arbre* (tree). From now on the green, secret retreat is the ultimate image of garden privacy, as in this verse by an anonymous woman poet, 'The Flower and the Leaf':

> And shapen was this herber roofe and all
> As a pretty parlour: and also
> The hegge was thicke as a castle wall.
>
> That who that list without to stond or go
> Though he would all day prien to and fro
> He should not see if there were any wight within or no.

The square enclosed gardens show the influence of Islam, and particularly the famous gardens of Andalusia and Granada, a taste brought from Spain, Sicily and southern Italy by the Normans. And with this eastern influence the garden enclosed became home to a more earthly, erotic spirit evoked in the ideal gardens of medieval romance.

Romances were the favourite reading of knights and their ladies, and the most famous of all was the long and leisurely *Roman de la Rose*. Begun around 1230 and completed forty years later, it was translated by Chaucer in the late fourteenth century, and gave its readers a nostalgic glimpse of the ideal garden of their forebears. The poem combines a humorous allegory of the Fall with the atmosphere of courtly love. In Maytime the Lover wanders from the flower meadows through a door in the wall, opened by Lady Idleness, wearing a rose garland. She leads him to the inner garden of the Rose, a version of the Garden of Eden which is notably formal, 'Right even and square in compasyng'. On a path of fragrant green fennel and mint, he walks beneath a canopy of intertwined branches. The exotic trees come from the East, 'the land of Alexandryne': pines and cypresses, olives and bays; pomegranates, nutmegs, figs and dates. Squirrels and deer and rabbits run free, and the birds sing without cease. In this 'paradyse erthly' he finds the owner, Sir Mirth, dancing with his friends and his heart leaps with joy. Although all gardens must die with the cycle of the year, nature is stable and orderly, and each spring the spirit of love will return, like the plants and leaves.

There were small courtly gardens echoing this ideal in England in the twelfth and thirteenth centuries, and as the *Roman de la Rose* suggests, they were not always inside the castle walls. Sometimes they were separate enclosed areas within the parks. At Woodstock, Henry II replaced the old menagerie by a maze, known as 'Rosamond's Bower'. In the middle, so story has it though there is no hard evidence, the king made a fenced and hedged arbour, fragrant with roses. It was skilfully built so that he could make love to his mistress, Rosamond Clifford, away from prying eyes, but a myth grew up that the jealous Queen Eleanor penetrated the maze and stabbed Rosamond to death with her dagger. (In fact, Rosamond died peacefully in Godstow Priory in 1176, with the queen miles away.)

Woodstock already had two other courtyard gardens near the castle, and in 1150 the king asked his bailiff to have the queen's garden enclosed 'by two good high walls so that no one may be able to enter, with a becoming and honourable herbary near our fishpond, in which the same Queen may be able to amuse herself'. The garden next door, called Everswell after its constant spring, was joined to Woodstock by a roofed alley, and its streams were used to make a water garden with ornamental pools and fountains, with 'Rosamond's Well' and 'Rosamond's Chamber'. Nearby the king planted a hundred pear trees for shimmering blossom in spring.

British gardening gained even more from the Continent when Edward I, remembered for his great concentric castles, like Carnarvon and Harlech, married Eleanor of Castile. She brought fashions from the East, like using carpet for floor covering instead of strewed herbs, and a new vogue for baths. She also brought gardeners versed in the Moorish style and is said to have introduced sweet rocket, a native of Castile, and hollyhocks, long called the 'Rose of Spain', brought back from her journeys with the king in Palestine. Whether this is true or not, she certainly ordered apple trees and special pears, the white fleshed 'Blandurel' – now 'Calville Blanc' – from Aquitaine for her orchard at Langley Manor in Hertfordshire. (There were sixteen varieties of pear by the thirteenth century, and orchards might also contain mulberry, medlar, quince and cherry, all planted in wide rows, with the earth carefully scraped back from their roots.)

At Guildford Palace Eleanor asked her Italian gardener, William Florentyn, to make a herb garden with a marble-columned cloister, and had a special staircase designed so that she could step straight from her apartments into the private garden. Nobles, rich officials and opulent bishops now followed the court in planting orchards and nutteries, creating gardens surrounded with quickset hedges and ditches, with turfed banks

Lady watering her pinks in a tub – she has removed her thumb from the hole at the top, to let the water flow – from a French tapestry, c. 1400.

and arbours to stop and sit in, often embellished with little buildings, a 'gloriette' or pavilion, a summer house or a fountain. Eleanor, Countess of Leicester, wife of the powerful baron Henry de Montfort in the mid-thirteenth century, had her own castle at Odiham in Hampshire, a moated manor in a marsh. Here she made a garden in the park, encircled by a fence of boards, with five doors and seats with turfed roofs, a sheltered retreat. Courtly women across Europe were depicted enjoying their arbours, watering their flowers and even digging the garden themselves.

Planning gardens became the vogue in high society. But almost at once a note of snobbery sounds, a tone that will often be heard in the centuries ahead. (I have puzzled as to why gardening, of all occupations, should be so prone to this, even more than house decorating, or collecting fine art – perhaps it is to do with the possession of land, the right to put your stamp on the countryside, however small the patch might be?) The designer of the Countess of Leicester's Odiham garden was the humbly born Sir Paulin Peyvre – also known as John Piper. A steward to Henry III, he was mocked as a nouveau riche social climber, cashing in on this craze. He was 'an insatiable buyer-up of estates and unrivalled builder of manor houses', wrote Matthew Paris, and 'he so beset one, named Toddington (in Bedfordshire) with a palisade, chapel, chambers and other houses of stone . . . and with orchards and pools, that it became the wonder of beholders', displaying to them 'the wealth and luxury of earls'.

There were many like Piper who enjoyed flaunting their new wealth. Despite the sporadic fighting both at home and abroad, England was relatively stable, becoming rich on its wool trade. The towns were expanding and a new breed of entrepreneurs and officials were prospering. After 1300, fortified houses sprang up across the country, usually built on a square round a central courtyard, with the great hall opposite the gateway, a private wing on one side and kitchen and servants' quarters on the other. Ightham Mote, set in a curve of wooded Kent hills, still keeps this layout, entirely surrounded by its moat whose banks are overhung today with valerian, cranesbill and irises.

We know more about the gardens of one manor because its owner, Henry de Bray, kept an 'estate book'. His home was Harlestone Manor in Northamptonshire, granted in return for his work as a royal officer. He built a hall house and in 1292 added a grange and a garden, 'the New Yerde', enclosing the outbuildings and gardens with a high wall, and diverting the stream to make fish ponds and power a watermill. Five years later he made a herber with a dovecote in the corner and built a fountain. His house and barns were whitewashed. (Garden palings were also often white, or sometimes painted green, as a sort of camouflage.) These old manors continue to be discovered, like the fourteenth-century moated garden at Whittington in Shropshire, which has the earliest known viewing mound in England, and seven of the nine medieval gardens still survive at Aberglasney Castle in Carmarthenshire, where the bard Lewis Glyn Cothi stayed in 1477 and wrote lyrically of its pleasure grounds, its vineyards and orchards and shady groves. There is still a yew walk tunnel too, a mass of intertwined branches centuries old.

The new houses had parks, fish ponds, kitchen gardens and enclosed herbers. The ladies of the manor were known for their healing, and their herb plots were often locked gardens, set in the south-facing angle of the wall near their apartments: the light soil required for herbs meant that women could do the hoeing and raking, staking and tying themselves, even in their pointed shoes and best clothes. They grew tall, frothy angelica, which was used to flavour drinks (it was good for flatulence), or could be candied as after-dinner sweets, while its seeds were burnt to perfume a room; lavender for perfume and bath oil; balm and marjoram to attract the bees and make posies and preserves. These too were gardens for enjoyment and were proudly showed off to visitors: the enclosed courtyards with their rose-covered trellis and flowery mead, evocative as they are, were not the only pleasure gardens of the time.

5

. . . and profit

DEARTH, WAR AND PLAGUE were the curse of the fourteenth and fifteenth
centuries. The famine of 1315 was followed by the start of the Hundred
Years War in 1340 and the Black Death nine years later. History rings with
the names of battles – Agincourt, Crécy, Poitiers – and only two years
after the Hundred Years War finally ended came the first battle of the Wars
of the Roses. If England was a garden, it was a sadly neglected one. But
although this was an era of strife, England was no mean offshore island: in
the late 1340s Edward III's lands in Europe stretched from the Channel to
the Pyrenees; his reign was a time of pageantry and art and music, when the
royal castles and gardens were made ever more beautiful. Edward's queen,
Philippa of Hainault, had a special herber with unusual flowering plants,
including a perfumed pink which, said the Dominican friar Henry Daniel,
was 'wonder sweet and it spiceth every liquor that it be laid in'. Philippa
also brought rosemary to England from Antwerp, raising it from cuttings

given to her by her mother along with a medical treatise on the plant's virtues, which Friar Daniel translated into English.

Friar Daniel was a remarkable man. In his garden in Stepney he claimed to have grown 252 varieties of plants – making this perhaps the first botanical garden in Britain and the friar our first gardening expert. He also quotes a certain 'Henry the Poet', whom John Harvey has identified as the author of lines of verse in a fourteenth-century manuscript. The poet lists the plants in each of the borders of his square garden – about twenty-five different plants on each side, growing in mixed borders, with the taller plants at the back, sloping to the smallest in front, to form an edging for the lawn, much more like a pleasure garden than the St Gall tradition of raising each herb in a separate bed.

Gardeners were becoming skilled specialists, knowledgeable in planting, grafting and pruning, carefully overwintering young plants and propagating seedlings in special earthenware pots. Friar Daniel, for example, tells us how to grow bottle gourds in quart-size pots set on thin stones, free of damp, and how to supply them with water very gently by putting a feather through a hole in a pot and hanging it over the gourd on a crooked stick. When the seedlings are planted, in April, a new method is used with the same hanging pot, dribbling the water down a straw, or a strip of cloth. Special pots were made for watering, one for sprinkling, shaped like a gourd, with a thumb hole at the neck and holes in its base, and another a great jug with a watering 'rose' on the side, like a forebear of our watering cans.

But all the knowledge of the monks and friars counted for nothing in 1348, when the Black Death came. As men, women and children died in their thousands, villages lay empty, abbeys were decimated, estates were abandoned, crops rotted in the fields. The plague returned three times in fifty years and took a particularly heavy toll on the peasants, whose suffering was made worse by heavy tithes and low wages, and Richard II's Poll Tax of 1381 was the spur to the Peasants' Revolt, with its violent risings and bloody executions. The century ended in civil war and the triumph of Henry IV.

The terror of these decades intensified the escapist lure of Arthurian chivalry with its courtly romance and fantasy gardens. Geoffrey Chaucer was an official at the court of Richard II and expressed the mood of his day in his celebration of gardens in *Troilus and Criseyde*, in the *Canterbury Tales* and many other places, as well as his translation of the *Roman de la Rose*. Chaucer suggested that it was not only courtiers who found the flowery meadow an erotic private space. January, the besotted elderly husband in the Merchant's Tale, has a garden he thinks far finer than that in the *Roman*, and a silver key to his wicket gate, and there he takes his young wife May:

> And thynges which that were nat doon abedde,
> He in the gardyn parfourmed hem and spedde.

For the poet himself, as for many busy men, his garden was chiefly a haven from toil. The simplest flower, the daisy, could give him untold pleasure:

> Hoom to myn hous full swiftly I me spedde
> To goon to reste, and erly for to ryse,
> To seen this flour to sprede, as I devyse.
> And in a litel herber that I have,
> That benched was on turves fresshe y-grave,
> I had men sholde me my couche make . . .

Chaucer was a realist too, and knew that poorer folk had no time to sit on a turf bench and admire daisies. The old widow in his Nun's Priest's Tale has a typical meagre smallholding: three sows, three cows, a sheep called Molly and the king of the yard, the cockerel Chantecleer. When Chantecleer has bad dreams his chief wife, the hen Pertelote, decides these stem from constipation and runs to find herbs 'growyng in our yeerd':

A day or two ye shul have digestyves
Of wormes, er ye take youre laxatyves
Of lawriol, centaure and fumetere
Or elles of ellebor, that groweth there . . .
Pekke hem up right as they growe and ete hem yn.

Gardening has always been a balance of poetry and practicalities. Most of the people of medieval England lived on the land as small tenant farmers or free labourers, or as villeins, the unfree peasants known as 'houseboundmen', which gives us the familiar term of husbandry. Nearly every peasant had a plot attached to his cottage – as early as 1086 thousands of such 'garths' or 'yards' are listed in the Domesday Book. They could be tiny, one or two metres square, or as large as four or five acres. After the Black Death many landlords could not find enough peasant labour so they leased off more plots to tenants: countrymen began to have cottages of their own – and with them came the birth of the English cottage garden.

Archaeologists have charted many deserted medieval villages, with their homestead plots marked by ditches and banks once set with hawthorn hedges. If we stepped back in time into those narrow lanes, radiating out from the new, stone-built church and the manor opposite, we would see thatched cottages with roughly finished walls, each with enclosed ground in front, planted with cabbages, onions, parsley and herbs. The flowers in these gardens were mostly brought in from the field and carefully cultivated – primroses, cowslip and oxlip, verbascums and mallows. And where the owner or his wife was lucky, they might have some true exotics, perhaps brought back from the Crusades by a soldier or a local knight, like Turks Cap and Madonna lilies, and the lovely *Rosa gallica*.

At the back, behind the rough lean-to sheds where they kept their home-made scythes and rakes and tools to work on the shared strip fields, lay another enclosed garth, a long rectangular plot, stoutly protected against wandering horses, cattle, sheep and geese with ditches and wooden palings, and prickly hedges of thorn and holly. Inside, the small patches

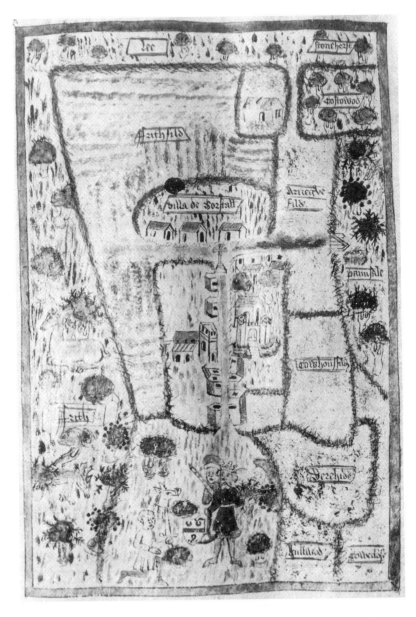

Plan of the village of Boarstall, Buckinghamshire, 1444, showing the moated manor opposite the church, and the peasant houses, open strip fields and woods.

were a jumble of herbs, vegetables and flowers, all mixed together with a few apple and pear and cherry trees: later in this period medlar and quince and plum were also grown in village gardens, and walnuts, chestnuts and filberts. The beds were enriched from the compost heap in the corner – or with dung, if you were rich enough to keep a cow or a horse. To add to the grain for bread and the beans and peas for their pottage which came from their strip fields, villagers grew cabbage and kale, onions and garlic and leeks (by far the favourite, tastiest, most fragrant vegetable), carefully spaced out according to the simplest measures, a 'hand span', or a 'foot'. Everything was thrown into the poor man's pottage: garlic, marigolds, dripping, nettles and docks, and herbs to give strong savour – the hotter the better. In his 'Vision' of 1394 Piers Plowman describes the harvest from his croft as peas and beans, leeks, parsley and shallots, 'chiboles [small onions] and chervils and cherries, half-red'.

Beyond the garden, near the stream, were the styes for the pigs and, for the wealthy ones, coops for the chickens or ducks and pasture for the cow. For peasant families, like those in the Forest of Arden in the fourteenth and fifteenth centuries, the gardens or 'curtilages' were a vital resource. They raised grain on their fields, grazed their animals on the common, collected faggots and wood and often hunted game in the forest. In their own yards some of them grew crops for sale, like osiers, hemp and flax. The occasional law case gives us a glimpse of their lives: a court case of 1390 brought by Richard Sharpmore of Erdington complains angrily of trespassing pigs trampling down all his vegetables, grass, beans and peas.

This was gardening as an adjunct of farming, purely for subsistence – we can see how it worked in the reconstructions at the Weald and Downland Museum in Sussex. But even in the years of plague and civil war larger landowners made a profit from their gardens, selling their produce in local markets – eels from the fish ponds, honey from the hives, hay from the park, fruit and cider from the orchard, wine from the vineyard, vegetables and herbs, and turf for fuel. Everything had its price, not only nuts and fruit, but even fallen branches, old hedges and nettles (young nettles were to eat, like spinach, the old ones were valued for their tough fibres to weave into cloth).

In the grander gardens the plantsmen working for the barons and merchants were a brotherhood of experimenters, developing technical knowledge, learning about plant structure and propagation, exchanging tips and passing on their skills to the next generation. Their names, hinting at their occupation, crop up in the account books: Thomas Daisy, John Park, John Springold. Many royal gardeners gave their work as their title, like William le Gardener and Roger le Herberur. They were nearly all men, but very occasionally you meet a woman gardener, like Juliana, at the manor of Little Downham, which belonged to the Bishop of Ely in the 1340s, a tough unmarried woman who organised the villeins and worked the heavy soil to produce enough vegetables and fruit for consumption and for sale. It could be a good life, although the pay ranged widely – from 1s a day for John Roche at Windsor castle in 1359, to 2d a day for women who did the weeding and even less for boys who planted leeks.

Merchants and landowners were as proud of their kitchen gardens, enriched with precious dove dung from their dovecotes, as they were of their pleasure grounds. The seeds ordered for the royal palace at Rotherhithe in 1354 sound positively excessive, twenty pounds of colewort, enough to sow two acres, and twelve pounds of seed each for onion and leeks. Grand recipes exist, as in Richard II's royal recipe book, the *Form of Cury*, for vegetable stew like the unappetising-sounding 'Compost', a mix of parsley, onions, cabbage, parsnips and peas, spiced with wine and honey, mustard and raisins. People also now ate vegetables on their own: parsnips were made into sweet fritters and even salads became fashionable.

One of the grandest medieval kitchen gardens belonged to the Earl of Lincoln at the end of the thirteenth century. It was an old monastic garden that had been owned by Dominican friars until they moved to a new site in Blackfriars, and the land stretched all the way down to the river, with ponds and vineyards and enclosed gardens for flowers, fruit and vegetables. The Earl sent abroad for 'slips' to graft on to his fruit trees – the new

Costard apple, and new pears of different kinds for eating, stewing and perry making. From this specialist garden little plants were sold and even precious roses. Law students were taken into the earl's house in 1310 and the present Lincoln's Inn Gardens are a reminder, a mere fraction of his old estate. Not far away, Gray's Inn also started life as a private house, with a fine estate of thirty acres.

In the city, behind the high, narrow-fronted houses were little alleys and yards where the townsfolk grew their own fruit and vegetables. The merchants who lived within the walls had large rectangular plots, with raised beds of herbs and flowers and sandy walks, and the halls of the city guilds each had their alleys and arbours and pleasure gardens, now buried under streets and offices. (The little courtyard garden, paved over now, is still there in the Merchant Taylors Hall, while the mulberry tree planted near the Drapers Hall in 1364 survived for six centuries until felled by a storm in 1969.) City churches also had their patch, for produce for the vicar and flowers for the services and for festival garlands. The Tower of London had a fine garden with blossoming fruit trees and the slopes of Tower Hill were terraced with vines. Nearby were market gardens, often rented by townsfolk to add to their income – the cause of a dispute in 1372, when the Tower Hill gardeners were sued for letting their garden rubbish pile up.

Smaller cities, like York, also had gardens in their suburbs and small plots at their heart. And where new towns were built, like Berwick-on-Tweed, Winchelsea, Salisbury and Hull in the reign of Edward I, each plot of land was specifically provided with room for a garden. Later, as the town's population grew, the plots were divided and sold for new houses and the gardens moved outwards: a plan of Hull from the mid-sixteenth century shows hedged plots circling the houses within the town walls.

Meantime, the herbals and the translations of classical authorities were copied and circulated, and we find recipes and short notes of advice about gardening jotted down in hundreds of medieval commonplace books and manuscripts – practical advice, handed on from father to son, mother to daughter, gardener to apprentice. Britain has nothing like the detailed

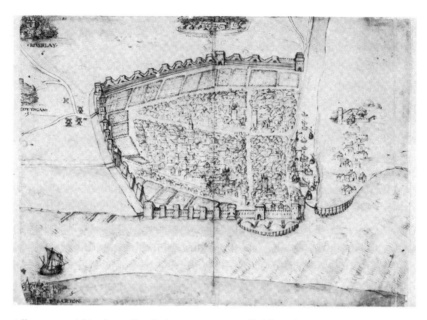

Allotments within the walls of Kingston-upon-Hull, fifteenth-century sketch. This is an impressionistic rather than accurate plan, showing hedged areas divided into plots, orchards and squares of pasture.

manual that the 'Goodman of Paris' wrote at the end of this century for his young bride to help him in his trade, but it is clear that gardening here was a wide-ranging subject, enriched by both theory and experience.

It was also becoming a recognised craft with differing ranks and status and specialisations. The Worshipful Company of Gardeners was founded in 1345, and among their honours was the right to present posies to the queen and princesses at coronations and royal marriages. In the same year, in London, 'the Gardeners of the Earls, Barons and Bishops and of the citizens' petitioned that they might stand in the same place 'where they have been wont in times of old', in front of the church of St Augustine by St Paul's churchyard, 'there to sell their garden produce of their said masters and make their profit, as heretofore'. The noise of their market had apparently caused great irritation to the priests in the church and they were given a new place at Baynard's Castle instead, but they had certainly made their presence felt.

There were now also commercial nursery gardens, selling seeds and plants and turf and trees. Young trees were needed not only for orchards, but for hedging and fencing, the most popular being willows and alders, aspens and poplars (the white poplar was a new introduction in this century). The saplings and grafts were called 'imps', and the nurseries, called 'impyards' were dotted about the country from Durham to Norwich. And around 1440 the first complete gardening book was written in English, *The Feate of Gardening* by Master Jon Gardyner. He lists a hundred herbs and gives tips on growing vines and grafting fruit trees on to stocks, covering the graft with clay and moss, and binding it with hazel strips. For vines, he decrees that each cutting should have three buds or knots, two set beneath the earth and one left to grow, with dung spread carefully around, and the young plants supported on forked sticks. Elsewhere he gives special tips on cultivating the newly introduced and immensely precious saffron. But Jon was also very keen on the basics: on onions and herbs, and especially – in my modernised spelling – on planting greens, the universal 'wurtes':

> Every month hath his name
> To set and sow without any blame
> May for summer is all the best
> July for harvest is the next
> November for winter must the third be
> Mars for lent so may I thrive . . .
> . . . And so from month to month
> Thou shalt bring thy wurtes forth.

At the opposite end of the spectrum from the queens and fine ladies in their bowers here is a no-nonsense man who tells us very helpfully how to have fresh greens to eat all year round.

6

Tudor conceits

W HEN THE FIRST Tudor, Henry VII, came to the throne in 1485 the old nobility had virtually vanished. The Wars of the Roses left lands abandoned, castles empty, their gardens and crops decaying. The new king, nervous of rivals, commanded that the outer walls of castles be torn down so that their gardens now spread outwards into the countryside. New men from the rising middle classes – Cecils, Cavendishes, Russells – took over the great estates, building new houses, bringing new ideas, new ambitions. Although the king was notoriously thrifty, he already introduced some elements of the lavish style of Burgundy: at Richmond Palace in 1501, under the king's and queen's windows, were 'most fair and pleasant gardens, with royal knots allayed and herbed; many marvellous beasts, as lions, dragons and such other of divers kind, properly fashioned and carved in the ground, right well sanded and compassed with lead; with many vines, seeds and strange fruit, right goodly beset'. This set the tone and when the eighteen-year-old Henry VIII became king in 1509 a great era of display began.

Henry loved pleasure. He admired the Burgundian court, with its feasts and jousts, mummings and masquerades, and envied the bold gardens of France, like those laid out at Fontainebleau for his rival, Francis I. He lured Continental artists to Britain, like Holbein and the architect John of Padua, who brought a host of Italian craftsmen. With their help Henry beautified his own palaces, while his favourites built great mansions. At Thornbury Castle in Gloucestershire the Duke of Buckingham made a fortified inner garden with a gallery leading out into a walled orchard: 'Full of young grafftes, well laden with frute, many rooses, and other pleasures; and in the same orchard ar many goodly allyes to walk ynne openly.' The orchard was surrounded by a bank, with arbours of white thorn and hazel, enclosed by palings and hedges and a ditch.

Buckingham was accused of treason and executed in 1521. And the man who engineered his downfall, Cardinal Wolsey, also expressed his ambitions in gardens. Wolsey's courtyards at York Place (Whitehall) and Hampton Court were like grand versions of the medieval gardens enclosed, a refuge from the smells and plague of cities. But Wolsey's own power soon trembled in the balance and in 1526, in a desperate attempt to keep the royal favour, he gave Hampton Court to the king. It was no good: four years later he was indicted as a traitor and died on his way to London to answer the charge. Much later, in *King Henry the Eighth*, Shakespeare gave the cardinal gardening metaphors to describe his fall: he was like a fine fruit tree, laden with blossoms and 'blushing honours', but then came a 'frost, a killing frost', nipping his root just when he thought his greatness was ripening.

Henry filled Wolsey's gardens with sundials and statues of heraldic beasts on poles, brightly painted and gilded, bearing the Tudor flag or coat of arms – dragons, greyhounds, lions and horses, antelopes and harts. Everything in this emblematic garden shouted, 'The Tudors are here! Henry is King!' And at Nonsuch, Henry's new Italianate palace on the Surrey downs with its forest of pinnacles, visitors describe a mass of arbours, painted benches, fountains, sundials and topiary beasts. The colours changed around the courtiers as they walked and the air was heavy with scent.

After the dissolution of the monasteries in the 1530s when their lands were surrendered to the crown, Henry VIII rewarded his followers with yet more great country estates. At the same time his new Chancellor, Thomas Cromwell, ruthlessly extended his garden in London, seizing his neighbours' land and digging ditches and throwing up high brick walls almost overnight. The man who later wrote the great *Survey of London*, John Stow, remembered how his father had an allotment there, with a garden shed or summer house, which was simply pulled up from its foundations and wheeled 'on rollers into my father's garden'. He was given no warning and no redress.

In court circles, at least, arrogance and gardening often went together. Over the years, however, other groups had begun to share in England's new prosperity: the wool industry in Norfolk and the West Country flourished, trading through the Merchant Adventurers company at Antwerp, and rich clothiers and merchants began modernising their houses, showing off their new wealth with tapestries and fine oak furniture within, and cunningly designed flower beds without. Peace brought a new outlook, literally. The elite now gazed admiringly at the sophisticated styles in the courts of Paris, the cities of Italy, the towns of Holland and vowed that their gardens, like their lives, would be modern and outward-looking.

After the short, troubled reigns of Edward and Mary, Elizabeth I seemed to embody this wide vision. Her fleets sailed the oceans, dealing in wine and tobacco, spices and silk. Her own long travels around the country spurred her courtiers to build ever grander houses to entertain her. At places like Burghley and Longleat, owners added long, formal façades, and elsewhere the medieval courtyard style gave way to linear buildings, high and airy, with huge windows catching the light, giving wide views over the countryside, as at Hardwick Hall. A house on top of a hill could be seen for miles and shone like a lantern at night. The gardens were just as grand. There was a new emphasis on variety, on striking visual effects, on making them almost sets for theatrical performances. For the first time people talked of gardens as if they were a form of self-expression, displaying not merely their owners' wealth, but also their reason and imagination. When Elizabeth visited her favourite Robert Dudley, Earl of Leicester, at Kenilworth in 1575 an ecstatic letter writer covered pages with descriptions of the festivities, the wonderful fountains, and 'many delectable, fresh and umbragious Bowers, arbers, seats and walks, that with great art, cost and diligens wear very pleasantly appointed'.

Among the greatest of the mansions, with a garden that inspired universal wonder, was Theobalds, built by Elizabeth's clever hunch-backed Secretary of State, Sir Robert Cecil, but there were also many smaller romantic new houses, glittering with glass. Montacute in Somerset was begun in 1580 with a raised courtyard enclosed by low walls ending in two elegant 'garden houses', and a vast sunken garden, with a raised terrace all around, later marked by clipped Irish yews. Another impressive building was the eccentric Wollaton Hall, built by Robert Smythson for Sir Francis Willoughby, Sherriff of Nottinghamshire in the 1580s, also to entertain the queen, in the shape of a symmetrical cross of squares. It was shockingly modern.

The basic rectangular design stayed in favour for a century but grew gradually more and more elaborate. A mount or a raised terrace made it easy to look down and enjoy the garden's shape and colour – the most dramatic focus at Henry VIII's Hampton Court was a huge mount planted with thousands of trained shrubs and topped with a vast summer house for outdoor banquets, 'the Great Round Arbour', three storeys high, glittering with glass. North of the border royal gardening was also undertaken in style. A park had existed since the eleventh century at Stirling Castle, but in 1502 the ground nearest the castle walls was made into the New Garden, later known as 'the King's Knot', further improved around 1540 when the new palace was finished for James V and his bride. Traces still remain of the turfed banks and terraces and ramps: the courtiers looked down from the castle on to a long rectangle, clearly patterned with turf terraces in the shape of an octagon, with a moated mount in the centre, probably with a fine summer house.

Although no subject would dare to copy such royal grandeur, the gentry of Scotland, England and Wales liked the fashion of eating outside, in special supper houses or rose-covered arbours, and enjoyed music and games in the garden, dalliance and flirtation. These lesser folk also had their 'mounts', which were usually in the angle of an outer wall, with a view both over the garden within and the country outside. Some, like the mount that still stands at Rockingham Castle in Northamptonshire, were turfed and terraced, with winding walks to the top.

Mounts were romantic places and Edmund Spenser understandably placed 'a stately mount', topped by a grove of trees forming a closely entwined arbour, at the heart of his vision of the garden of Adonis in *The Faerie Queene*. The mount remained in fashion for several generations. 'In the very middle' of the ideal garden, Francis Bacon decreed in his famous essay 'On Gardens' of 1625, there should be 'a fair mount, with three

The mount at New College, Oxford, from David Loggan, *Oxonia Illustrata*, 1675.

ascents, and alleys, enough for four to walk abreast; which I would form in perfect circles, without any bulwarks or embossments; and the whole mount to be thirty feet high and some fine banqueting house with some chimneys neatly cast and without too much glass'. When the gardens of New College, Oxford were completed in the 1640s, a mount still took centre stage, and in the colleges and elsewhere they may actually have been used as a stage for masques and plays.

Another way of looking down on the beauties of the garden was from galleries, like the Duke of Buckingham's at Thornbury, which led from the house to the chapel and parish church, a substantial structure built of stone, with a timber arcade, roofed with slate. In all weathers, tripping to divine service in their curly-toed shoes, the family could keep dry and cast admiring glances at the patterned garden. In the Cloister Garden at Aberglasney you can still see the rough stone three-sided cloister with a parapet above and a summer house where the walks meet. Not all galleries were so grand. Most were one-storey timber structures, with plants trained up them, running along the side of a courtyard garden. Sir Thomas More had a gallery at his manor house near the Thames in Chelsea and in houses within the city they led out from the parlour at the back.

At different points along the galleries were arbours, or 'roosting places', to sit and gaze, or take a breath: occasionally similar arbours were built in low branches of old trees and were popular meeting places for the ladies. Sometimes low earth terraces, or 'mount walks', had a gazebo (a 'gaze-about') at each end, like the charmingly squat, octagonal, red-brick towers at Hales Place in Kent, with a room below, perhaps to store tools, and a heated room above, for entertaining and admiring the view.

On country estates these mounds and arbours looked out onto the park that stretched beyond the walls. The deer park was a status symbol, and many men who rose to power under the Tudors stamped their will on their tenant farmers by enclosing land to create more woods and open space for hunting. Sometimes the cost, in terms of lost rents and yield, proved too heavy and parks shrank again as farmers were given rights to plough. But around many grander houses one can imagine them expanding, contracting and spreading again as fashion and wealth decreed.

The parks held no curving lakes (those would come two centuries later), but there were decorative fish ponds and other bold, watery ventures, like the 'Water Orchard' of the eccentric Sir Thomas Tresham at Lyveden New Bield, Northants, a mass of blossom surrounded by raised walks with mounts at each corner, enclosed by a broad deep canal. Tresham's Catholic beliefs landed him in prison for a quarter of his life and from Ely jail he sent detailed letters, ordering 360 trees, one for almost every day of the year: apple, damson, walnut, pear and cherry trees – in the end all were sold to pay his debts (the National Trust are restoring it with the original cultivars, and their aerial photographs have shown that there were seventeen rows running north to south and eighteen east to west). One complete Tudor water garden still survives in England, at Bindon Abbey, Dorset, 'a garden of haunting melancholy whose shadowy waters are deep and wide enough to row a boat along'. Water was everywhere, sparkling in jets from the newly fashionable fountains, which grew more fantastic as the century wore on. These were sometimes adapted for practical jokes, which the Elizabethans loved. In 1591 the German visitor William Platter commented on a white marble fountain at Hampton Court, 'with which one may easily spray any ladies or others standing about and wet them well'.

Water was a key feature of Robert Cecil's innovative garden at Theobalds, which had canals for guests to row upon. In 1597 the German visitor Hentzner marvelled at the variety of plants, the cunning labyrinth and the columns and pyramids of painted wood, and the fine 'jet d'eau with a basin of white marble'. The gardener showed Hentzner a summer house with the statues of twelve Roman emperors and a water-driven revolving table. The building, he added, was 'set round with cisterns of lead into which the water is conveyed through pipes so that the fish may be kept in them, and in the summer time they are very convenient for bathing'. This mix of sensual luxury and classical allusion, surrounded by shimmering, rainbow-making water, echoes the fantasy delights in Sir

Philip Sidney's *Arcadia*, published in 1591, the most popular romance of its day.

Surprise and delight have always been the charms of a good garden. In Tudor England gardens were for games, archery and tennis for the great, bowling for almost everyone. The people of the day took particular delight in intricacy, as we can see in their embroidered clothes, their jewels and the witty conceits of their poetry. At Hampton Court, by the end of Elizabeth's reign the geometrical gardens included chess-board-like squares, marked in different colours with red-brick dust, white sand, green grass. The crowning glory was the topiary, described by another German visitor, Platter, in 1599 as being 'all manner of shapes, men and women, half men and half horse, sirens, serving maids with baskets, French lilies and delicate crenellations all round'.

There were flowers in raised beds, and arbours to sit in the shade. Hornbeams and pleached limes were also trained to form alleys and tunnels to keep women's complexions fashionably pale (Theobalds had over two miles of covered walks). Many Elizabethan comedies make use of these, like *Much Ado about Nothing*, where Hero sends her maid Margaret to lure Beatrice into the orchard while they talk about Benedick:

> . . . say that thou overheard'st us,
> And bid her steal into the pleached bower
> Where honeysuckles, ripen'd by the sun
> Forbid the sun to enter . . .

One illustration of the love of puzzles and secret places was the maze, or labyrinth. Turf mazes may have ancient, pagan origins and British mazes have been linked with the symbolic 'Routes to Jerusalem', paths of penitence laid out on the floor of churches, and with the ancient turf circles, mistily allied in imagination with tales of the Trojan War and 'Troy games': one turf maze, made as late as 1688, still exists on the village green at Hilton, near Huntingdon. As a garden ornament they became popular in Italy, then

THE SECOND PART OF THE

Gardeners Labyrinth , vttering ſuch skilfull experi=
enceſ and worthie ſecretes,about the particular ſowing and re-
moouing of the moſt Kitchin Hearbes, with the wittie ordering
of other daintie Hearbes , delectable Floures , pleaſant Fruiteſ,
and fine Rootſ,as the like hath not heretofore been vttered
of anie. Beſides the Phiſicke benefits of each Hearbe
annexed , with the commoditie of waters
diſtilled out of them , right ne-
neſſarie to be knowen.

Title page of the Second Part of Thomas Hill's *The Gardener's Labyrinth*, 1577, showing
men training climbers over the arbour and planting flowers in raised beds with wooden
edges and carved finials: notice the table in the shade, and the neat squares of grass.

in France in the late fifteenth century and they first appeared in England as circular designs of low shrubs, not the high thick hedges we think of today. Henry VIII seems to have had mazes at Hampton Court and Nonsuch, and in 1557 Princess Elizabeth is described as visiting her sister, Queen Mary, in a pavilion at Richmond hung with rich tapestries and set 'in the Labyrinth of the gardens'.

Mazes were really more like knot gardens, another favourite feature. These were usually set out on square plots near the house, divided by paths into quarters, with patterned arrangements in each compartment. The motif of interlinked lines (a symbol of infinity) may have reached the West in the fifteenth century through the designs of oriental carpets, and the most complex patterns seem to have been provided by professionals who also made designs for embroidery, carpets, calligraphy and marquetry. (A late pattern, from William Lawson's *The Country Huswife's Garden*, of 1617, appears at the head of this chapter.) Box, thyme, rosemary and hyssop were clipped into little hedges arranged so that they seemed to run over and under each other like a woven ribbon, an evergreen pattern clear all year round. There were two kinds of knots, 'open' and 'closed'. In the first, the spaces were marked with different coloured earths – yellow clay, crushed red tiles, and coal dust – while the second were usually filled with flowers of a single colour, especially carnations and pinks. Some patterns were plain, others were genuine 'knots', like those made with string; others were pictorial, with shields or initials.

The fashion was peculiarly British and stoutly long-lasting. In 1613, when more intricate patterns based on embroidery (*parterres de broderie*) came in, Gervase Markham in *The English Husbandman* maintained that old-fashioned knots were still rightly more popular with 'the vulgar'. But the far grander Francis Bacon, in his essay 'On Gardens' twelve years later, dismissed them, and the topiary figures that often went with them, as old hat and trivial – 'they be but toys,' he wrote, 'you may see as good sights many times in tarts. I for my part do not like images cut in juniper or other garden stuff; they be for children.' He was right about the

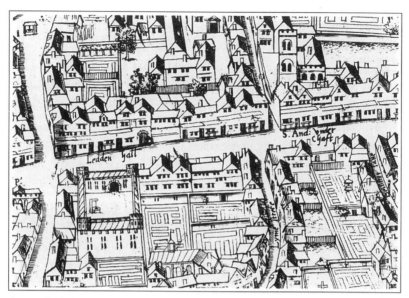

The Leadenhall sheet from a copperplate map of London around 1559, showing the courtyard gardens with wells and fountains and rectangular beds.

tarts – intricate pastries and marzipan knots were smart desserts – yet he still designed knots for his own garden. Squires and their wives in small manor houses and country houses clung to their knots, and patterns were still being published up to the Civil War.

In time, simplified versions of the knot garden and topiary reached the farms and cottages and smaller town gardens. The 'copperplate maps' of London, drawn between 1553 and 1559, just when Elizabeth came to the throne, show market gardens and fine suburban plots outside the walls, and small public pleasure gardens with 'banqueting houses' and bowling alleys: women spread washing on the meadows of Moorfields while men practise archery in Spitalfields, and in the crowded streets around Leadenhall the gardens have neat beds, summer houses, trees and wells.

All across the country well-off families extended their gardens. (We would be astonished, I think, at the bright colours of the painted trellis, benches and miniature wooden mounts.) Even in smaller houses the

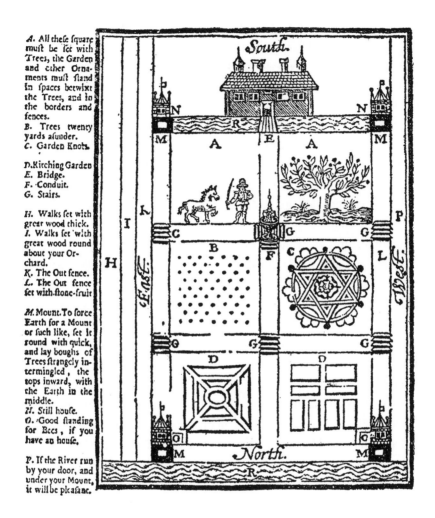

A. All thefe fquare muft be fet with Trees, the Garden and other Ornaments muft ftand in fpaces betwixt the Trees, and in the borders and fences.
B. Trees twenty yards afunder.
C. Garden Knots.

D. Kitching Garden
E. Bridge.
F. Conduit.
G. Stairs.

H. Walks fet with great wood thick.
I. Walks fet with great wood round about your Orchard.
K. The Out fence.
L. The Out fence fet with ftone-fruit

M. Mount. To force Earth for a Mount or fuch like, fet it round with quick, and lay boughs of Trees ftrangely intermingled, the tops inward, with the Earth in the middle.
N. Still houfe.
O. Good ftanding for Bees, if you have an houfe.

P. If the River run by your door, and under your Mount, it will be pleafant.

Garden plan from William Lawson's *A New Orchard and Garden*, 1618.

windows looked out on to a symmetrical plot, with big trees cleared to each side and a straight central path to the door. Flanking the gravelled walk lay knot gardens, or perhaps an avenue of topiary or pollarded trees, and balancing each other on each side of the main garden lay the kitchen garden and the orchard.

We can see something of the beauty of these symmetrical Tudor gardens at places like Little Moreton Hall in Cheshire and in reconstructions like that at Mosely Old Hall, Wolverhampton, the Old Palace at Hatfield, or Sylvia Landsberg's garden at the Tudor Museum, Southampton, with its painted railings and patterns of box, santolina, savory and germander, and double buttercup. But the geometric plan and the many different features show most clearly in a book from the end of this period: William Lawson's *New Orchard and Garden*, drawing on a gardening career of 'forty and eight years'. The mounts, marked M, each with its summer house, are there in each corner. The squares marked A and B are for trees, including a topiary knight and his horse; C is for 'Garden Knots', while D is the 'Kitching Garden' and K is the outer fence with fruit trained against it. I is a shaded walk before the 'Walks set with great wood thick' on the outer edge; N is the still house, for distilling the essences of flowers and herbs; O is 'good standing for bees' and P is the river to laze by and to fish. Elsewhere, Lawson suggests, there might be a maze, a bowling alley and an orchard, and raised banks of sweet-smelling camomile studded with daisies and violets to relax on – if you ever got tired of all these glorious, intricate delights.

7

The plantsman cometh

IN THE 1580s, THE years leading up to the Spanish Armada, William Harrison found much to complain of in his native country, but one thing to gladden him. 'If you look into our gardens annexed to our houses,' he wrote, 'how wonderfully is their beauty increased, not only with flowers, but also with rare and medical herbs.' In comparison the old gardens 'were but dunghills':

> How art also helpeth nature in the daily colouring, doubling, and enlarging the proportion of our flowers, it is incredible to report: for so curious and cunning are our gardeners now in these days that they presume to do what they like with nature, and moderate her course in things as if they were her superiors. It is a world also to see how many strange plants and annual fruits are daily brought

unto us from the Indies, Americas, Taprobane [Ceylon],
Canarie Iles and all parts of the world.

These immigrants survived their change of climate and soil so well that they
were now like 'a parcel of our own commodities'.

Plants were big business at this time and a whole culture grew up
around them. New arrivals prompted an interest in naming, classifying
them, and finding the best means of growing and propagating. The classical
texts and ancient herbals had been circulated since the advent of printing in
the middle of the fifteenth century, but now botanical gardens were founded
in Pisa, Padua, Montpellier and Leiden, and pioneering botanists like
Clusius in Vienna and the Flemish l'Obel (after whom lobelia is named)
were trained as physicians in European universities, where collections of
dried plants, 'herbariums', acted like preserved libraries of nature. Several
of these scholars came to London, including l'Obel, who became King's
Botanist to James I.

The new scholarship widened the herbals' scope. Renaissance
scholars began to study plants for their own sake as well as for their medical
virtues. In England, the lead was taken in Elizabeth's time by William
Turner, Dean of Wells. His book, *The Names of Herbes* (1548), was
followed by *A New Herball* (1551–63), the first full British herbal. At the end
of the century in 1597 appeared the most famous of all, Gerard's *Herball*.
John Gerard was a friend of l'Obel and of the French royal botanist, Jean
Robin, and like many British men he learnt from the refugees and travellers
from the Continent, where plant cultivation and botany were more
advanced. A practical, sociable, inquisitive man, he often went out collecting herbs with his friends, botanising on Hampstead Heath or in the
meadows by the river.

Earlier, Gerard had worked for William Cecil at Theobalds. In the
sixteenth century such gardeners to the great became men of stature with a
livery of their own, hiring labourers to dig and plant, boys to rake the
gravel, bricklayers to make new walls, carpenters to build trellis. Preparing

for a visit from the king in May 1515, Wolsey's head gardener at York Place, John Chapman, employed four undergardeners, eight labourers and twenty-two women weeders: the men got 6d or 4d a day, but the stooping women took away only 3d. After their toil from dawn to dusk they disappeared again into the alleys of Whitehall.

Men like Chapman needed good suppliers. New plants were handed on as gifts or provided by other gardeners and once rare species now spread across the land. Many plants were also bought from nursery men, like those needed for the three borders of rosemary and six borders of lavender ordered by Henry VIII in 1543 from 'Henry Russell of Westminster, gardener', with three loads of sand for his bowling alley. On the outskirts of Oxford and York and London, Protestant refugees from Catholic Europe set up small market gardens, sometimes in the kitchen gardens of the newly dissolved monasteries. Once the owners had capital they began supplying trees, plants and seeds as well as selling their fruit and vegetables. Conscious of their skills, in 1605 the market gardeners and flower growers, toolmakers and herbalists of London joined in a formal Company and two years later they received a Royal Charter. A second charter in 1616 gave the Company the power to inspect and destroy seeds or plants on sale, if they were 'unwholesome, dry, rotten, deceitful or unprofitable', and decreed that men had to serve a seven-year apprenticeship before they could trade in plants. The sign of completing this was the right to wear a dark-blue apron – the gardener's badge for many generations.

Well-known nurserymen handed on the business to their families. One was Henry Banbury of Westminster, who stocked innumerable varieties of apples and pears, and became famous as an 'excellent grafter and painful planter'. Another was his neighbour, Ralph Tuggie, a great 'florist' who died in 1632 and was renowned for his carnations, but also for his colchicums and auriculas. The new plants in British gardens were sometimes varieties of familiar species improved by selection: nurserymen and country housewives were known for producing double varieties of many common flowers, a wonder that was put down to our damp, lush climate. By 1600 there were doubles of columbines, daisies, buttercups and primroses, violets and marigolds. The Huguenots were credited with introducing auriculas, 'Beare's Eeres', originally from the Alps, and there were many other fresh arrivals, collected by gardeners and by the merchants and seamen. From Holland came the hop, in 1524, transforming British beer. From Italy Jehan le Leu, or 'John Wolf', brought back apricot stocks in 1542. From France around 1525 Leonard Mascall introduced the 'pippin'. In *Henry IV, Part II*, Shakespeare's doddering Justice Shallow proudly invites Falstaff 'to see mine orchard, where, in an arbour, we will eat a last year's pippin of my own graffing, with a dish of caraways and so forth'.

Within forty years the boast of men like Shallow, amateurs with claims to horticultural skills, was so common that it had become the butt of satire, listed among the courtly skills of George Gascoigne's 'The Green Knight's Farewell to Fancy', in 1575:

> To plant strange country fruits, to sow such seeds likewise,
> To dig and delve for new found roots, where old might well suffice;
> To prune the water boughs, to pick the mossy trees,
> Oh how it pleased my fancy once to kneel upon my knees,
> To griff a pippin stock, when sap begins to swell;
> But since the gains scarce quit the cost, *Fancy* (quoth he) *farewell.*

Fruit tree growing was highly specialised, requiring skill and the expensive, well-kept tools beautifully illustrated in Leonard Mascall's *Art of Planting and Grafting* of 1572. The Huguenot nurserymen had brought new techniques, like dwarfing, developed in French monasteries. After the 1530s standard fruit trees were often grafted a few inches from the ground on to French dwarfing stock – like the tiny *pomme de Paradis* – and then trained as a horizontal espalier, while a fan shape was preferred for peaches, apricots and almonds. All these fruits, and even pomegranates, were established in Tudor gardens in the 1550s.

Ambassadors and emissaries like William Cecil and Francis Carew

Illustration of woodcraft and grafting on the title page of Lawson's *A New Orchard and Garden*, 1618. Note the carefully drawn tools, and the paling fence around the orchard.

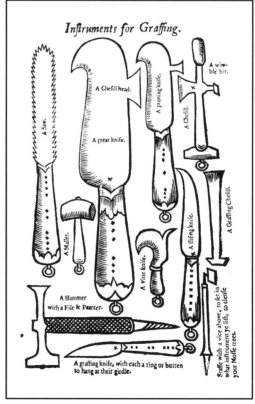

Instruments for grafting, from Leonard Mascall's *Art of Planting and Grafting*, 1572.

often took time off on their trips abroad to collect seeds and cuttings and trees. Carew planted the first Seville orange at his estate at Beddington around 1580. These oranges had been brought from south-east Asia by the Arabs in the tenth century and grown in Spain and Portugal, but they had to be carefully tended in our northern climate. Cecil built a special shelter for his oranges at Burghley in 1561 but Carew's were the most famous – a century later they were still full of fruit. Carew was so adept that he could delay the ripening of his cherries by keeping the tree cool in summer, 'by putting on a canvas cover and keeping it damp' so that Queen Elizabeth could eat them in the autumn, out of season. In 1600 another skilled plantsman, Sir Hugh Platt, presented the Lord Mayor with fresh oranges and green artichokes for Twelfth Night, 6 January, grown in his London gardens. He used his own methods of manuring, forcing and delaying, and suggested special walls with alcoves to catch more heat, as well as piling manure on the outside, so that the slow fermentation warmed the bricks through.

Flower beds were transformed too. Flemish settlers in Norfolk brought the carnation; in the 1550s keen growers collected French lavender, cistus and aconite, and ten years later the graceful laburnum, golden rain, and soon the rambling *viticella clematis*. All these came from southern Europe. The first *Echinops*, ornamental globe thistles, came from Siberia, the snowdrop and several new species of campanula from the eastern Mediterranean, the starry love-in-a-mist, *Nigella damascienca*, from the Middle East.

Many new plants came from Turkey, which had a tradition of fine gardening, including different irises, grape hyacinth, hibiscus and philadelphus. The most famous of these was, of course, the tulip. The story of its arrival has many versions, but the favourite tells how the Emperor Ferdinand's ambassador to Turkey, the Fleming Ogier Ghiseli de Busbecq, was travelling from Adrianople in midwinter when he saw a plain full of flowers – narcissi, hyacinths and 'tulips'. The name came from mishearing his guide's explanation of their shape, *tulipand* – like a turban. At great cost,

Busbecq sent bulbs to the emperor in Vienna in the 1570s and from there the court botanist, Carolus Clusius, brought some to Holland when he took over the botanic garden at Leiden in 1594. Many bulbs were stolen and within forty years they were the prize of Dutch gardeners. As tulip mania swept Holland, fortunes were won and lost over a single bulb, especially if it could 'break' (the accidental result of a virus) to provide new colours, or striped petals. In 1629 the botanist John Parkinson described a great variety of different tulips, mentioning among others:

> A white Duke, that is parted white and crimson flames, from the middle of each leaf to the edge.
> A Dutchess, that is like unto the Duke, but more yellow than red, with great yellow edges, and red more or less circling the middle of the flower on the inside, with a large yellow bottome.

A little later again and Andrew Marvell, speaking in the conservative persona of the countryman in 'The Mower against Gardens', took the tulip as one example of the way plantsmen had distorted 'the wild and fragrant innocence' of nature:

> With strange perfumes he did the roses taint;
> And flowers themselves were taught to paint.
> The tulip white did for complexion seek,
> And learned to interline its cheek;
> In onion root they then so high did hold,
> That one was for a meadow sold:
> Another world was searched through oceans new
> To find the marvel of Peru . . .

All the new tubers and bulbs – including the anemones and the great crown imperial, first grown in Britain around 1580 – glorified the gardens. Knowing their history gives them an extra magic. The first plant from the New World, the Peruvian climbing nasturtium, had been planted in Britain around 1535, its leaves and seeds a peppery, piquant addition to a salad. America yielded more exotics, like the fiery canna and climbing passion flower. The promise of the East was still to come, but from India in 1596 arrived the first impatiens, our 'Busy Lizzie', and a year later the wonderful hibiscus 'Rose of China'.

The *Yucca gloriosa*, the 'Spanish Bayonet', had come from America in the 1540s but it was half a century before its majestic spike burst into a cream fountain of flowers to delight the plant collector William Coys in his Essex garden in 1604. Coys also managed to grow the sweet potato, and the common potato, that novelty which later became a staple of British diet. Gerard mentions the potato in his herbal, and suggests it be eaten roasted and boiled, and served with oil, vinegar and pepper. The potato's close relative, the tomato, the 'Love Apple', is said to have arrived in 1596; again, Gerard had one growing in his garden, having got seeds from Spain and Italy. Tomatoes were supposed to be good for 'the Itch', but weren't much favoured at British tables until the mid-nineteenth century.

Gerard had his own special garden at Holborn and in 1596 he published a careful list of all the plants, over a thousand, including the laburnum, persimmon, the Judas tree, white mulberry, laurestinus and yucca. In 1597 a walk in a fine garden, so the frontispiece to his herbal implies, offered the entertainment of seeing others work for your delight, as well as the pleasure of fresh air, flowers and trees. The inset oval shows a couple strolling among the raised beds of the kitchen garden, perhaps at Theobalds itself, with an orchard and cornfield behind, ducks on the moat and a church spire in the distance. But pride of place is given to the emblematic figures holding the exotic introductions: the goddess Flora at the top holds a 'White Mountain Pinke', a 'Lillie of the Valley' and a sunflower from America; under her rule the rather unlikely classically garbed gardeners clutch an *anemone pulsatilla*, a Madonna lily, a daffodil and a head of maize (which Gerard himself grew successfully).

The herbals were not primarily gardening books, but they are a treasure trove of knowledge about what was actually in the gardens of the day, including new flowers and vegetables. In the next generation there was more stress on pleasure than on medicine, especially in the work of John Parkinson, apothecary to both James I and Charles I. Charles gave him the title of Botanicus Regius Primarius – the King's First Botanist – after the publication in 1629 of his massive, beautiful *Paradisi in Sole Paradisus Terrestris* (a pun on his name 'Park-in-Sun, Park-on-Earth'). Like Gerard's herbal, this was a book for the rich connoisseur, dedicated to the French Henrietta Maria, the 'Rose and Lily Queen'. Its very title seems full of respect for the natural world and its use by man:

PARADISI IN SOLE
Paradisus Terrestris
or
A Garden of all sorts of pleasant flowers which our
English ayre will permitt to be noursed up:
with
A Kitchen garden of all manner of herbes, rootes, and fruites,
for meate or sause used with us,
and
An Orchard of all sorte of fruitbearing Trees
and Shrubbes fit for our Land
Together
With the right orderinge, planting and preserving
of them and their uses & vertues

On its title page Adam plucks the apple in an Eden surrounded by tongues of fire from a kindly sun. In this little paradise with its winding stream we find the cyclamen, the Crown Imperial and the tulip, the date palm and vine and the pineapple – and the legendary 'vegetable lamb of Tartary', looking rather stiff as it grows from its straight stalk.

The title page of John Parkinson's *Paradisi in Sole, Paradisus Terrestris*, 1629.

In the marvellously rich language of his day Parkinson tried to convey how every plant looked – an extremely difficult task – so that even readers who had never seen it could appreciate its charm and see precisely how it grew. In over 600 folio pages illustrated with 800 woodcuts, he described 1000 plants, many of them new introductions, and gave realistic instructions on planting. He grew many rare plants in his own garden at Long Acre: tobacco and nasturtiums, canna and passion flower, and a treasured yucca, taken from a cutting of Gerard's that had been raised in Paris and had now returned to London.

In the 1620s Parkinson moved to the suburb of Lambeth, where his neighbour was another garden hero, John Tradescant the Elder. Tradescant had worked as gardener to Robert Cecil at Hatfield, travelling to France and the Low Countries to buy hundreds of fruit trees – cherry, pear, quince and medlar – many shown in the beautifully coloured drawings he commissioned for Cecil, a collection known as *Tradescant's Orchard*. Cecil valued him so much that he had his image carved on the newel post of the Hatfield staircase, spade in hand. After Cecil died in 1612, Tradescant worked for Lord Wotton in the old monastic gardens of St Augustine's, Canterbury, and in 1618 he accompanied a diplomatic voyage to Russia, landing whenever he could to collect plants, among them the Muscovy briar and a new type of angelica. Two years later he was on board ship again, this time sailing south against the Barbary pirates and continuing his plant foraging on the coast of North Africa. His next post was with James I's dangerously charismatic favourite, George Villiers, Duke of Buckingham, for whom he travelled to the Low Countries for trees and planted a famous avenue of double limes.

Finally, after Buckingham was murdered in 1628, Tradescant started his own business. He was famous by now for his rare and delicate plants and although he was lured back to work for Charles I and the queen, his Lambeth nursery remained his first love. Inspired by Parkinson, who called him 'my very good friend', he noted the plants in his own garden in the back of his copy of the *Paradisus*, with the date of their acquisition, and in 1634 he published a catalogue of his own, helped by his son John (better educated, and able to cope with the botanical Latin). Their portraits, painted by Emmanuel de Critz, suggest how the hearty spade-wielding young man has taken over from his grey-haired father, sitting back wreathed in a garland of his produce. John the younger travelled to Barbados and three times to Virginia. From each voyage he brought back more new species: the Virginia creeper, American sycamore, tulip tree, maidenhair fern and the first asters, or Michaelmas daisies, as well as the popular spiderwort, *Tradescantia virginiana*.

At Lambeth the Tradescants also displayed the collection of curiosities they had made on their travels: carvings and clothes, feathers and fish, coins and charms. The 'Ark', as it was known, has been called our first public museum, and after it was rather dubiously acquired by their neighbour, Elias Ashmole, the collection formed the core of the Ashmolean at Oxford. In the little courtyard behind the Museum of Garden History in St Mary's Church at Lambeth a knot garden surrounds the monument to father and son, inscribed with these verses:

> . . . Know stranger, e'er thou pass, beneath this stone
> Lie John Tradescant, grandsire, father, son . . .
> These famous Antiquarians that had been
> Both gardeners to the rose and lily Queen,
> Transplanted now themselves, sleep here; and when
> Angels shall with their trumpets waken men,
> And fire shall change the world, these hence shall rise
> And change their gardens for a Paradise.

II

LEAF

8

Stuart fantasies

THE JACOBEAN GENTRY, on the whole, held to the old style of Tudor days. Doors or long windows led from their houses out on to the terrace and the garden extended in squares to each side, each square with a different style. But the really grand gardens were at once more fantastical and more 'scientific' than their Elizabethan predecessors. James I, who took the throne in 1603, was interested in all things new in the arts and sciences – including gardening. He gave the London gardeners their charters and saw horticulture as a means of boosting national wealth, planting vineyards in St James's Park and commanding that mulberries be sent for sale to all county towns in the hope of establishing a new silk industry.

By now gardening was so entwined with courtly culture – and so familiar, too, to the merchants and country gentry, and even to the artisans of the time – that it provided a common language, an easily accessible imagery. It's startling to find Shakespeare, for example, couching a central scene in *Richard II*, where the queen learns of Richard's deposition – entirely in gardening terms. 'Why should we in the compass of a pale', the servant asks the gardener,

> Keep law and form and due proportion,
> Showing, as in a model, or firm estate,
> When our sea-walled garden, the whole land,
> Is full of weeds, her fairest flowers chok'd up,
> Her fruit-trees all unprun'd, her hedges ruin'd
> Her knots disorder'd and her wholesome herbs
> Swarming with caterpillars?

At court, collaboration overlapped with intense rivalry and this, too, was expressed through gardens, which became a key sign of status: innumerable portraits were painted in this reign and the next, showing languid courtiers posing with their new gardens in the background. In these intimate circles, where everyone was linked by family or marriage or favours, people were always exchanging gifts, swapping leases, handing over houses. When Sir Robert Cecil reluctantly relinquished his beautiful garden at Theobalds to the admiring king, James granted him the neglected Hertfordshire estate of Hatfield. Over the next five years Cecil built a new house and created a new garden, with the help of his old gardener, Mountain Jennings, and the young John Tradescant. It didn't hurt that he also received splendid gifts, including 30,000 vines from the wife of the French ambassador, and 500 fruit trees from the queen of France (diplomacy through horticulture).

    Yet London was the seat of power and many landowners – gentry as well as nobility – were away from their estates for several months each year. Between 1550 and 1660 the relationship between landlords and the rural community underwent a huge change. Land was enclosed, old customary tenures turned into 'rack rents' and traditional charity cracked under the strain, to be replaced by stern new vagrancy laws. This caused anxiety at court – James and his successor Charles I both issued proclamations, urging

1. Detail of a wall painting from Pompeii, 1st century AD.

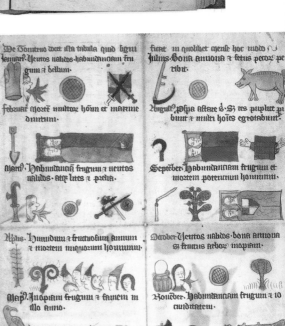

2. (*top left*) Aelfric's Glossary to *Grammatica Latin-Saxonia*, 995.
3. (*facing page, left*) Peasants harvesting, from the *Aelfric Pentateuch*, 1025-50.
4. (*facing page, right*) Hand tools in a late 14th-century calendarial and astrological manuscript, showing riddles, a glove, scythe, one-sided iron spade, sickle, billhook, flail, pail, axe, weeding hook and forked stick.

5. (*right*) Adam digging, stained glass window from Canterbury Cathedral, c.1178.

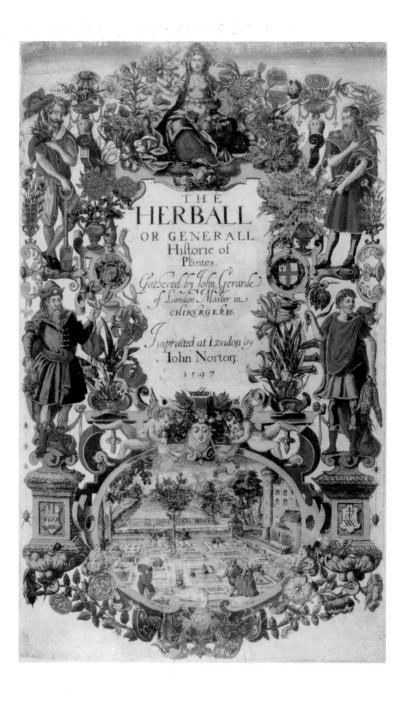

THE
HERBALL
OR GENERALL
Historie of
Plantes.

Gathered by John Gerarde
of London Master in
CHIRVRGERIE.

Imprinted at London by
John Norton.
1597

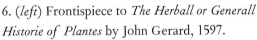

6. (*left*) Frontispiece to *The Herball or Generall Historie of Plantes* by John Gerard, 1597.

7. (*above left*) Rose and garden pea from *Herbal and Bestiary, an ABC for Children*, 16th century.

8. (*above right*) Christine de Pisan digging in a garden, from *Le Livre de la Cité des Dames*, 1475.

9. (*right*) *The Lover Attains the Rose*, illuminated by the Master of the Prayer Books, Bruges, c.1500.

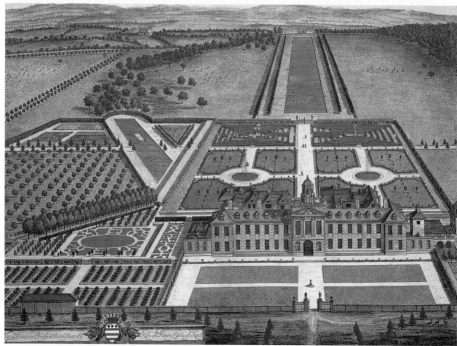

the gentry to leave London and live on their estates. And a generation of poets, beginning with Ben Jonson in his praise of Penshurst in 1612, talked up the country house, stressing the freedom from corruption of the city, the combination of personal fulfilment with hospitality, of simplicity with generosity, an ideal embodiment of natural order.

In fact, as far as design went, the gardens were not natural at all. Since the end of the seventeenth century the taste of the elite had made them look abroad, not at home, for inspiration. Admirers of Italy, like Sir Philip Sidney, were struck by the great hillside gardens, divided into terraces and ornamented with sculpture and fountains. As early as the 1560s Sidney's father flattened the land in front of the old family castle at Penshurst to make a splendid garden for fruit and vegetables. The most dramatic feature was 'the Great Terras' overlooking the vast walled garden: the walls were planted with yellow peaches, apricots, cherry and plum, and the excavations from the enormous earth-moving operations were used for a 'Great Pond'. After Philip Sidney's early death his brother Robert finished the walling of the orchard and used yew hedges to create a series of compartments and walks. Today, this is one of the most evocative of all Elizabethan gardens, as you gaze down from the terrace over the tops of the low fruit trees and realise how greatly they were valued for their blossom in spring, their shade in summer, their glowing fruit in autumn.

The Italian taste grew. From 1604 until the start of the Thirty Years War in 1619 there was peace in Europe: the roads were open and aristocrats like Lord Arundel and his countess, with Inigo Jones in tow, set off for Italy, returning with collections of treasures. Travellers sent open-mouthed reports of Italian villas, with their staircases, cypresses, grottoes and fountains. In his pioneering *Elements of Architecture* in 1624, Sir Henry Wotton, who had been ambassador to Venice, recommended that a garden should be entered from a high terrace, looking down on a plot that was not regular but 'rather a delightful confusion', so that as the viewer walked down the steps to different levels, he moved through different regions of scent and sight, as if he had been 'magically transported into a new Garden'. Variety and surprise could be contained in a harmonious whole. This is the pattern at Haddon Hall in Derbyshire: high buttressed walls, now covered with roses, hold back the hillside and great flights of steps lead down from the terrace to the rectangular pleasure garden. And a lovely painting of 1662 shows us Massey's Court, Llanerch, near Wrexham in Denbighshire, with terraces falling away down to the river, gazebos and arbours, lead flowerpots on top of the walls, and an ornamental circular pool with a Neptune on his rock. Architectural features took prominence – sturdy yet elaborate Italianate gates (much loved by Inigo Jones), carved balustrades, posts and stone balls. The old geometric knots were under siege from the new French fashion for curving patterns of island beds with sanded walks between, as shown in an illustration for a summer garden in the English edition of a new French book.

Like the elaborate court masques – whose painted backdrops so often depicted gardens – the elements of Stuart gardens often had a symbolic

An early summer garden viewed from the terrace, with tulips and peonies and an elegant tunnel arbour and classical gateway, from the English edition of Crispin de Passe, *Hortus Floridus*, 1614.

value. Trees, terraces, statues and water all had their role to play, and since their many allusions presupposed a cultivated education, gardening sometimes formed a private, exclusive language of the elite. Francis Bacon's ideal estate, described in his essay 'On Gardens' in 1625, four years after he fell from grace as Lord High Chancellor, expressed a nostalgic ideal: 'God Almighty first planted a garden', runs his famous opening line, 'and indeed, it is the purest of human pleasures; it is the greatest refreshment to the spirits of man; without which buildings and palaces are but gross handy-works.' Bacon looks back to the gardens of his youth and his glory days at court, praising the old mount and the arbour, and including a formal 'wilderness' or 'heath', with thickets of sweet-briar and honeysuckle, a ground speckled with violets, strawberries and primroses, and 'little heaps, in the nature of mole-hills', with wild flowers or standard bushes 'pricked upon their top'.

The garden could be a place of contemplation, carrying many codes more contrived than Bacon's. Some were religious: Catholics who could not worship in public planted knots embodying eternity, filled with flowers representing the Madonna and saints and now forbidden festivals. Some were scientific, like Twickenham Park, where the brilliant and extravagant Lucy Harington, Countess of Bedford, a close friend of James I's queen, Anne of Denmark, took over the lease from Francis Bacon in 1607. This garden was designed in concentric circles. In each corner, steps led to view points where you could look down on the pattern, representing the Copernican universe, with Earth in the centre and then Luna, Mercury and Venus in circles of birch, followed by lime circles for Sol and Mars, and a fruit tree circle for Jove, with Saturn beyond. (A similar circular garden, replanted in Victorian times, exists at the Chastleton house in north Oxfordshire.) In Scotland, the garden at Edzell in Angus belonging to the Lindsay family was as substantial as Hatfield, with stone walls of an unusual design, divided between 'flower boxes' and emblematic sculpture illustrating the planetary deities, the liberal arts and the cardinal virtues.

Other patterns were more metaphysical: when Philip Sidney's sister Mary married the Earl of Pembroke in 1577 she employed Walter

Raleigh's brilliant half-brother Adrian Gilbert to help her with her alchemy and her garden at Wilton. Gilbert made walks, said the poet John Taylor, who met him as an old man in 1623, 'resembling both divine and moral remembrances, as three arbours standing in a triangle, having each a recourse to a greater arbour in the midst, resembleth three in one, and one in three'. His patterns were fantastically complex: 'Such deal of intricate setting, grafting, planting, innoculating, railing, hedging, plashing, turning, winding, and returning circular, triangular, quadrangular, orbicular, oval, and every way curiously and chargeably conceited.' Now a very old man, Gilbert called the garden Paradise, with himself as a 'true *Adamist*, continually toiling and tilling'.

While the old Adamist toiled on, a new fashion arrived, a blend of Italianate design and French fashions (the Luxembourg Gardens in Paris were laid out at roughly the same time). This style was favoured by Charles I's French queen, Henrietta Maria, for whom John Tradescant the Elder installed an Orange Garden and a bowling green in 1636 at the new palace of Oatlands. In the next decade, at St James's Place and Wimbledon she employed the French gardener, André Mollet, to lay out extravagant beds or 'parterres' in the scrolling French manner. The British soon took to parterres, and developed a style of their own. In the smartest gardens, the new parterres were not edged, but cut in grass itself, verdant plain *plats*, scythed short and rolled and beaten smooth. Later, French writers would define this fashion as *parterre à l'Anglaise*. There were four kinds of parterres, explained John James at the start of the next century in *The Theory and Practice of Gardening*, translating a French text: the intricate, magnificent 'parterres of embroidery' laid down in box; 'parterres of compartiment', which were more symmetrical; 'parterres of cut-work', with box-edged flower beds, and 'Parterres after the English manner'. These, wrote James, 'are the plainest and meanest of all. They should consist only of large Grass-plots all of a piece, or cut but little, and be encompassed with a border of Flowers, separated from the Grass-work by a Path of Two or Three Foot wide, laid smooth and sanded over, to make

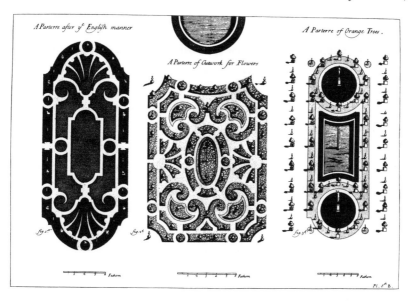

A Parterre after y^e English manner

A Parterre of Orange Trees.

A Parterre of Cutwork for Flowers

Three designs for a parterre, an often reproduced plate from John James's 1712 *Theory and Practice of Gardening*, translated from Dézallier d'Argenville. The unusual parterre of orange trees was for summer display.

the greater Distinction.' Thus was the classic small British garden born.

The gardens of the Stuart court, which mixed geometric control with luxuriant plants and the fantasy of sculpture and fountains, suggest a godlike assumption of control over nature. A central element in all this display was the use of water, in which Sir Robert Cecil once again took the lead: he had excelled in this at Theobalds, and now he was busy adorning his new garden at Hatfield with fountains and grottoes, glistening with shells. The Hatfield wonders were created by the current star, Salomon de Caus, a Huguenot from Normandy, who had visited Italy, studied the classics and worked on the palaces of Brussels, before coming to England in 1607 to work for the then queen, Anne of Denmark. He was both an artist and an architect-engineer, who wrote on perspective and machines moved by water and air, including silver balls balanced upon jets of water. The garden de Caus created for Anne at Somerset House was emblematic of her royal status, incorporating a great 'Parnassus' fountain, an artificial 'mountain' encrusted with shells, with Apollo and the Muses in the centre, and reclining river gods representing the four main rivers of Britain. His waterworks reflect the fantastical side of Jacobean life, involving elaborate automata, grottoes with statues, islands with giants on rocky outcrops and fountains in the shape of a nature goddess with plumes of water spraying from a cornucopia.

Salomon's younger relative (possibly his brother) Isaac de Caus was also a genius at garden design. In the 1630s it was Isaac who designed the new garden at Wilton – sweeping away Gilbert's intricate alleys – for Philip Sidney, fourth Earl of Pembroke. Wilton was the greatest garden of the first half of this century. The squares of the traditional Tudor design were now ranged in three divisions, contained within a vast rectangular space, well over half a mile long and quarter of a mile wide. As they strolled down from the terrace, visitors would enter the first section, arranged

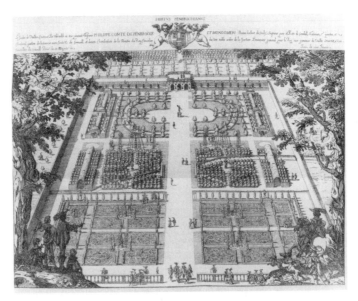

A bird's eye view of his plan for Wilton garden, by Isaac de Caus, 1715, looking towards the grotto.

around four fountains, with mythological statues in the middle of curling parterres, so ingeniously cut in box, said John Evelyn later, that they made 'a stupendious effect'. This, too, was an emblematic garden, planned around themes of love and chastity, its parterre ruled by statues of female deities and biblical and classical heroines: Venus, Diana, Susanna, Cleopatra. At the far end, in the middle of the lower terrace dividing garden from park, was a spectacular grotto, full of joke fountains and devices.

In country houses large and small, grottoes were usually at the lowest level of the terrace, as at Wilton, with the stream running down the hill below ground and issuing as a fountain. A grotto became *de rigueur* and many were very elaborate. The one designed by Isaac de Caus for Lucy Harington still exists in the basement of Woburn Abbey, a virtual banqueting room with dolphins and putti prancing across its walls beneath the shell-encrusted vaulted ceiling. In a quite different style Francis Bacon's old servant, Thomas Bushell, the 'Enstone Hermit' – an adherent of the mystical, quasi-magical schools of Renaissance thought – created a bizarre house and grotto with curious waterworks in Oxfordshire, which became so famous that it was visited by Charles I in 1636. (Almost thirty years later John Evelyn visited the ageing hermit and discovered he had two mummies in his grotto, and 'lay in a hamoc like an Indian'.)

In 1677 John Worlidge told readers of his *Systema Horti-culturae*, which was aimed at the owners of 'fair Estates and Pleasant Seats', that a grotto was essential for coolness in summer. It could be vaulted with brick, with secret rooms and passages and, of course, waterworks 'for your own and your friends' divertissements. It is capable of giving you so much pleasure and delight that you may bestow not undeservedly what cost you please on it, by paving it with Marble or immuring it with Stone or Rock-work, either Naturally or Artificially resembling the excellencies of nature.' The most famous in the kingdom, he added, was the grotto at Wilton 'wherein you may view or might lately have done so, the best of waterworks'.

The grotto had a long afterlife. It was still part of aristocratic gardens after the Restoration and enjoyed a new popularity in the eighteenth century. Alexander Pope, who built a tunnel under a road to link his riverside house at Twickenham with his much loved garden, made this into a grotto, its emphasis changing over time from a place of fancy and meditation to a 'scientific' site, showing fossils and minerals, the inanimate wonders of nature. At Stourhead Henry Hoare's cave included statues of nymphs and river gods; at Painshill William Hamilton's vault was designed to look like caves near Naples where Virgil set the entrance to the underworld. But the grotto was also very much a woman's place, linked to the fashion for shell collecting. Pope's friend, Lady Mary Wortley Montagu, made one, sniffed at by her younger contemporary, Mary Delany, as far too regular, with the coral all painted: 'Mine shall not be made after that model.' Mary herself became a grotto addict: she had been married at seventeen, against her will, to the sixty-year-old Alexander Pendarves and endured seven years of miserable marriage until his death. Ten years later in Dublin she met Dr Patrick Delany, who shared her interest in gardens and in 1743 they married. She began shell collecting, made a 'shell-grotto' for her uncle in Fulham, sent shells by the barrel to friends, designed a grotto for her brother and, when she was nearly seventy, helped her friend the Duchess of Portland ornament hers at Bulstrode in Buckinghamshire. Even her own bedroom was starry with shells.

Many women's grottoes were more like fine rooms than watery caves. At Goodwood in the 1730s the Duchess of Richmond worked with her daughters, Caroline and Emily, using local flint and fossils and thousands of shells in elaborate flower patterns and swags. Mother and daughters worked for seven years, it was said – making it sound like a task from a fairy story. When one daughter, Emily, married and moved to Carton in Ireland, she and her sister Louisa created a fantastic domed shell cottage, its walls bulging with conches and sponges from distant seas among the scallops and winkles of Dublin Bay.

9
———

'Wife, into thy garden'

FAR FROM THE VISTAS and grottoes of Wilton and the plant hunting of the Tradescants, up and down the country ordinary people got on with their gardening, simply as part of their daily routine. For many – particularly the wives of the small gentry, yeomen and farmers of England, Wales and Scotland – it was a source of sustenance for their families and considerable personal pride. Foreigners remarked with amazement on the independent manners of Englishwomen, despite their legal subservience to their husbands. At all levels of country life, a woman's days were packed. The mistress of a large country house had to entertain guests, run a large staff and take care of the whole estate when her husband was away – even defend it by force, in many instances, during the Civil War.

At the other end of the scale the labourers' wives undertook extra work, sewing or lace- or basket making, or seasonal work in the fields to add to the family store. In between these the prosperous farmer's wife had fewer social duties or desperate needs, but her workload was huge. She was responsible for the kitchen, stillroom, laundry and dairy, and looked after pigs and calves, and the pigeons, poultry and geese, including their slaughter and dressing for market. She supervised the brewing of the ale and the heavy, time-consuming task of washing and drying of all the linen and clothes, sending her maids scurrying to spread the heavy sheets across the bushes in her garden. She was also in charge, as Richard Surflet noted in *The Country Ferme* in 1600, not only of the 'oven and cellar', but of clipping the sheep and weaving and spinning, of making the clothes, and 'of ordering the kitchen garden; and keeping the fruits, herbs, roots and seeds; and moreover of watching and attending to the bees'. Many must have wilted under the load, especially given constant childbearing, yet others still found time to embroider fine work, to read and make music, and sing and dance.

The houses of the gentry, often with the church nearby, expressed their role as centre of the community. In Elizabethan and Stuart times, old manor houses and farms were smartened up, and prosperous squires and yeomen built houses in sheltered valleys, in black and white timber or all of stone, sometimes moated but now often simply set in their meadows and orchards. The kitchen gardens were not yet hidden away, but were usually in front of the house, screened behind high hedges, with vegetables on one side of the gravel path and fruit on the other. On a smallholding the square kitchen garden would probably be about three 'perches' wide – about fifty feet – and double that on larger prosperous farms.

An engraving made around 1570 after a well-known painting by Pieter Bruegel shows all the hard labour of spring, with the lady of the house, hat in hand, urging on her busy servants. And the writings of gentlewomen show that women were indeed setting and sowing. In Oxfordshire Elinor Fettiplace scrupulously noted in her Receipt Book all the best times for sowing and transplanting herbs and vegetables in her garden at Appleton, so that they would be ready for each season: in midsummer, at the waning of the moon, one should sow 'all manner of potherbs, & they wilbee greene for winter; also Lettice seeds sown at this time and removed when they bee of a

Spring work in the garden, with a well-off housewife on the right, urging on her servants. English engraving, 1570, after Pieter Bruegel.

prettie bignes at the full wilbee good and hard Lettice at Michaelmas'. Elinor's relative, Lady Hoby from Yorkshire, put up her feet to write her diary after 'allmost all the after none in the Gardene sowing seed'.

Grandmothers and mothers handed on country skills, aunts instructed nieces, cooks taught new maidservants, neighbours helped neighbours. Many women kept their own household books, filling the creamy pages over the years with recipes, details of cures and tips for the garden. An elegant version, purporting to be Henrietta Maria's own (hardly likely) household book of secrets, was published as *The Queen's Closet Opened* in 1655. But long before this women were copying out tips from the printed books of advice that were often given to new brides. Marriage, in the country, was a partnership and several authors link the woman's role in the garden firmly to that of the husband in running the farm.

In gardening, the great innovator was Thomas Hill, whose *Briefe and Pleasant Treatyse, teaching how to Dress, Sow and Set a Garden* of 1563 grew into *The Gardener's Labyrinth* of 1577. Hill asserted solemnly that though 'The husbandman or Gardener shall enjoy a most commodious and delectable Garden', this could not be done unless he knew 'what to begin and follow'. And although he addresses the husband (men took charge of the orchard), he also speaks to the wife and gives a vivid sense of the way a kitchen garden, in particular, must have looked. He begins from scratch, stressing the importance of choosing the right site, preferably sloping very slightly and facing south-east, to catch the full morning sun. The garden is divided in quarters, each containing a number of raised beds, four or five feet wide, separated by channels through which the water could run. In the centre there might be a fountain or a shallow 'dipping pond' to submerge watering pots easily in, but he also illustrates other methods of watering, from his round-bellied pot with its narrow neck and double handles to

Watering with a 'great Squirt' powered by a pump in a tub, from Thomas Hill, *The Gardener's Labyrinth*, 1586 edition.

steady it (the forerunner of the modern watering can) to 'a great Squirt' used so that 'the water in breaking may fall as drops of raine on the plants'.

The Elizabethan reader, elbows propped on the solid oak table in the kitchen, might also mark the places which spoke of the spreading of dung, or the clearing of the beds 'both of the stones and unprofitable roots' before digging, or the best way to make straight beds using twine and sticks. Hill shows tools, too, and lists all 'The skilful inventions and helps against the Garden Moles, Ants, Gnats, Flies and Frogges, everting, harming and wasting, as well Kitchen hearbs, as trees and fruits'. His lovely illustrations show the kind of garden a well-off countrywoman or London merchant's wife might have enjoyed. He has a special section on 'sowing, planting and setting of most delectable Flowers and Hearbs in use, for adorning a Summer Garden, or a Garden of pleasure and delight'. And amid the old favourites he includes the new and modish, like the tulip, subjected to his sturdy common sense (although his surprisingly late planting instructions seem to make them a summer, not a late spring, bloom):

> Tulips are very beautyful flowers, but have no sent. They adorn a garden wel, or the house: their roots are like Onyons, which you must set out in January if there be no frost; and after they have done bearing, about Michaelmas take up the roots out of the ground, which will be double, and keep them dry in a Box or Paper against the next year.

In reality, country gardens were probably far more untidy than Hill's fine plans. While the nobility and gentry enjoyed their new Italian gardens, the farmers' wives and cottagers paid less attention to design, yet many loved their flowers and showed off happily to admiring neighbours. One such neighbour made a record of all the flowers blooming around Goodwife Cantrey's house in Northamptonshire on 28 July 1658: double and single larkspurs, sweet williams, three kinds of spiderwort, four colours of lupin, 'the great blew, the little blue, the yellow and the white', purple and white scabious, marigold, London pride and hollyhocks. Among Goody Cantrey's herbs were fennel for weak eyes, camomile for headaches, white lilies for 'bile', feverfew against the shaking fever.

In most gardens these herbs grew nearest the door, while the beehives lined the furthest hedge or stood safely on the other side of the wall. Flowers grew among the vegetables, fruit bushes rambled over the walls, nut trees took up space in the middle of the beds. Alongside the paths ran borders full of flowers, pinks and daisies and columbine, hollyhocks and peonies and irises. The hedges had shady arbours made of ash poles and willow, covered by vines, melons or cucumber, as well as scented climbers. Everything was mingled together although in 1618, in *The Country House-Wife's Garden*, William Lawson heralded a change, decreeing that 'it is meet that we have two Gardens; a Garden for flowers and a kitchen-garden'. Yet this was mostly for ease of gathering the vegetables and even Lawson did not advocate a fierce separation. He acknowledged, too, that women might have a hand in designing all parts of the garden, and since there were so many diverse forms of mazes and knots, 'I leave every House-wife to her self to design it.'

Housewives read Hill and Lawson, but also the simpler, more democratic verse tract of Thomas Tusser, *A Hundred Good Points of Husbandry* of 1557, which had swelled by 1573 into *Five Hundred Points of Good Husbandrie*. The Cambridge-educated Tusser had tried farming, not very successfully, in Suffolk and Essex, and he set out his points month by month in a jogging, humorous, easy-to-read verse. The rhymes made it easy to remember and he condensed his longer text into an 'abstract' for each month in snappy short lines, as for March:

> For garden best
> Is south south-west
>
> Good tilth brings seedes,
> Evil tilture, weedes.

Poor Tusser did not make much money – indeed, he died in a debtor's prison – but his books were extremely popular. His readers were yeomen and gentry who saw the garden very clearly as the woman's realm. In *A Hundred Good Points*, in the middle of his section on 'March', he stops to add 'A Digression from Husbandrie: to a Poynt or two of Huswiferie':

> In Marche, and in Aprill, fro morning to night:
> In sowing and setting, good housewives delight.
> To have in their gardein, or some other plot
> To trim up their house, and to furnish their pot.

'Wife, into thy garden,' he orders in the spring, while in September she and her servants are busy finding strawberry roots and planting soft fruit bushes for the next year. Even in December they tend to their beehives and in January plant hedges to throw the washing on to dry when the finer weather comes again.

Tusser gives his tips for each month, rather like a modern columnist in a Saturday newspaper. In November he suggests,

> If Garden require it, now trench it ye may,
> One trench not a yard from another go lay.
> Which being well filled, with mucke by & by
> Go cover with mould, for a season to ly.

There are good full lists of fruit and seeds and herbs, which include all the old 'pot-herb' vegetables and salad, as well as herbs for medicine, and others to strew on the floor or distil for perfume or cordials. Every month is busy. Under 'January', for instance, he lists twenty-seven fruit and nut trees to be 'set or removed', including different kinds of plums, peaches and pears, and new fruits brought over by the Flemish settlers like 'barberries' and the pale gooseberry. In September:

The Barberry, Respis [raspberry] and Gooseberry too.
Look now to be planted as other things do
The Gooseberry, Respis and Roses all three,
With strawberries under them, trimly agree.

The rhymes are bad and the advice pretty standard, but there is magic here, as a modern editor has said, as we follow the life of the farm through the year; the spring arrives, the level fields dry beneath the wind, the clouds pile high; in summer the land is golden with corn, scarlet with poppies; in autumn the crisp frost comes and then the winter sun, rimmed with white mist, the earth sleeping until spring returns again.

Not surprisingly, Tusser's little book was a hit and was constantly reprinted before he died in 1580. There were more and more such books as time went by: Surflet's *Country Ferme*, Gervase Markham's *Country Contentments* (1611) and *The English Huswife* of 1615, and then Lawson's *Country Housewife's Garden*. But Tusser's was found on country bookshelves until the Napoleonic Wars and beyond. In one of his poems John Clare describes a Nottinghamshire cottager whose library was the Bible and Prayer Book, *Pilgrim's Progress* and 'prime old Tusser'.

By the early seventeenth century, as the old pattern of the hall house with its high-ceilinged central chamber was being replaced by new styles with more private rooms, some of the old communal living disappeared, but on the farms the family, maids and labourers still ate together in the roomy farmhouse kitchen. Sometimes all the cooking and preserving was done in the 'house room' over an open range, hung with coppers and spits and hooks and pots, but in larger houses there was a separate kitchen at one end of the house, a veritable factory surrounded by the pantry and larder and dairy and stillroom, where all the preserving took place, and the concocting of potions and lotions, ointments and salves.

Apart from spices and sugar and wine, nearly all the food for the table came from the land: game from the copses and fish from the streams, meat from the herds and flocks, chickens in the yard and ducks and geese on the pond; cheese from the dairy; bread from their own grain, ground at the mill; ale from the brew-house and honey from the hive. As Gervase Markham put it sternly, the housewife 'must proceed more from the provision of her own yard than the furniture of the markets'. Cookery books and household accounts show how imaginative they could be: for roast mutton, one mistress made a sauce of spearmint and sugar, or broom-buds, French beans, clove-pinks or cucumbers, while for goose she tried sorrel and (appropriately) gooseberries. Summer salads – with violets and cowslips as well as green herbs and leaves – grew in popularity: in 1699 John Evelyn, like a foodie of today, wrote a whole 'Discourse on Sallets', even laying down the right way to toss them and the ingredients for their oil-and-vinegar dressing. And in winter Henri Misson could report that the English ate boiled beef with 'five or six Heaps of Cabbage, Carrots, Turnips, or some other Herbs and roots, well pepper'd and salted and swimming in Butter'. For winter sauces the housewife opened her store cupboard, taking out the pots of vegetables pickled in the summer, the candied flowers and conserves of fruit.

Fruit was a staple all year round, fresh stewed and preserved. Apples, pears and cherries, red- and blackcurrants, gooseberries, rasp-berries, quinces, and occasionally the new peaches and apricots, were all grown in country gardens, the surplus being sold at the market in the nearby town. The apples were good for cider and the pear for perry, and recipe books were full of recipes for wine: cowslip, cherry, elder, gooseberry.

In the garden the housewife also found almost all the ingredients for her stillroom. Here she worked like a scientist with glasses and alembics, distilling the purges and cough medicines and potions, preparing her conserve and pickles, and making perfumed oils for scents and soaps. Everything was useful, even plants that we now consider purely ornamental. Marigolds and violets were candied for sweets, peonies were preserved as a remedy. Elderflowers and irises and mallow were made into

The still room, from the *Dictionarum Domesticarum*, with bees to provide honey, herbs drying on strings, and pestles, mortars, jars and distilling equipment.

lotions for softening wrinkles, rhubarb in white wine was used for dying your hair blonde, strawberry and watercress were pounded into a cream to remove the much-disdained freckles. Sir Hugh Platt (who was knighted for services to science) insisted that to get rid of freckles you should wash your face at dawn and dusk at the wane of the moon with the distilled water of elder leaves – which *must* be distilled in May. For a general clearing and cleansing, prescriptions included a milk bath with a boiled mixture of rosemary, feverfew, origanum, fennel, mallow, violet leaves and nettles added to two or three gallons of milk: 'then let the party stand or sit in it an hour or two, the bath reaching up to the stomach, and when they come out, they must go to bed and sweat, and beware taking of cold'. Among less alarming favourites were the 'Queen of Hungary's Water', a tonic for beauty and health, made for thyme, sage and savory, marjoram and rosemary, distilled in 'spirits of wine', or a 'honey of roses', made of red-rose petals and bean-flower water, which 'taketh away the spots of the face'.

Most countrywomen, and the gardening experts whose books they read, firmly believed that all planting and sowing and reaping should be governed by the phases of the moon. (And if this seems eccentric, I did see a gardener on television in 2002 arguing persuasively that if the moon ruled the tides, then why not the level of sap, or juice in the fruit?) Following the familiar rhythm of the seasons, our housewife gathered the herbs and flowers and roots: the leaves of herbs, it was said, were strongest in flavour and power if picked between mid-April and early July; stalks and stems from July to October, roots from October through to April again. At all times of the year, wrapped in a cloak against the wind or tying her bonnet to shade her from the summer sun, we can see her – perhaps, like us, despairing at the slugs among the lettuces or cursing the birds in the redcurrants – but still setting off down the tidy gravel paths and returning with her overflowing basket.

10

Swords into pruning hooks

IN THE 1630s THE grandiose layout of Wilton set a pattern for the future, but so did a much smaller garden made around the same time in the village of Chelsea by Sir John Danvers (the brother of Sir Henry Danvers, who created Britain's first Physic Garden in Oxford in 1621). The Chelsea garden was a broad rectangle with a terrace at each end, a small idyll of patterned compartments, still managing to contain a grotto with a banqueting house above, and a miniature wilderness of shrubs and fruit trees, with coloured statues of the gardener and his wife to surprise the guests. This rectangular model — without the coloured statues — was adaptable to town and country gardens of two acres, or even half an acre, and its symmetrical beds, neat topiary, statues and splashing fountains suggested calm, harmony and ease. But in the 1640s, right across Britain, all harmony was shattered by the onset of the Civil War — and in conflict, as well as peace, gardening played a powerful symbolic role.

In April 1649 the small revolutionary group known as the Diggers took over common land on St George's Hill in Surrey, sowing it with parsnips, carrots and beans. The Diggers' leader, Gerrard Winstanley, taught that God made the earth for all and that private property came after the Fall – although it has to be said that it was not the parliamentary troops but angry local householders who destroyed their crops and allotment-like sheds. Then, in the spring of 1651, two years after the execution of Charles I, the parliamentary forces ransacked the royal gardens at Oatlands, ripping up the orange trees, removing the roses, despoiling the beds. It was as if lavish gardening were a symbol of the indulgence of the monarch and the aristocracy, whose privileges were no longer rooted in the earth but could be torn up and reclaimed for the people.

Yet a garden could be a retreat from strife, as well as a symbol of struggle. Two of Cromwell's generals stepped back and retired to their gardens. One was General John Lambert, whose botanical passion was satirised in a pack of cards, where the eight of hearts showed him holding a bloom, captioned 'Lambert Kt of ye Golden Tulip'. The other was General Fairfax, who left the limelight for his estate at Nunappleton House in the lush Ouse valley south of York. In 1650 the twenty-nine-year-old Andrew Marvell became tutor to Fairfax's daughter Maria, writing poems that express the conflict between the retired, contemplative life and the life of action needed to build a nation. The soldier was still there, Marvell felt, in Fairfax's garden, in the military ranks of flowers, which stood like regiments at parade under their colours, 'That of the tulip, pink and rose'. There is a hint, too, that the garden plan even contained the figures of the 'star forts', which Civil War generals copied from ones they had seen on the Continent, with jutting bastions and terraces. Fairfax had left war behind,

> But laid these gardens out in Sport
> In just the figure of a Fort
> And with five Bastions it did fence
> As aiming one for ev'ry Sense.

Now and in the next century, garden planners did indeed adopt the fortress designs, using the 'bastions' as viewpoints, both terraces and barriers against the fields without.

In the aftermath of war violent themes took softened horticultural shapes. In the 1690s, at Kensington Palace, William III commissioned a garden known as the 'Siege of Troy', with yew and variegated holly, 'to imitate the lines, angles, bastions, scarp and counter-scarps of regular fortifications'. Old military men often followed suit, like the second Earl of Stair at Castle Kennedy near Stranraer, who called in the Royal Scots Greys and Inniskillen Fusiliers in the 1730s to build ridges and rides like battle encampments. And a favourite, if fictional, military garden is created by two old veterans wounded in William III's Continental wars: Uncle Toby and his servant Trim in Sterne's *Tristram Shandy*. To bolster Toby's spirits, when his wound fails to heal, they lay out the fortifications of Dunkirk on an old bowling green, facing the walls and parapets with sods.

Back in the Commonwealth, gardening was either strictly practical – Cromwell was a great promoter of agriculture – or it stressed the Eden-seeking, contemplative mood. Sometimes a gardener managed to do both. In his *Treatise of Fruit Trees*, the Calvinist divine Ralph Austen proposed a national initiative in fruit tree planting (supplied by his own nurseries, naturally), an idea also favoured by the radical Samuel Hartlib, who suggested that all waste ground should be planted with apples, pears, quinces and walnuts 'for the relief of the poor, the benefit of the rich, and the delight of all'. England would thus become 'The Garden of God'.

Ralph Austen, too, linked his faith and his fruit growing. After his main text he added an essay on 'The Spiritual Use of an Orchard'. His title page shows a mystical orchard, a square embraced by a circle and the quote 'A Garden inclos'd is my sister my spouse; Thy plants are an orchard of Pomegranates, with pleasant fruits'. The world was 'a great Library', he maintained, and fruit trees were some of God's books: he had sent us 'the *Booke of Nature* before he sent us the *Book of the Scriptures*'. At the Fall, mankind had been cut off from the good apples of Eden and banished to bitter crab apples: the good Christian must regain paradise by planting the best trees. It was an optimistic message:

> The joy of the Husbandman is not a flash and so away, but it is *a settled and habituall* joy . . . which also keeps the spirits cheerful and lively: for there are *many renovations, and a continual progress to the more benigne, and things mending and growing to the better.*

This was also the view of the pamphleteer William Prynne, who wrote, 'If Bibles fail, each garden will descry the works of God to us.' For many Puritans gardens were books of emblems: God was the husbandman, tending his orchard, the world; man was the gardener, tending his own soul. 'Christians are like flowers in a garden', wrote John Bunyan, 'that stand and grow where the gardener hath planted them' and are 'jointly nourished and nourish one another'. In the Celestial City in *A Pilgrim's Progress*, land is rent-free, 'plums and figs and grapes and apples will be open to every passenger, in common and free for all'.

Running through this rhetoric was a murmured rebellion against the artifice of contemporary gardening, embodying the fallen world. In Milton's Eden,

> . . . the crisped brooks
> Ran nectar, visiting each plant, and fed
> Flowers worthy of Paradise which not nice art
> In beds and curious knots, but Nature boon
> Poured forth profuse on hill, and dale, and plains.

And Marvell, who had been Milton's secretary, expresses this too through his down-to-earth Mower in 'The Mower against Gardens':

'Tis all enforc'd the fountain and the grot
While the sweet fields do lie forgot
Where willing Nature does to all dispense
A wild and fragrant innocence.

You didn't have to be a Puritan to see the garden in contrast to the corruption of the world. In 1650 John Evelyn bought a copy of Parkinson's *Paradisus* and perhaps this book, combined with his nostalgia for Italian sunshine, inspired his search for evergreen trees and the illusion of a perfect, perpetual spring. In his *Kalendarium Hortense* he proposed that gardens should be 'as near as we can contrive them to the garden of Eden'. The royalist Evelyn and the republican Hartlib became friends through their shared interest in tree planting, yet their backgrounds and tastes could not have been more different. Evelyn was only twenty-two when the conflict began in 1642. During the Commonwealth he travelled often to France and Italy, observing and comparing their gardens and farms and, back home in 1651, he adapted the Italian style at his brother's house at Wotton, Surrey, designing a terrace, a grotto and a classical portico. Then, in 1652 at his own home, an old gabled Elizabethan country house near Deptford that had belonged to his wife's family, he laid out an oval garden, 'which was before a rude orchard, and all the rest one entire field of 100 acres'. (The only disaster came years later, in 1698, when he leased the house to Peter the Great of Russia, who 'enjoyed being wheeled through the holly hedge in a wheelbarrow' and caused general devastation.)

Evelyn was an idealist: his futuristic tract *Fumifugium* suggested that London's smoky atmosphere might be helped by a band of flowery fields, shrubs and herbs on the outskirts; his greatest work, *Sylva*, on forest trees, influenced the planting of many new avenues and woods. Over the years he translated the leading French works on gardening, and for half a century from the 1650s he collected his gardening lore in a great book, which he planned to call *Elysium Britannicum*, but never managed to organise and finish – a third of it, unearthed at Christ Church, Oxford, has

John Evelyn's drawings of tools from his *Elysium Britannicum*, c. 1660. As well as basic forks and spades, hoes and rakes, ladders and watering cans these include water barrels, bell-glasses and cold-frames (58), a knife-grinder and a cart, a book to write down plant names and 'a Bed-Stead furnished with a tester and Curtaines of Green' to protect choice flowers 'from the parching beames of the Sunn' (53).

recently been published. His practical side shows in his own 'Direction for his Gardener', his drawings of garden tools and his *Kalendarium Hortense*, which allocated tasks to each month, with a rather lyrical, swinging approach to the job. In May, for example:

> Observe the Mulberry-tree, when it begins to put forth and open the leaves (be it earlier or later) bring your Oranges &c boldly out of the Conservatory.
>   Cleans vines of exuberant Branches and tendrils.

Not surprisingly, many people at court and in the new Royal Society asked Evelyn for advice. He planned a 'philosopher's garden' at Albury in Surrey in 1667 for Henry Howard, later Duke of Norfolk, with a tunnel through the hillside and vineyards on the slopes, and suggested the fine avenues of Euston Hall in Suffolk. He gave advice to the Chancellor, Lord Clarendon, to the Earl of Arlington and the Earl of Essex at Cassiobury in Hertfordshire.

Arthur Capel, Lord Essex, came from a well-known garden-making family. (His father, a devoted royalist, was executed in 1649.) Lord Essex's youngest brother, William, had a garden at Kew, later taken over by the royal family to become the world-famous Kew Gardens. One of their sisters, Elizabeth, Countess of Carnarvon, was an excellent flower painter and the other, Mary, was one of the most influential plant collectors of the day.

It is a commonplace in garden histories that around this time 'flowers disappeared from the garden' and instead found their way inside the house, carved on panels, embroidered on tapestries, woven into carpets. Certainly, John Worlidge complained in 1677 of 'many stately Country residences, where they have banish'd out of the Gardens Flowers, the miracles of Nature, and the best ornaments that ever were discovered to make a real pleasant'. Yet Worlidge himself writes at length on flower growing and everywhere I look I find mention of flowers. At Sayes Court Evelyn had a special walled garden laid out on old-fashioned lines, running along the back of the house, with an arbour under two old elms. On a roughly sketched plan he labelled this as 'My Private Garden of choice flowers and Simples'.

In *Lady's Recreation*, his contribution to a trilogy called *The Art of Gardening Improved*, Evelyn boldly suggested that woman might cultivate exotics as well as simple flowers, like the 'Noli me Tangere', whose pods suddenly snap open 'and fly to pieces to the great surprise of the person molesting it'. Lord Essex's sister Mary Capel was not one to be put off such warnings. In 1657 she married the Duke of Beaufort and, while he laid out his sixty criss-crossing avenues at Badminton, she concentrated on rare plants. She created an orangery, a 'stove' 100 feet long, to rival the queen's, and competed with her in gathering thousands of specimens from the West Indies, Virginia and the Cape of Good Hope, including nerines, guava, pawpaw, bananas, aloes and hibiscus. At Beaufort House in Chelsea she had a huge sunken flower garden, surrounded by a terrace. There were special beds for spring flowers – anemones, jonquils, tulips, crown imperials – others for gillyflowers, polyanthus, carnations and peonies, and another area was divided into wide rectangular beds for her prized auriculas. She corresponded with leading botanists, including Sir Hans Sloane of the Chelsea Physic Garden, and Badminton she created a special botanic garden, where a speciality was the mass of 'geraniums' from South Africa: one of her introductions was the ivy-leaved geranium, *Pelargonium peltatum*.

Flower gardening was by no means an exclusively aristocratic pursuit. During the Commonwealth many royalists simply kept their heads down for the duration, as Sir Thomas Hanmer, the husband of one of Henrietta Maria's maids of honour, did at Bettisfield in Flintshire. Here he wrote his own *Garden Book*, packed with descriptions of the gardens of his time, discussing the taste for French or Dutch parterres, the new fountains and groves full of singing birds.

Hanmer's main flower garden seems to have contained circles of beds or knots within square areas outlined by walks, an Italian style suggested in the generation before by Parkinson. It was next to the house, surrounded by walls with espaliered fruit trees and borders, grassy walks and central beds surrounded by boards. In 1660 he wrote a list of the 'Flowers in the Great garden, Bettisfield'. His real joy, however, was his 'little private seminary' where he raised his flowers and trees, with a 'wynter house' to shelter exotics, and a collection of 'such treasures as are not be exposed to everyone's view'. These included an exceptional range of tulips, irises and anemones, but also new plants from the West Indies, among them the amaryllis, which he watched, holding his breath in amazement in 1656 as its tall stalk with the two heavy buds suddenly exploded into the huge lily-like trumpets of orangey pink.

Hanmer was a close friend of John Rea, from Norton's End at Kinlet on the Shropshire–Worcestershire border, a plant-collecting country gentleman (not to be confused with the naturalist John Ray). He found the Commonwealth years grim, 'our Long Winter', he called it, looking back, and spent the years gathering a store of knowledge for his own three-part book, named after the Roman goddesses of flowers, corn and fruit, *Flora, Ceres and Pomona*, which he felt able to publish only in 1662, when the Restoration had brought spring back again. The title page was crowned by Flora between two overflowing urns. 'It is knowledge that begets Affection, and Affection increaseth Knowledge,' he wrote in his preface. 'It is chiefly that, which hath made my Flowers and Trees to flourish, though planted in a barren Desart.'

In *Flora, seu de Florum Cultura*, 1665, Rea included detailed plans for flower gardens, walled enclosures with geometric beds, bounded by pole hedges of trained trees, or lattice with roses. As a nurseryman he has a good grumble at the gentlemanly plant scroungers who pretend they love flowers but are 'unwilling to part with anything to purchase them'. (At his death in 1677 Rea left his nursery to his daughter, Minerva, who married another plantsman, the Revd John Gilbert, who wrote *The Florist's Vade*

Mecum, 1682.) Rea liked birdsong, and scent, and flowers among the vegetables; he adored his plants and, as many historians have noted, may have been one of that long line of people who actually talked to them:

> Into your garden you can walk
> And with each plant and flower talk;
> View all their glories, from each one
> Raise some rare meditation.
> Recount their natures, tell which are
> Vertuous like you, as well as fair.

Rea demonstrated the new empirical approach of his age, the ethos of the Royal Society, founded in 1660. Basing his advice on observation and experiment he rejected the old lore of planting by the moon. Yet he was also a conservative, proud of his forty years with his trowel, and disdainful of artifice, fountains and grottoes. They might be marks of magnificence, but 'all such dead Works in Gardens, ill done, are little better than Blocks in the way to intercept the sight, but not at all able to satisfy the understanding. A choice collection of living Beauties, rare Plants, Flowers and a Fruit, are indeed the Wealth, glory and delight, of a Garden.'

Everyone had slightly different ideas about design: often there were existing gardens near the house, laid out in the old Jacobean style of grass squares and walks, which people were reluctant to replace, so their new flower gardens were slightly away from the house, entered through a special gate. Most landowners did not bother to 'plan' their gardens at all. Instead they simply added the features that most took their fancy. They might erect a new fence right across the front, with no apparent purpose; build a rash of garden houses of different styles; plant an avenue going nowhere or stopping short of the house so that carriages then had to slope off round the back. They would dig a canal that cut oddly through their old Elizabethan rectangular garden and plonk a 'temple' at the end; fill a square with wooden obelisks; cut every tiny tree into fantastic shapes. The lovely

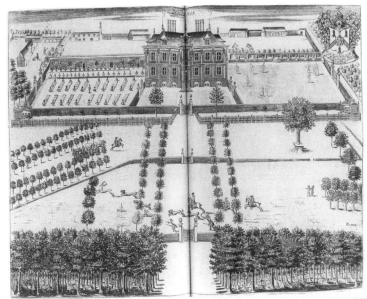

John Drapentier's drawing of 'Stagenhoe', from Sir Henry Chauncey, *Historical Antiquities of Hertfordshire* (1700), with flower garden and orangery on the left, bowling green on the right, and farmyard behind. It is mystery where the carriages go after the final gate. Below is a detail from 'Little Offley', showing the curious topiary work, and a bustling farmyard with dung-heap and dove-cote.

illustrations by John Drapentier to Sir Henry Chauncey's *Historical Antiquities of Hertfordshire* of 1700 are full of these oddities and they also show how important hunting and shooting and care of the farmyard were to the country gentry. But they did like their flowers: as Timothy Mowl has pointed out, the drawing of 'Stagenhoe', a house built about 1650, shows bowls being played to the right, while on the left is 'the garden of a flower enthusiast', with twenty rectangular beds and forty flowerpots on the terrace, following Worlidge, who recommended that such pots 'painted white and placed on Pedestals in a straight line on the edges of your Walks or Walls or at the corners of your Squares, are exceeding pleasant'.

In our terms, these gardens would have still been too bright – like their Elizabethan forebears the gentry of the seventeenth century loved dazzling colours, and since the current flowers were over so early they got out their paintbrushes. John Rea, for example, advocated multicoloured fences 'coloured green in oil, with Pink and Verdigreese, or Ortment [bright yellow] and Indico'. And in summer, in those pots on the terrace and beside the house, the flowers were ablaze. But everyone benefited from the expertise gathered in the new botanic gardens and the greater understanding of plant physiology. Slowly this knowledge was disseminated in little practical books like *The Flower Garden* by William Hughes, of 1672, written for working gardeners and florists 'but chiefly for more plain and ordinary Country men and women as a perpetual Remembrancer'.

In the towns new houses tended to be built in terraces, with long patches of garden behind – sometimes just a dark scrubby yard, but often filled with small trees, geometric flower beds, standard roses in tubs and blooms overflowing from terracotta vases. City gardeners tried anything that would grow in the polluted air, and disguised their high walls with trellis and even *trompe l'oeil* paintings, and set up a summer house, fountain or sundial. There were larger gardens, too, in the capital and in provincial towns like Shrewsbury, Gloucester and Nottingham, the 'garden city', where the garden of the well-known Hallowes family, not the largest in the town, covered 12,000 square feet.

Profpectus domus ab horto, oppidum verfus.

William Stukeley, pen and ink wash of his house in Grantham, 1727.

A good garden, as Timothy Nourse wrote in the last years of the century, could have 'Flowers for every month or season of the Year', including a wilderness with wild strawberries, and little banks planted with thyme and violets and primroses. It might not be Eden, but the smart town ladies and impoverished country landowners, and the scholars and antiquaries like William Stukeley walking proudly down the gravel drive at Grantham, just as much as General Fairfax and John Evelyn and the Duchess of Beaufort, could all feel their garden was a work of art and a place of peace.

11

Points of view

VISTAS, POINTS OF VIEW, grand formality, infinite distance. These were what the elite of the Restoration wanted. For them, the garden would break its bounds, melting into the park, leaping outwards to the country.

Charles II admired the absolutist style of his cousin, Louis XIV, exemplified in the great new *parc* designed by André Le Nôtre at Vaux le Vicomte in 1657, a style that would rise to its height at Versailles. Le Nôtre's signature was the avenue, one main axis speeding from house to horizon, cutting across the broad parterre, with its elaborately patterned beds and gravel paths, forging ahead into the park, dividing to pass a formal pond or fountain or canal, extending ever onwards through the woods. Smaller avenues fanned out at certain points, like green starbursts from the main avenue, each V-shaped division marked by fountains, statues, pools. Strapped for cash, Charles imitated Louis as best he could, even requesting that Le Nôtre might come to England: his request was declined, as the master was somewhat 'occupied at Fontainebleau'. Instead, André Mollet, the French gardener who had worked for Charles's mother Henrietta Maria before the Civil War, accompanied by his nephew Gabriel, brought Gallic chic to Charles's parks. Their favourite device was the *patte d'oie*, avenues radiating from a semicircle, like the foot of a goose: when Charles II married Catherine of Braganza in 1662 he took her to Hampton Court, where she could step out of her suite on to a gilded balcony, looking down on his glinting new canal, the Long Water, and at the new avenues driving outwards from the formal curve of limes.

Landowners like the Duke of Buckingham at Badminton followed the king's lead, laying down a network of radiating avenues. Ralph Montagu, who had been Charles's ambassador at Versailles, spent twenty years – and a fortune – creating his own version of Versailles at Boughton in Northamptonshire, with parterres, a formal 'wilderness', groves with statues, an octagonal basin with an eighty-foot jet of water and orderly avenues progressing for miles in all directions. It was rumoured that Montagu planned an avenue marching to London, over seventy miles away – an astonishing assumption (even if apocryphal) that one could dispose of swaths of countryside at will. Other aristocrats built fine canals, like the beautiful stretch of water created by the Earl of Kent at Wrest Park in Bedfordshire. Many of these formal late-seventeenth-century estates can be seen in the paintings and engravings of Kip, Knyff and Badeslade, clear as a diagram in the early years of their planting with their straight lines, bobbly young trees and crisply cut canals. Few exist today, swept away by the landscaping of the next century, although there are survivors, including the lime avenue at Kingston Lacy in Dorset, planted in 1668. The beech avenues springing from their *patte d'oie* at Bramham, in Yorkshire, lasted from around 1700 until a gale of 1962, but they have now been replanted. At Bramham, too, in 2002 researchers from Leeds University used ground-penetrating radar (the kind water companies employ to find broken pipes) to rediscover the pipes linking its historic water features – showing just how hard it can be to puzzle out what these old gardens looked like.

Edmund Waller's plashed avenues and canal at Hall Barn, Beaconsfield, c. 1700.

The pattern of canals and linked avenues still endures at Hall Barn, near Beaconsfield, a garden of great calm and charm, begun by the poet Edmund Waller in the 1600s and completed by his grandson seventy years later. Here and in similar gardens, as the new trees grew they were 'plashed', cut down one side so that they became like a high hedge, with trees 'set very thicke and so shorn smooth to the top', which, as Celia Fiennes noticed at Ingestre in Derbyshire, 'makes the length of a walk look nobly'. At Badminton the ash and elm trees were plashed even in the so-called Wilderness.

The lure of the vista of an avenue of trees or topiary, radiating from a semicircle and ending in statuary, obelisks or a small building or temple, and the appeal of a long glistening canal view, endured well into the middle of the eighteenth century. Both were features of the Earl of Burlington's first garden at Chiswick and a set of enchanting pictures by Balthasar Nebot of 1738 show imaginative views of the proposed gardens for Hartwell House, near Aylesbury in Buckinghamshire, laid out in this way. On a smaller scale are the avenues begun in 1695 at Inkpen Old Rectory in

Berkshire. But the most perfect surviving garden in the Mollet style was started much later, in the 1730s, at St Paul's Walden Bury in Hertfordshire. Here the long lines of clipped hedges hold back the groves of trees on each side of three broad, undulating green walks, radiating from the lawn, and giving views of monuments, statues, or the local church spire. Within the wood, where the paths cross, are secret glades like the oval 'Theatre of the running Footman', with a pool and a temple, its odd name deriving from a central statue of the discus thrower, the Discobolus.

St Paul's Walden Bury gains its magic from blending formality with naturalness and mystery. As some writers have noted, the pure French style did not really transfer well across the Channel: the light was too soft to do justice to the crisp perspectives, the landscape too undulating to show avenues stretching into infinite distance. And the British actually liked the 'natural' look of clumps of trees, the intimate feel of small enclosures. An updated version of the old terraced Italian style fitted better with hillside sites, like the amazing Powis Castle in North Wales, where the terraces march downhill like hanging gardens, to what must once have been grand

Samuel and Nathaniel Buck, *View of Powis Castle*, from *Buck's Antiquities*, 1774.

formal gardens below. Powis was designed by William Winde, who had just finished work at Cliveden in Buckinghamshire, where George Villiers, second Duke of Buckingham, now looked down from his new terrace out across a parterre that stretched right to the brow of the hill, like a headland above the blue wooded distances beyond, giving, as John Evelyn said, 'a circular view to the utmost verge of the horizon'.

Evelyn took a particular delight in the new passion for tree planting: indeed, he can be said to have helped in promoting it. A keen member of the new Royal Society, he published his *Sylva: A Discourse on Forest Trees* in 1664. He had been horrified at the loss of trees in the years of the Commonwealth: whole areas of the Midlands had been denuded, as the new blast-furnaces for working iron devoured the wood. He was anxious, too, that the British oak on which the Navy depended would be lost: 'A timber tree is a merchant adventurer,' he wrote in *Sylva*, 'you shall never know his worth till he be dead.' He persuaded people that tree planting was patriotic and also that it would increase the value of their estates, but his book expressed spiritual values too: trees could bring wealth to the soul, as well as to the pocket. It covered decorative as well as useful trees and introductions, like the Virginian walnut and the acacia (the *Robinia pseudo-acacia* from America). Evelyn was still wary, though, of the 'Constantinople', the new horse chestnuts, which had arrived from Turkey in the time of Tradescant, recommending that avenues of these should be planted 'where the winds come not fiercely, which is apt to take off whole branches'.

Sylva was one of those rare books that are a genuine spur to action. Thousands, perhaps millions, of trees were planted and Charles II himself, as Evelyn remembered proudly, was 'sometimes graciously pleased' to remark on it and say 'that I have by that booke alone incited a world of planters to repair their broken estates and woodes, which the greedy rebels had wasted & made such havoc of'. Yet he could not stop the roaring charcoal furnaces of the early industrial revolution and, by the time of his death, swaths of natural woodland were lost, including almost all of the great Forest of Arden in the east Midlands. The appeal to his 'better-natured countrymen' to preserve existing woods and replace those that had been destroyed is one that still speaks to us strong today.

When James II fled into exile in 1688 his daughter Mary took the throne with her husband, William of Orange. William made the riverside palace of Hampton Court his chief residence, employing Christopher Wren to carry out the alterations, his friend Hans Willem Bentinck as garden supervisor and Le Nôtre's pupil, Daniel Marot, to lay out the Great Maze and the marvellous Privy Garden, which has been so superbly restored in the 1990s. In Charles I's 'Fountain Garden' the style was that of swirling *'parterre de broderie'*, but in the Privy Garden – which was sunk between terraces, so that you could see the barges of the river through the beautiful wrought-iron screens – William chose the *parterre à l'Anglaise*, with shapes cut out of the turf and filled with coloured gravels. On the terraces were yew pyramids and hollies and scented shrubs, and around the edge were thin borders of flowers, with bulbs in spring, and marigolds, snapdragons, cornflowers and yellow lupins in summer. To make the Privy Garden an old hornbeam arbour was removed, but it was quickly replaced by a wych elm bower curving over a long wooden structure, where Mary and her ladies sat and sewed. (The Queen's Bower, which survived until felled by Dutch Elm disease in the 1970s, was also restored in the 1990s.)

William was a keen botanist and in Holland, in 1675 he had revoked the restrictions on the Dutch East India Company's carrying of exotic plants. At their famous gardens at Het Loo, he and Mary planted each new species in extraordinary pots – stone, Delftware, terracotta, lead and bronze. Mary brought her rare plant collection with her from Holland, and with her garden staff she built three walled gardens and a sequence of three hothouses, each with four stoves providing underfloor heating, the 'Glass Case Garden'. One walled garden was for auriculas, one for flowers in containers and one for exotics. She sent her own collectors to the Americas, and organised the gathering of seeds from the Cape, Barbados, Canaries and East Indies, germinating them on manure and tanner's bark in her melon ground. Until her early death from smallpox at thirty-two she cosseted her treasures, bringing them out in their great pots in the summer months: cacti and succulents, palms, aloes, agaves and yuccas, orchids and bulbs, climbing campsis and passion flowers – a scented, sensual delight, a royal collection to be proud of.

Mary loved her little enclosed flower gardens. The old polarity between the small and enclosed as opposed to the great vistas, the inward-looking garden versus the park, was now expressed in terms of 'Dutch' versus 'French' style. People argue about what this implied, but it's clear that certain gardens definitely gave people a feeling of 'Dutchness', with courtyards and ornamental canals, intricate topiary and oranges, myrtle and oleander in tubs. One garden that historians disagree over, some swearing there is not a jot of Dutch influence and others claiming it as a superb model, is Westbury Court in Gloucestershire. The garden here was made between

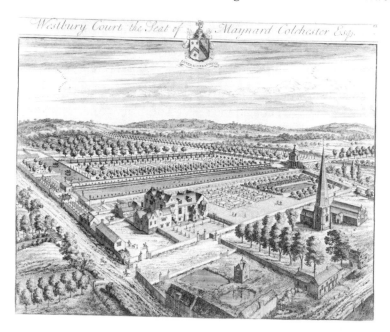

Westbury Court, Gloucestershire, engraving by Johannes Kip, 1720.

1690 and 1702 by Maynard Colchester (who had a friendly Dutch neighbour) and it contains a canal stretching from a fountain at one end to the Tall Pavilion at the other, giving a view of the whole pattern. The garden was bordered by a wall, with hedged enclosures and walled spaces, and the gravel paths were separated from the grass by clipped pyramids of yew and silver holly globes. There were more clipped shrubs, laurestinus and daphne, and trained fruit trees: apricots, cherries, plums, nectarines and peaches, and in one compartment a fine parterre was filled with hundreds of bulbs brought specially from Holland. In the 1960s it was one of the first garden restoration projects of the National Trust, who turned to the original account books and planted seventeenth-century varieties of espaliered apples with evocative names: Court Pendu Plat, Calville Blanc d'Hiver, Golden Reinette and Catshead.

Dutch gardens broke up wide spaces into happily crowded enclosures, with trellises and hedges and curling parterres mirroring the grilles of the popular ironwork gates. When Celia Fiennes rode across England in 1697, she found this pattern everywhere, even at stately Woburn, which boasted 'all sorts of pots and flowers and Curious greens, fine orange, Cittron and Lemon trees and myrtles, stiped ffileroy [probably the popular *Phyllyrea latifolia*] and ye fine aloes plant'. And it suited smaller gardens, too. In the little spa of Epsom Celia visited Mrs Booth, who had a walled garden, 'the breadth of the dwelling-house, the dining room and drawing room look into it', where she had managed to pack in a small canal between two mounts, and had trained apricot, peach, plum and nectarines in fans, with cherries, stripped of their lower branches, forming arches between them. Just down the road lived Mrs Steevens, who 'has a very pretty neat house and gardens', with six grass walks, 'guarded by dwarfe fruit trees'. From the main walk her visitors strolled through gates in a palisade of painted and gilded ironwork into another garden where there were cleverly cut areas of grass (*parterre à l'Anglaise*), box-edged knot gardens filled with flowers, smart topiary, and 'on the left side a coddling hedge secures a walk of orange and lemmon trees in perfection'.

The orange and lemon trees, admired since Elizabethan times, now really came into their own. In winter, proud owners carried their trees carefully into glasshouses, which were no longer merely glassed-in shelters against the wall but heated by the new stoves developed in Holland. Evelyn had suggested this in 1670 and he was particularly impressed by Henry Capel's new glasshouses at Kew, the 'orangerie and Myrtelum', which were 'most beautiful and perfectly well-kept'. As the century wore on the glasshouses filled with other tender plants – jasmine and oleanders, myrtles and pomegranates – and became elegant, decorative buildings to entertain guests amid the steamy fragrance. One of the most prized features of Burlington's Chiswick garden in the 1720s was the charming Orange Tree Garden, with its obelisk and pool in the centre and little temple behind.

Topiary, or 'Curious greens', was another Dutch passion. The yews and hollies were clipped into more fantastic shapes than ever before, with simple balls or pyramids giving way to birds and beasts and crowns and sailing ships. That said, one of the most enduring topiary gardens in Britain, at Levens Hall in Cumbria, was not designed by a Dutchman but by the French gardener Guillaume Beaumont in the 1690s. Several of the old trees may have lasted since then and Levens itself has hardly changed – the story is that a gypsy woman cursed the house, saying there would be no male heir until the river stopped flowing and a white faun was born. And, certainly, for centuries – until, indeed, a frost stopped the stream and a white faun was born – the owners were women with no funds for garden improvements. There have only been ten head gardeners since Beaumont himself, most of them working there for decades into extreme old age. Perhaps the Westmoreland air kept them going (and apparently it's easier to clip box if the shears are wet). The topiary was added to in the nineteenth century and the trees have burgeoned into huge, bizarre bumps and towers, casting weird shadows over the low box hedges.

French and Dutch and Italian styles blended into a combination that could be transplanted with ease to any country home or castle, however distant – one of the finest, now reconstructed, was the demesne of canals, formal parterres and wilderness surrounding Antrim Castle in Northern Ireland. But for planning and planting on the grand scale professionals were required and the founding of Brompton Park Nursery in 1681 answered this need. This nursery exercised a virtual monopoly for years. It was massive, spreading across a hundred acres in Kensington, in the area now ruled by the V&A and the Natural History and Science Museums. Its founders had all been gardeners to the nobility – Joseph Looker (or Lucre) to the queen, Moses Cook to Arthur Capel, Earl of Essex, and John Field to the Earl of Bedford – while the youngest partner, George London, had been apprenticed to Charles II's gardener, John Rose, and had worked for the famous plant collector, Bishop Compton, in Fulham.

Their first big project was Longleat in Wiltshire but in 1685, with the founders now dead or retired, George London joined forces with a new partner, Henry Wise. London and Wise had perfect connections among the Whig magnates, brilliant publicity (John Evelyn devoted pages to their praise in *The Compleat Gard'ner* of 1693) and stupendous energy. London rode across country lugging his maps and plans, and wooing high-born clients from Yorkshire to Cornwall, carrying metropolitan fashions to the regions. From the Brompton nursery trees and shrubs, clipped yews and hollies and osier baskets of bulbs and flowers were sent out by carrier and cart and barge. For twenty years London and Wise built pools and cascades, and planted mile upon mile of avenues and hedged walks. Millionaires by today's standards, they worked on all the major gardens, including Chatsworth, Badminton, Melbourne and Blenheim. Under their regime the grand vistas and formal parterres continued to hold sway – but already the tide of taste was shifting. Change was on the way.

THE TEMPLE.

12

Arcadia

WHEN QUEEN ANNE CAME to the throne in 1702 she told Henry Wise to take out the elaborate parterres in the Fountain Garden at Hampton Court, so the story goes, because she could not bear the smell of box: a more likely reason was her determination not to overspend on her gardens, as William III had done. The cost of grand formality was horrific. Hundreds of labourers were needed to plant the trees, to move the soil, to build the bastions; hordes of weeding women to keep the beds spruce; scores of seasonal labourers to pick the fruit from the great orchards; tens of skilled mowers to scythe the grassy walks and beat them smooth; dozens of boys to plant bulbs by the thousand – at Blenheim the Brompton Court nursery planted 1600 elms in the avenues, ordered half a million bricks for the walls of the massive kitchen garden and supplied 18,500 yellow crocuses alone, as well as tulips and anemones and narcissi. Even rolling the gravel could become a neoclassical Labour of Hercules – John Evelyn noted that the best rollers 'are made of the hardest marble, and such as are procured from the ruines of many places in Smyrna when old columns of Antiquities [are] being saw'd off'.

Luckily for aristocratic purses, tastes were changing. The landed class had felt the impact of the Continental wars severely and as new land taxes were brought in to pay the armies, small estates suffered and were often swallowed up by great ones. Landowners could not afford the labour to maintain the avenues and parterres, and when the topiary planted by their fathers grew too big and blocked the view they simply chopped it down. It was expensive, too, to keep the lush fruit trees in tip-top condition. In 1718, when William Cotesworth, the owner of Park House in Gateshead, was in London, his friend Colonel Liddell was supervising some alterations: if he hadn't feared offending the head gardener, declared the colonel, 'I would have whipt over with my Gardner and pruned all your trees and have slasht them rarely – I know you would have thanked me two years hence.'

It was time for a more natural style. Here the drive for economy was combined with a new 'patriotic aesthetic'. Since the Act of Union with Scotland of 1707, Britain felt it deserved a cultural style of its own, one that linked it to the classical past but was more informal than the absolutist court styles of Europe. At the same time the cost of the wars of the past twenty years had shifted power from the court to Parliament and the City, and the whole atmosphere of debate was changing; the 1690s saw the founding of the Bank of England and the first national newspapers; public opinion began to matter and the chatter of coffee houses cut across the classes. One of the subjects they talked about was gardening. 'Our British Gardeners,' wrote Joseph Addison in a much quoted essay in the *Spectator* in 1712, 'instead of humouring Nature, love to deviate from it as much as possible. Our Trees rise in Cones, Globes and Pyramids. We see the marks of the Scissars upon every Plant and Bush.' Give him a tree in its natural form any day, he claimed, rather than one 'cut into a Mathematical Figure', and an orchard in bloom compared with 'all the little labyrinths of the most finished parterre'.

'I may be singular in my opinion,' Addison wrote rather proudly, but he was not singular at all. The twenty-five-year-old Alexander Pope slashed away at topiary in an essay in late September 1713 for Addison and Steele's new periodical, the *Guardian*, which ends with a 'Catalogue of Greens to be disposed of by an Eminent town-Gardiner':

> *Adam* and *Eve* in Yew; Adam a little shattr'd by the fall of the Tree of Knowledge in the great Storm; Eve and the Serpent very flourishing.
> *St George in Box*; his Arm scarce long enough, but will be in a Condition to stick the Dragon by next *April* . . .

It was evident, decided Pope, that 'Persons of genius' liked nature, whereas 'People of the Common Level of Understanding are principally delighted with the little Niceties and Fantastical Operations of Art'. He knew 'an eminent Cook', he sneered, 'who beautified his Country Seat with a Coronation Dinner in Greens'. Haven't we heard this tone before in Francis Bacon and his disdain for 'pastry cook' knots? And it is there in Pepys's diary, when he turns up his nose at the 'Cockney Gardens and plotts', which look as if made of 'past board and March pane [marzipan], and smell more of paynt than of flowers and verdure'. Now that topiary was in every shopkeeper's backyard, the only thing for a man of taste to do was to turn his back.

With the new Hanoverian dynasty in 1714 came the birth of a different, very British, Arcadia. The following year the professional gardener Stephen Switzer, who had worked at Brompton Park, called for a 'Natural Rural' style of gardening. In the 1720s the cry was taken up by another professional, Batty Langley, when he asked, 'is there any Thing more shocking than a *stiff regular garden*?' But the change did not happen all at once: formal gardens continued to be made throughout the century, and the actual plans that Switzer and Langley published are full of stiff designs (Part I of Langley's book was actually titled 'Of Geometry').

Ideas of what was natural differed. What we now call 'landscape gardening' would move, roughly, through three phases in this century; the straightforward softening of formality and opening of the garden to the country; then a pictorial, classical, allusive style; and finally the radical parkland of Capability Brown and his followers. In the first phase people still clung to the idea of the garden as separate from the wild – Switzer promoted 'belt' or 'ribbon walks' leading through different scenes, with clumps of trees, decorative buildings and views. But the clear boundary wall between garden and fields was already disappearing with the introduction of the sunken ditch or ha-ha (so astonishing at the time, said Horace Walpole, that 'the common people called them Ha! Ha's! to express their surprise at finding a sudden and unperceived check to their walk'). Beaumont used this at Levens Hall in the 1690s and Charles Bridgeman, soon to be royal gardener, made it a key feature at Stowe in 1714.

The Ha-ha.

Fountains and grottoes gave way to curving ponds and S-shaped serpentine streams (the actual Serpentine in London's Hyde Park was created in the 1730s), and designers also began to exploit every rise and dip and striking feature. Vanbrugh liked to set his dramatic buildings on 'eminences', like the Temple of the Four Winds at Castle Howard in Yorkshire, and at Blenheim he tried vainly to persuade the Duchess of

Malborough to keep the ruined manor: it would make 'one of the most agreeable objects that the best of landscrip painters can invent', he pleaded.

As these gardens were seen more and more as works of art to be admired, so references to landscape painting crept increasingly into discussions. Addison had already suggested that by planting trees, opening up views into nearby cornfields and improving by a little art 'the natural embroidery of the Meadows', 'a Man might make a pretty Landskip of his own Possessions'. But then, 'At that moment,' wrote Horace Walpole, looking back to his youth, 'appeared Kent, painter enough to taste the charms of landscape, bold and opinionated enough to dare and to dictate':

> He leaped the fence and saw that all nature was a garden. He felt the delicious contrast of hill and valley changing imperceptibly into each other, tasted the beauty of the gentle swell, or concave scoop, and remarked how loose groves crowned an easy eminence with happy ornament. . . . Thus dealing in none but the colours of natures, and catching its most favourable features, men saw a new creation opening before their eyes. The living landscape was chastened and polished, not transformed.

William Kent was far from solely responsible for creating the British landscape garden, but Walpole was right to see him as a trendsetter, since he helped to create a particular garden ideal that gripped the contemporary imagination. Kent was a burly Yorkshireman painting in Rome where he met Richard Boyle, third Earl of Burlington, then on his Grand Tour. After Burlington's second trip to Italy in 1719 the two men returned home together. Kent lived at Burlington House until his death in 1748 and their relationship, and that of later coteries of gardeners (including the gossipy, flamboyant Walpole), lends depth to the feeling that gardens were a refuge and often a kind of code for men who had secrets, sexual or political or both. The taciturn Burlington, for example, was a leading

Whig aristocrat and dictator of taste, yet had deeply hidden Jacobite loyalties.

The new mood in gardens was also coloured by admiration for seventeenth-century painters like Poussin, who filled his luminous landscapes with groves of trees, gleaming rivers, temples and processions, and this influence was soon intensified by the different forms of romantic wildness British patrons discovered in the paintings of Salvator Rosa and Claude Lorrain. At Burlington's new Palladian villa in Chiswick, which had only recently had its fine formal avenues, canal and orangery installed, Kent swept away some of the groves to make a spreading lawn with a circular hedge and statues in niches (a shape known as an *exedra*). He also 'serpentised' the canal into a winding river, made a cascade within a specially built ruin and thinned the trees to give tantalising glimpses beyond.

Such gardens, alas, proved just as costly as formal parterres and work at Chiswick came to an end in 1738, when Burlington's debts reached over £200,000. But Kent also worked on Lord Cobham's gardens at Stowe, following in the footsteps of Vanbrugh and Bridgeman. This astounding garden tells a story. The powerful Cobham, fallen from grace and now leader of the opposition, used every aspect of his estate to declare his staunch Whig loyalty to the Protestant Succession of 1688, celebrating the heroes of English 'liberty', the old Saxon worthies as well as the humanistic ideals of ancient Greece and Rome. His gardens were an ostentatious display of wealth, hugely labour-intensive, employing hundreds of men over many years to remould the landscape, digging lakes and hills and building temples. Here, in a sheltered valley, Kent laid out the 'Elysian Fields', complete with a rushing River Styx. Nearby he placed a Temple of Ancient Virtue, standing opposite a ruined Temple of Modern Virtue, to show the corruption of the age, and a Temple of British Worthies, with statues of Elizabeth I, Drake, William III, Milton and Newton.

All the different scenes in a garden like this were planned for entertainment. Guests could be taken on a tour, which was why the circular layout of paths was important, a circuit on which you might stop at a temple to take tea, or read the inscriptions, or gaze at the view through a telescope. After dinner coffee might be served in the rotunda, or special boating expeditions arranged on the lake, while the gentlemen could take a cold plunge in a special Roman-style pool. Stowe was the 'garden circuit' par excellence, the first British garden to have a guidebook.

At Rousham, near Oxford, Kent planned another landscape circuit, but here he had no political programme to follow. Instead, he reworked Bridgeman's earlier designs into the extraordinary groves and walks we can still follow today, using every slope of the ridge along the sinuous bank of the river to create surprises and mystery. A narrow serpentine rill runs through the wood into an octagonal pool, then down to the huge pond in the 'Vale of Venus' where shoals of goldfish dart among the water-lilies. An arcaded Roman 'praeneste' in golden stone looks down across the river to the misty fields beyond. From the bowling green on top of the slope (now

William Kent's drawing of the cascade in the Vale of Venus at Rousham shows his romantic use of slopes, streams and luxuriant trees.

a croquet lawn) it's hard not to laugh with delight at the Gothic 'eye-catcher' on the hill across the vale. But Kent's touch is felt most strongly in the trees framing the view, the contrast between different shades and textures of green, the subtle use of water. 'Adieu to canals, circular basons and cascades tumbling down marble steps,' wrote Walpole admiringly 'The gentle stream was taught to serpentine seemingly at its pleasure.' Kent was a painter in gardens, a master of mood.

Part of the joy of visiting Rousham is that although Kent's groves seem held in a timeless spell, the garden as a whole has grown with the centuries. Behind a thick yew hedge and brick wall lies the old kitchen garden: in June 2003, spied through the wrought-iron gate, four peacocks paraded between a tumbling double border rich with the scent of honeysuckle. Gardens never stand still.

In the eighteenth century gardens like Rousham, or Euston Hall in Suffolk, encouraged men in the illusion that they were retiring from the corruptions of the town to a rural scene imbued with innocence – the pastoral life Virgil recommended in the *Georgics*, and Horace in his odes. Although it was relatively small compared with a country estate, Alexander Pope's garden at Twickenham, which he began in 1719 and worked on for the next thirty years, was typical of this Arcadian vision. It had a formal grove of lime trees, two small mounts, urns and statues, and the famous tunnel grotto, and eventually a line of cypresses leading to an obelisk, a memorial to his mother. Into his five acres he also packed a lawn (his 'bowling green'), a vineyard, a kitchen garden and fruit trees, and 'stoves' where he grew pineapples.

Amateur gardeners with wealth and panache shared this pastoral dream, retiring either to a garden or to a 'farm'. Often they were men who for some reason were excluded from the public sphere. After the disaster of the South Sea Bubble the prickly Chancellor of the Exchequer, John Aislabie, was sent to the Tower. Once out, he skulked home to Yorkshire to turn his estate at Studley Royal into one of the most famous gardens of the age, with its beautiful 'Moon Ponds', planes of water against a backdrop of trees framing a temple and a vista crowned by the ruins of Fountains Abbey. Far to the south, at Wooburn near Weybridge, in the 1730s the Catholic Philip Southcote, barred from office by his religion, transformed the land around his farm into an ornamental garden, a *ferme ornée*. At West Wycombe Sir Francis Dashwood, founder of the 'Hell-Fire Club', made a garden in the shape of Leda and the swan – the lake was swan-shaped and the garden's central point was the Mound of Venus, its temple rising above a grotto called 'The Gate of Life'.

For others gardening was a way in, not out. The banker Henry Hoare laid claim to the old aristocratic culture by devoting thirty years and a fabulous fortune to perfecting his beautiful setting at Stourhead in Wiltshire, with its Virgilian walk around his new lake. The path led from temple to temple among the trees, with a series of scenes that the educated stroller would recognise as quotations from the *Aeneid*. The grotto, or Nymphaeum, was Virgil's underworld and the crowning glory was his chief temple, the Pantheon, filled with statues of heroes and thinkers. Just as Aeneas had built Rome, Hoare implied, so he had created this landscape kingdom. He and his friend and fellow enthusiast, Charles Hamilton, who lavished all his money on his garden at Painshill, were among the most faithful followers of the idyllic landscapes of Poussin and Salvator Rosa. In

Stourhead, sketched by S.H. Grimm in 1790.

Scotland, too, landowners began to see through the eyes of the artists. Sir John Clerk, of Penicuik in Midlothian, had been gardening from the start of the century but after a trip south around 1735 he changed his approach, turning his estate into a *ferme ornée*, with a bastion and high wooded walks. He redesigned his park to contain classical and poetic allusions, which could be followed on a circular walk, as at Longleat, and incorporated some of the same elements as Hoare, contrasting the pastoral landscape to a dark grotto, deliberately recalling the cave of the Cumaean Sibyl.

Less well-off folk also sank all their wealth into their gardens. One of these was the benignly eccentric William Shenstone in Staffordshire. His parents died when he was young; he was shy, depressive and gawky. At twenty-one he gave up the idea of the Church, and dedicated himself to his garden at the Leasowes, near Halesowen. Here the required rural walk led the visitor through different enclosures, offering constant 'surprises', marked by statues, obelisks and plaques garlanded with classical inscriptions. One of Shenstone's gardening friends was Henrietta, Lady Luxborough. Half-French, the half-sister of Viscount Bolingbroke, Henrietta was older, grander, livelier, but she had separated from her husband – not the thing to do – and lived away from society at Barrells, near Henley-in-Arden: gardening always cheered her up, and friendly neighbours supplied seeds and cuttings and gossip. Her letters to Shenstone over the years are full of shared enthusiasms, new books, visits to the gardens of others. Both saw themselves as picturesque hermits in their rural retreats.

And while great gardens like Rousham or Stourhead were 'works of art', quite separate from the house, when this kind of gardening was applied on a smaller scale, something interesting happened to the relation between house and garden. The perspective of the landscape garden demanded not that you look *down* on patterns, as in Tudor and Jacobean gardens, but actually walked *through* a series of pictures. As the century wore on, the main rooms were increasingly on ground level, and their doors and windows opened directly on to the artistically arranged 'natural' world outside.

13

The citizen's box

THE SUPPOSEDLY NATURAL gardens of the early eighteenth century were as full of conceits and elliptical codes as the elaborate gardens of the Stuarts. It was the dawn of garden visiting and the tourists certainly needed a guidebook to appreciate the glories of Stourhead or Stowe. But the allusions were not only classical: the new aesthetic language of 'old Albion' enshrined in Britain's medieval past was also creeping into the garden. The first Gothic garden building, 'Alfred's Hall', was constructed in the 1720s by Pope's friend, Lord Bathurst, at Cirencester Park, and priories and rustic temples followed. In the 1730s Kent built a summer house called 'Merlin's Cave' for Queen Caroline at Richmond Lodge at Kew, complete with wax figures of famous Britons and a turf-covered hermitage occupied by a real hermit, the 'thresher poet' Stephen Duck. Ironically, Duck had won fame by attacking fashionable pastorals and now here he was, writing poems for the queen about blissful bowers and nymphs: a few years later he drowned himself in a fit of despair. Poor Caroline was mocked for her gardening passion and her lack of taste. Yet the hermitages spread relentlessly, though not always successfully: Hamilton's resident hermit at Painshill went on strike after three weeks.

A little later, in 1748, Mrs Delany described Lord Orrery's garden near Dublin where, in an acre of shrubs and 'little winding walks',

> is placed an hermit's cell, made of the roots of trees, the floor is paved with pebbles, there is a couch made of matting and little wooden stools, a table with a manuscript on it, a pair of spectacles, a leathern bottle . . . *Four little gardens surround his house* – an orchard, a flower-garden, a physick-garden, and a kitchen garden, with a kitchen to boil a teakettle or so: I never saw so pretty *a whim so thoroughly well* executed.

With a sigh of pleasure she summed up the mood that inspired this whole landscape movement: 'the rurality of it', she wrote, 'is wonderfully pretty.'

These artificially arranged rural landscapes with their ruins and hermitages could indeed seem rather absurd. This was especially true when devotees lacked the spreading acres and tried to cram all their features into a small space. By mid-century the fashion for serpentine walks and classical inscriptions, as well as pretty rococo gazebos and hermit's cells, was reaching the aspiring middle classes. Thomas Wright ('the Wizard of Durham') published an enticing pattern book of summer houses and arbours in 1755, and three years later added one on grottoes, described by John Harris as 'the most beautiful and rarest of all 18th century garden pattern books'. Almost inevitably, the intelligentsia and the quality turned against the Arcadian ideal. It had become debased, they felt, a language of the suburbs, as topiary had been a generation before.

A different kind of garden owner, agog to imitate the glories they saw, had slowly emerged during this century. As long ago as 1715 Stephen

'An Ornithon, or Arbour of the Aviary Kind, Chiefly contrived for the Reception of singing and other beautiful Birds', from Thomas Wright, *Universal Architecture*, 1755. The arbour should be made of 'rugged Timbers of Oak, the more fantastical and robust the better', with a thatched roof, finished inside with ivy and moss, and the floor 'may be either Sand, Gravel or Pebbles agreeable to the Builder's Fancy'.

Switzer had addressed himself to a new emerging class: the merchants, parliamentarians and civil servants whose work kept them in London but who longed to escape the stench of the crowded streets, especially in summer. A decade later Defoe declared with astonishment, 'How many noble seats, superior to the palaces of sovereign princes, do we see erected within a few miles of London, by *tradesmen*.' Some, he said, 'still taste of London' and 'live both in the city and in the country at the same time'.

Over the years these 'middling classes' had come to associate the suburbs with health, clean air and water. There were efforts to make the cities green – Soho Square in London, Old Square in Birmingham and Queen Square in Bath all had gravel paths, geometrical grass plots, flowering shrubs and clipped trees. Some people pleaded for these to be more informal: 'I think some sort of Wilderness Work will do much better,' wrote Thomas Fairchild in 1721, 'and divert the Gentry better than looking out of their Windows upon an open Figure.' Gradually the hard lines were softened and tall elms and flowering shrubs began to spread in the little enclosures. Fairchild was the first to address himself to town-dwellers, and the title page of his book, *The City Gardener* (seen at the start of this chapter), shows his own nursery, with its parterres, new greenhouses and tubs of exotics. In 1691, Fairchild also produced the first recorded hybrid by pollination, crossing a gillyflower with a sweet-william to breed what was mockingly-called 'Fairchild's Mule', a sensation in its day, ancestor of the modern border carnation.

Some wealthy folk began to buy flower gardens (a grand form of allotments) on the edge of the city, with summer houses in place and water laid on. And from the 1730s little spas and pleasure gardens blossomed around London. The most famous was Vauxhall, but there were many others, where the emphasis was firmly on the rural. At Bagnigge Wells, for example, there were several walks:

> ornamented with a great variety of curious shrubs and flowers, all in utmost perfection. About the centre of the garden is a small round fish-pond, in the midst of which is a curious fountain, representing Cupid bestriding a swan, which spouts the water through its beak to a great height. Round this place, and indeed over the whole garden, are genteel seats for company . . .

The White Conduitt House, Islington, offered gardens with a fish pond, and boxes adorned with paintings, but especially 'a most agreeable view of the metropolis'. (Hampstead and Belsize Park had rather a bad name for gallantry and were to be avoided by 'ladies who value their reputation'.)

There were, of course, still numerous private gardens in the heart of the city and many were laid out on formal lines, like old Roman gardens, in keeping with the Georgian respect for the classics, with rows of pots and straight box-edged borders filled with special flowers, as strongly scented as possible, to disguise the city smells: myrtle, mignonette, damask roses and honeysuckle. In the early eighteenth century the special varieties known as 'florists' flowers' (which star in a later chapter of this book as the flowers of the industrial artisan) were still newly fashionable, prestigious and expensive: tulips, auriculas, carnations, pinks, anemones, polyanthus, hyacinth and ranunculus, a kind of ornamental buttercup. These groups of flowers, had become popular by 1683, when Samuel Gilbert published his book *The Florist's Vade Mecum*: by the end of the seventeenth century there were already over 800 named ranunculi, for example, their colour ranging from pale yellow to deep purple, plain and mottled and streaked.

While the beds were filled with stiff but sweet-scented blooms, the plots were also ornamented by clipped shrubs and fruit trees and lead statues, often with a bold feature at the end like an arbour or obelisk. These precious spaces were cherished even more as the eighteenth century progressed and began to reflect the new landscape style, with curving walks, untrained trees and rustic arches. Todd Langstaffe-Gowan, writing on London gardens, quotes Mrs Delany indignantly rebutting the idea that her garden there was not up to her sister's in the country, even if keeping it spruce was hard work:

> You think, madam, I have no garden, perhaps? But that's a mistake; I *have one* as big as your parlour in Gloucester, and in it groweth *damask-roses*, stocks variegated and plain, some purple, some red, *pinks, Phillaria*, some dead some alive; and *honeysuckles* that never blow. But when you come to town to weed and water it, it shall be improved after the new taste, but till then it shall remain disheveled and undrest.

Mrs Delany, like gardeners before and since, could never resist a beautiful new plant even if she had no room for it: when she visited the botanist Dr Fothergill in Essex, she moaned that she 'crammed my tin box with exotics, overpowered with such variety I knew not what to chuse!'. She was not the only extravagant town gardener: Eliza Robertson's bills for her 'improvements' at her house in the Paragon, Blackheath, were so huge that she was arrested. This big spending was excellent news for the nursery gardens springing up all over town: there were already fifteen nurseries in London in the late seventeenth century and at least one in all the large provincial towns.

The longing for more space and fresher air drove many Londoners out of town. Successful actors and artists bought houses in the suburbs. William Hogarth had a small house in Chiswick, with a long lawn, an alley to play skittles or bowls and a huge mulberry tree, beneath which the children from the Foundling Hospital, of which he was a governor, came to play on sunny afternoons. David Garrick, the greatest star of the contemporary stage, had a villa at Hampton, complete with a riverside temple devoted to Shakespeare. Richer men – merchants, lawyers, bankers – built more substantial mansions. The ideal was a large house on a hill with a fine view, like Streatham Park, owned by Dr Johnson's friends, the Thrales (Henry Thrale ran a brewery in Southwark). Gradually many merchants made these country houses their main home, but while they wanted to live like aristocrats they did not want the burden of huge estates: they had no intention of giving up their profitable trades, shifting their capital into land and abandoning the proud traditions of their class. They merely wanted large, park-like gardens.

These were men for whom the new experts wrote. There was no need, Switzer said, to level hills or build canals, or to spend money on wall building or labour-intensive topiary. One could ignore the 'Clipt Plants, Flowers and other trifling Decorations fit only for little Town-gardens, and not for the expansive Tracts of the Country'. Here, all that was needed were woods, coppices and groves, a smart kitchen garden on the elegant lines Batty Langley suggested, and a 'small' cultivated area of around twenty acres looking out on to the country beyond, with its pretty – but profitably productive – woods and cornfields.

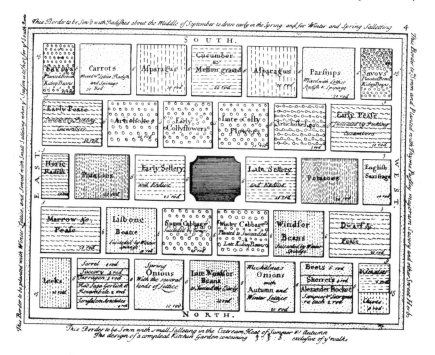

Batty Langley's plan for 'a compleat kitchen garden'.

Batty Langley's books, too, had some handy ideas on how to create a suburban Arcadia, including short-cuts for classical vistas:

> Views of the *Ruins of Buildings*, after the *old Roman Manner*, to terminate such Walks that end in *disagreeable Objects*; which Ruins may either be *painted upon Canvas*, or actually built in the manner with *Brick* and cover'd with *Plaistering* in Imitation of Stone.

By the mid-eighteenth century lesser tradesmen, professionals and shopkeepers were buying 'boxes' on roads out of London, which they remodelled and called 'Villas'. Satirical prints showed merchants with fat wives, living in tiny villas crammed with outrageous items of latest fashion in very bad taste. The new suburban dwellers were seeking a dream pastoral. Dr Johnson, in *The Idler*, introducing an essay on the vanity of human wishes, tells the story of a tradesman who

> thought himself rich enough to have a lodging in the country, like the mercers of Ludgate Hill . . . I found him at Islington, in a room which overlooked the high road, amusing himself with looking through the window, which the clouds of dust would not suffer him to open. He embraced me, told me I was welcome into the country, and asked me, if I did not feel myself refreshed.

What these critics really attacked was aping the genteel. There was already much derision about the comically poor quality of pretentious garden statues – acidly mocked in Hogarth's prints – although the statues

Matthew Darly, *The Flower Garden*, 1777, satirising extravagant horticultural coiffure.

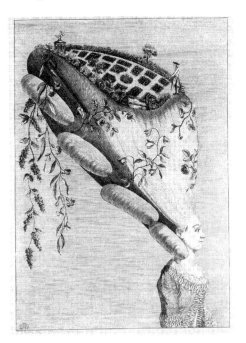

did improve when the redoubtable Eleanor Coade set up her artificial stone company in the 1770s. In the same decade, when the flower-garden craze coincided with the maddest height of hair-dos, Hannah More claimed to see 'eleven damsels' at a dinner, with 'amongst them, on their heads, an acre and a half of shrubbery besides slopes, grass plats, tulip beds, clumps of peonies, kitchen gardens and green houses'.

In the mid-eighteenth century the young, well-heeled metropolitan wags quickly pitched into the fierce battles about taste, especially the satiric papers, the *Connoisseur* and *St James's Gazette*. Rather like our modern imitations of estate agent language they indulged in a fierce mock pastoral. Here is one villa:

> pleasantly situated about three miles from London, on one side of a public road, from which it is separated by a dry ditch, over which is a little bridge, consisting of two narrow planks leading to the house. The hedge on the other side of the road cuts off all prospect whatever, except from the garrets, from whence indeed you have a very fine vista of two men hanging in chains on Kennington Common.

In the house is a spanking new portrait of the lady in the parlour, 'in the habit of a shepherdess, smelling of a nosegay and stroking a ram with gilt horns'. This association of pretension with the feminine, and with the acquisitive, dominating voice of 'her indoors', would also be an enduring element of anti-suburban mockery.

In 1753 the new periodical, *The World*, started by a circle of virtuosi including the Earl of Chesterfield and Horace Walpole, led a sustained attack on imitators of Kent, personified by 'Squire Mushroom, the present worthy possessor of Block-hill', who has made his fortune and bought 'a VILLA'. Taken with the rage for taste, he has a 'yellow serpentine river, stagnating through a beautiful valley, which extends near twenty yards in length', a Chinese bridge, a 'grove perplexed with errors and crooked walks', a hermitage and 'pompous clumsy and gilded building said to be a temple and consecrated to Venus; for no other reason which I could learn, but because the squire riots here sometimes in vulgar love with a couple of orange wenches, taken from the purlieus of the theatre'. All these clichés appear too in the nouveau-riche Mr Sterling's garden in Garrick and Coleman's play *The Clandestine Marriage*, as he shows off 'my walks and slopes, and my clumps and my bride and my flow'ring trees and my bed of Dutch tulips' to the astonished Lord Ogle. Even the ruins are here: 'Ay, ruins, my Lord! And they are reckoned very fine ones too. You would think them ready to tumble on your head. It has just cost me a hundred and fifty pounds to put my ruins in thorough repair. – This way, if your Lordship pleases.'

Many Lords no longer chose to go this way. Turning their backs on the temples, they reverted to the pure and simple – and productive – landscape.

14
———

Miller & Co.

THE GARDENER'S GAZE NOW reached to far horizons. Henry Compton, Bishop of London for forty years from 1675 to 1713, packed his Fulham garden with over a thousand rarities, using his missionaries as plant hunters. The most successful, John Baptist Banister, sent back many plants from Virginia, especially trees, including the 'sweet bay' (*Magnolia virginiana*, Britain's first magnolia) and a black walnut, which was photographed in 1894, its girth reaching seventeen feet. Banister himself died at thirty-two, falling to his death, or being accidentally shot – the stories vary – while collecting on the banks of the Roanoke river.

Medical men were quick to experiment with the new plants. In 1673 the Worshipful Society of Apothecaries had leased a riverside site among the market gardens of Chelsea and in 1722 the wealthy doctor, Hans Sloane, who had once been an apprentice here and now owned the manor, handed over the lease of the Chelsea Physic Garden to the Society in perpetuity, for an annual payment of £5. Fifty samples of dried plants were to be given to the Royal Society each year, a collection now in the Natural History Museum: many are the first record of cultivation in Britain.

Sloane also recommended a new gardener, Philip Miller, a market gardener's son who ran a nursery in St George's Fields south of the Thames. The Oxford Physic Garden and the Edinburgh Botanic Garden, founded in 1670, were by now important centres for the exchange of plants, but in his half-century reign Miller made Chelsea the leader, corresponding with plant collectors and experts in Europe and America. A solid, red-faced man, Miller was combative and difficult (so many gardeners are!), but a brilliant experimental gardener who grew pawpaw and melons and pineapples, and nurtured plants from across the globe. All his practical knowledge was poured into his *Gardener's Dictionary*, the bible of eighteenth-century plantsmen and the ancestor of all later horticultural encyclopaedias: it ran though sixteen editions before 1830, and was translated into Dutch, German and French, and each printing was updated to include newly cultivated plants. Compared with the rich, poetic descriptions of Parkinson, his prose was a model of sense, infused by the belief in reason and experiment of this new century.

Miller was one of the group who joined the Quaker draper, Peter Collinson (who had his own botanical garden at Mill Hill), in sponsoring the Philadelphia Quaker, farmer and self-taught botanist John Bartram to collect plants for them. Soon Bartram was commissioned to send twenty boxes a year, being paid five guineas a box: he continued his plant gathering for over thirty years until the start of the American War of Independence. The consortium that funded him also included Sir Hans Sloane, Dr John Fothergill (yet another Quaker), the Duke of Richmond and the rich young Lord Petre, an outstanding collector who began when he inherited his estate at fifteen: when he died, tragically young, at twenty-nine, 200,000 plants were sold from his Thorndon estate. About 2000 new species came from Bartram's boxes, including phlox and helianthus, the first ceanothus, balsam fir and the luscious evergreen *Magnolia grandiflora*, which he found

16. (*above*) *The Topiary Arcades and George II Column, Hartwell House* by Balthazar Nebot, c.1738.

17. (*left*) *Pineapple Grown in Sir Matthew Decker's Garden, Richmond, Surrey, 1720* by Theodorus Netscher.

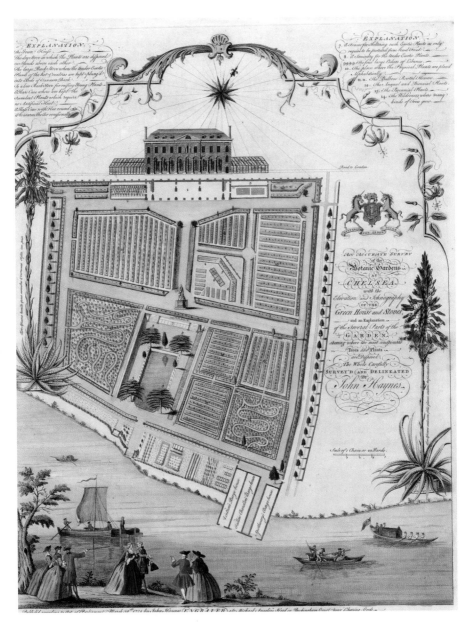

18. Plan of Chelsea Physic Garden, engraved by John Haynes, 1751.

19. (*top*) Vegetable Garden, detail of *Panoramic View of Charlton Park*, c.1745 by Thomas Robins.

20. (*above*) *Chiswick, View of the Orange Tree Garden*, Pieter Andreas Rysbrack, 1728-32.

21. (*top left*) *In the Library, St. James' Square, Bristol* attributed to Thomas Pole c.1805-6.
22. (*top right*) *St. James' Square, Bristol: The Potting House*, attributed to Thomas Pole c.1805-6.

23. (*left*) *Back Garden of Mr. Paul Sandby's House at 4 St. George's Row, Tyburn*, c. 1773 by Paul Sandby.
24. (*above*) *Shewing a Garden*, engraved by Isaac Cruikshank after George Woodward, 1796.

25. (*top*) *Conversation Piece before a House in Monument Lane*, c.1780 by W. Williams.
26. (*above*) *Pierrepont House, Nottingham*, c. 1708-13, English School.

27. (*left*)
Melbourne Hall,
Derbyshire.
28. (*below*)
Studley Royal,
Yorkshire.

29 – 30. Overlay (*above*), showing planned improvements to The White Lodge, Richmond Park (*top*), from Repton's *Fragments on the Theory and Practice of Landscape Gardening*, 1816.

31. Flower paper mosaic of *Physalis*, Winter Cherry, by Mrs Delany, 1770s.

in South Carolina. The excitement must have been boundless – imagine watching a magnolia unfurling its great buds against the glossy dark leaves for the first time, or seeing the white and crimson camellias which flowered at the Thorndon greenhouse in 1739.

Other colourful garden favourites came from the Americas: the azure morning-glory, the rudbeckia, 'Black-eyed Susan', the glamorous Turks-cap lily, the sweet-smelling heliotrope and elegant purple *Verbena bonariensis*. And all the time new plants were also arriving from the East and from the Cape. Between 1730 and 1770 the number of species grown at Chelsea rose from 1000 to 5000. Among the new plants were heleniums, phlox, cornus, helianthemums and evening primrose. Some helped with common ailments, like *Gaultheria procumbens*, which gave us oil of wintergreen to ease sore muscles. Others later proved even more valuable, like *Catharanthus roseus*, the source of major anti-leukaemia drugs.

Miller and Collinson offered seeds to good nurseries, particularly James Gordon of the Mile End Nursery to the east of London, who had been Lord Petre's gardener and was gifted at germinating the seeds of newly arrived problem plants, like kalmia, gingko, gardenia and the Tree of Heaven. In 1760 James Lee and Lewis Kennedy started another great nursery in Shepherd's Bush to the west. The nurserymen's beautifully decorated and illustrated catalogues were themselves works of reference which helped the plants to spread across the land. In the 1720s the yearly seed bills of Henry Ellison and his brother-in-law Carr from Northumberland showed that they placed orders in London not only for bulbs from Holland, 'sweet-scented peas' and carnations, but for 'Battersea cabbage', 'Hackney', 'Cockermuth' and 'Early Dutch' turnips, 'Brown Dutch' lettuce. One letter requested 'lettuce and cucumber seed from Turkey, Melon from Marseilles and some Dutch Asparagus . . . There is a new fashion'd Melon called (I think) Cantaloup.'

Gardeners could not wait to get new seeds. Many common garden flowers were grown in Britain for the first time, including asters and coreopsis and phlox from North America, giving late-summer colour, after the native flowers had finished. The fuchsia arrived from Central and South

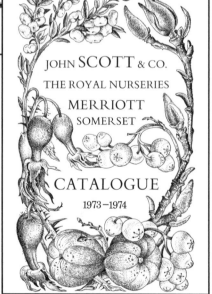

An advertisement for James Scott's nursery at Turnham Green in the mid-eighteenth century, promising fine pineapples and 'new invented Fire Walls to raise early Melons & Cucumbers free from the Watery quality they have in wet Seasons'. The long life of this style of decoration is shown by the John Scott catalogue of 1973.

America, and the nurseryman James Lee scooped one from a sailor's wife in Wapping after he was tipped off that a plant resembling the precious *Fuchsia coccinea* was growing on her windowsill: within a year he had 300 plants. But was this really *coccinea*, or was it (as Kew experts decided in 1790) *Fuchsia magellanica*, a variety that looked very similar?

Identifying and classifying were problems with so many new species. Miller was clerk to the Society of Gardeners, a club of twenty top London gardeners and nurserymen found in 1725 (Thomas Fairchild, author of *The City Garden*, was a member), who met monthly not only to talk plants, but to systematise their names. In 1730 Miller helped with the Society's *Catalogus Plantarum* and in his own *Dictionary* he identified species by the long, elaborate names given by the French botanist, Pitton de Tournefort. It was partly because the *Dictionary* was so popular that many of these names – like Acacia, Malus, Pulsatilla and Ananas – stuck firmly even though they were briefly replaced by new Linnaean titles. The Swedish Carl Linnaeus, who visited Holland, France and England before becoming Professor of Botany at Uppsala, revolutionised plant taxonomy in the 1730s. He divided plants in an orderly fashion into twenty-four classes according to the number of stamens, then into orders, families (genus) and species, with innumerable 'varieties', and he replaced the long descriptive labels by two names only: the genus, plus a 'trivial' name. Linnaeus prepared lists of species worldwide, and publishing them in his *Species Plantarum* (1753) and *Systema Naturae* (1758). The names were often tributes to friends, pupils, fellow botanists and the tradition continued.

By the mid-eighteenth century botany was already a fashionable pursuit among the quality, following the model of George III's mother, Princess Augusta, who created the Botanic Garden at Kew. Now Linnaeus's easy binomial names made it simple for everyone: primers were published and natural history societies sprang up like mushrooms. James Lee used the new system in his popular *Introduction to Botany* of 1760, while the massive 1774 catalogue of plants from his nursery used both the Latin

The etched frontispiece to the Society of London Gardeners *Catalogus Plantarum*, 1730: the plate, also used in Miller's *Dictionary*, shows how you can make a fine and varied French-style garden even where space is lacking.

and familiar English names. Miller himself took to the new terms very slowly and only used them in the later editions of his *Dictionary*. Dubbed 'the dictator of English gardening', he resigned from Chelsea in 1771, aged seventy-nine (to be replaced by William Forsyth, who brought us 'forsythia'). Soon all the plants in his famous garden were being rearranged 'according to the system of Linnaeus', including 3000 plants from the voyages of Banks and Captain Cook. The gardeners complained loudly at the increase in labour created

> by the numerous Collection of new Plants raised and cultivated in the Garden; and as many of them are of foreign Production, of tender natures and especially such as are raised from seeds, in Hot Bedds; and require frequent Shifting and changing of situation and constant watchfulness, attention and care to preserve them . . .

The traffic was not all one way. After the *Endeavour* landed in Tahiti in 1769, Joseph Banks noted that Captain Cook 'planted divers seeds which he had brought with him in a spot of ground turned up for the purpose. They were all bought of Gordon of Mile End and sent in bottles seald up, whether or no that method will succeed the event of this plantation will show.' Banks was particularly interested, since he was closely involved with the Royal Gardens at Kew (he was appointed unofficial director in 1771), and he was concerned with how seeds survived the ocean voyages. They might be carried in airtight bottles, dried in papers or preserved in beeswax, while plants and whole trees were packed in peat, or in tubs. The plants suffered badly from the variation and extremes of temperature – on the voyage from China, for example, the sailing ships had to cross the Equator twice.

One of the people who consulted Miller at Chelsea was the Revd Gilbert White, who asked him about growing melons in his garden at The Wakes

in Selbourne in Hampshire. Melon growing was one of White's particular
passions: his hotbed was forty-five feet long and gobbled up thirty cartloads
of dung every year. He grew squashes, and green and yellow cantaloupes;
he swapped seeds, fretted about frost, mildew, rain, baking sun; and
eventually harvested them from late August on, roping in his neighbours to
share the treat. On 12 September 1758 he noted, 'Held a Cantaloupe-feast at
the Hermitage: cut-up a brace & a half of fruit among 14 people. Weather
very fine ever since the ninth.'

The Wakes was built by Gilbert White's grandfather, vicar of the
parish for forty-five years. Gilbert himself was never actually the vicar, but
he lived here all his life apart from a short spell at Oxford. For years he
observed the natural cycle of the seasons, keeping a meticulous diary and
finally publishing his vivid, thoughtful letters in 1788 as *The Natural History
of Selborne*, one of our best-loved classics, reprinted in over 200 editions.
All the natural life is here – the tame bat that ate from his hand, the field
mice hanging their nests on the waving stalks of corn, the mating habits of
toads, the summer and winter birds of passage. And almost incidentally in
these pages, White broods on odd garden problems that still bother us
today, like the way new garden pests steal into the country from abroad. He
groans at the invasion of wasps in his orchard, sets boys to find the nests and
catches thousands 'with hazel-twigs tipped with bird-lime'. He notes how
his shrubs react to the fierce winters, especially what happens to the new
imports in late-March frosts and deep snows: contrary to what one would
think, he advises, plants from hot countries – and plants from Siberia –
should not be planted in 'hot' corners of the garden, because in both cases
they shoot away too early at the first touch of sun and the frost catches them
hard. (I came across similar advice in an RHS pamphlet of 2003.) In an
unexpected cold snap, 'it highly behoves every planter, who wishes to
escape the cruel mortification of losing in a few days the labour and hopes
of years, to bestir himself on such emergencies; and, if his plantations are
small, to avail himself of mats, clothes, peas-haum, straw, reeds, or any such
covering, for a short time.'

From 1751 to 1768 White also kept careful notes on his own garden in his *Garden Kalendar*. The Wakes had a small ornamental garden with a lawn edged with flowers and a bed of bulbs by the house. Beyond, stretching to the wooded hill called the Hanger, lay meadows and fields, grandly known as 'the Park', and on the northern side was a natural mound, Baker's Hill, on whose warm, gently sloping soil White planted his orchard, vegetables and melon beds. He produced a massive amount of vegetables – enough, one sometimes feels, to feed the whole village – asparagus, artichokes and endives, white broccoli, scorzonera, marrowfat peas, leeks and cucumbers, a whole variety of lettuces, maize, wild rice and potatoes and seakale from seeds that he collected on Devon beaches. Later he planted fruit trees and made espaliers for his apples. He hired villagers to help with the digging and paid Goody Hampton as a weeding woman, such a hard worker, White thought, that 'indeed, excepting she wears petticoats and now and then has a child, you would think her a man'.

The Old Hermitage on the Hanger at Selborne, watercolour by S. H. Grimm, 1777, with Gilbert White's brother posing as the hermit, and a 'rustic bench' behind.

White was a sociable gardener. He exchanged seeds and plants with friends and neighbours, visited Physic Gardens and corresponded with botanists and nurserymen. He also indulged in the current Arcadian fashion, in a rather ad hoc Shenstone-like way, making his little park a picturesque place. Between the garden and the park he built a ha-ha to keep the cattle out. He dug 'basons' in the chalky meadows and filled them with loam and manure to raise flowers; he set up urns on nine-foot pillars, cut vistas through hedges to end in a statue of Hercules and laid a zigzag path through the Hanger to the top of the hill, decorated with sandstone 'obelisks'. He even had an old thatched hermitage, where his brother Harry posed as a hermit with great success, and gave a tea party where his friends came dressed as shepherds and shepherdesses. It was all hard work, but when spring came round, White was always bursting with optimism. On 13 April 1759 he was making a bed for his annuals:

> Planted two rows of slips of a very *fine sort* of double-bloody-wall-flower from my Dame Scot's of Harting. Made the ground very mellow with lime-rubbish. Sowed a plot of Holy-oak [hollyhock] seed, & leek-seed. Planted some rose-campions, & Columbines in the new Garden.
>
> A Perfect summer's day, that fetched ye beds finely to their heat after such gluts of rain. Saw seven swallows, the first this year.

*

The Lichfield doctor, Erasmus Darwin, also used Miller's *Dictionary* and quickly adopted the new Linnaean names. Erasmus was the grandfather of Charles Darwin and himself the author of the first British theory of biological evolution. In his poem *The Botanic Garden* (1791) he put the sexual system of the Linnaean orders into fanciful rhymed couplets, linking the plant world to all kinds of progress from the 'big bang' at the beginning of time to the thrusting industrial world: his notes to the poem quote horticultural authorities from Thomas Fairchild to Hans Sloane and Miller, and he often refers admiringly to 'White's History of Selborne'.

Darwin had been at university in Edinburgh in the heyday of the Scottish Enlightenment and shared its progressive scientific approach to horticulture. From the 1720s Scotland had a Society for the Improvement of Knowledge, whose leading spirit, the Duke of Atholl, laid out 'irregular' plantations on his estate in the style recommended by Bridgeman and introduced the larch into Scotland in 1737. Another Society member was Lord Haddington, owner of the finest eighteenth-century garden in the region at Tyninghame, East Lothian. Invariably, the most go-ahead writers in the field came from Scotland and it is not surprising that in the next two centuries the country would provide the most skilled professional gardeners and adventurous plant hunters. Already, by the mid-eighteenth century the head gardeners on leading English estates were Scottish, men like Thomas Blaikie, who went on to promote the English style in France, and William Forsyth, gardener to the Duke of Northumberland and became Miller's successor at Chelsea.

In a little valley near Lichfield, Darwin had his own botanic garden, rather on the model of Shenstone, who lived not far away. At the end of his life, in 1800, he published a vast tome, *Phytologia: or the Philosophy of Agriculture and Gardening*, which examined, among other things, the new discoveries of photosynthesis, and the key roles of nitrogen, phosphorus and carbon in plant nutrition. He was a keen 'scientific' gardener himself and when his friend Richard Lovell Edgeworth wrote from Ireland for advice about hothouses in 1788, Darwin had plenty to say:

1. My Hothouse has fire 4 months in a year only. 2. consumes about six tons of coals by conjecture. 3. it is about 82ft. long and about 9ft. wide. 4. it has only oblique sashes, no perpendicular ones. 5. it is divided in two, that one half may be a month forwarder than the other. 6. it produces abundance of Kidney-beans, cucumbers, Melons, and Grapes, not pines.

*

He explained that he kept pots of flowers between the vines, and that even now, in February, his beans were already eight inches tall, melons one inch high, and vine-shoots five inches long. His greenhouse had cost him about £100, he said, a great sum 'and I don't repent the expense'.

In his own garden Darwin conducted experiments on the germination of seeds, or the respiration of leaves and their sensitivity to light. Fellow botanist-gardeners sent him information, part of that great body of forgotten amateurs who subtly influenced the way that skills and knowledge developed. 'Miss —' showed him her intricate dissection of the offsets of 'leaf-bulbs' of tulips; 'Mr Wheatley', a London surgeon, vividly described the way the leaves of the sundew, *drosera*, bent upwards when an insect landed on them, tipping their 'globules of mucus' to the centre to entangle and destroy it; Mr Eaton, 'an ingenious florist of Derby', showed him the different ways hyacinths and tulips form new bulbs.

Darwin was also a great admirer of our old friend Mrs Delany, explaining how, when she was seventy-four and her eyesight was no longer good enough for her to paint well, she began making her famous 'paper mosaics' of flowers, 'according to the Linnaean classification', completing 970 before she gave up at the age of eighty-two. Many of her specimens came from the Chelsea garden that Philip Miller had ruled so proudly for so long. For her, as for so many of her contemporaries, the garden was a realm of both experiment and art.

III

FLOWER

15

_____

Brown and his foes

W HILE THE ASPIRING London tradesmen were filling their plots with statues
and the amateur botanists were poring at plants through their microscopes,
something strange was happening to Britain's larger gardens and estates.
The parterres were vanishing. Great swaths of lawn began at the house and
swept into the distance, dotted with clumps of trees, sloping down to wide
curving lakes. It was a rude shock to the system. Gardening was an art, but
this – at least at first glance – was all nature.

Most landowners were less inspired by ideals of nature than by the
desire to improve their land, drain marshes and bogs, raise better livestock.
But the two could go hand in hand: you could value the landscape for its
beauty as well as its wealth. And the person who could best bring out the
aesthetic 'capabilities' of the setting was Lancelot 'Capability' Brown. He
was born in 1716 into a well-off farming family from Northumberland and
from 1741 he worked at Stowe under Kent, taking charge since Kent was

hardly ever there. Stowe made Brown's name and in 1751 he set up on his own, advising on estates across the country. He would visit his clients, charging ten guineas for the initial consultation and sending a junior to make a technical survey and detailed plans, and he brilliantly offered the whole package, subcontracting and supervising the actual work, which often amounted to thousands of man-hours of digging, building and planting. His fees were enormous, his clients were the top aristocracy and in the 1760s he was also gardener to George III at Hampton Court, where he planted the Great Vine and imposed his will on his monarch by refusing, for once, to tear down the old avenues. 'I very earnestly wish I may die before you, Mr Brown,' someone is supposed to have said.

'Why so?' asked Brown.

'Because I should like to see Heaven before you have improved it.'

Brown's landscapes were broad and open, with the deer or sheep in the park grazing as near as the ha-ha would allow. They were also predominantly green, with an 'infinite delicacy of planting', as he put it, 'so much Beauty depending on the size of the trees and the colour of their leaves to produce the effect of light and shade'. These shady trees were sometimes placed as grand single specimens (huge old trees, oaks and chestnuts, were moved into new positions), but more often they were grouped in clumps, with fences to stop the deer nibbling the bark, or as belts hiding jarring signs of genuine rural life like the home farm or kitchen garden. Contemporary paintings can make this style look hauntingly empty, even bleak, but in reality it might not have been as stiff as it appears. We don't associate Brown with flowers, but he did suggest using flowering shrubs, tangles of honeysuckle and roses, walks through laburnum and lilac – touches of romance and scent. The extravagant list of plants ordered for the wilderness at Petworth in 1757 is far from austere: syringas, Persian jasmine, 'Virginia Shumacks', tamarisks, acacias, almonds and cherries and peaches, and a mass of roses: sixty sweet briar, five Rosa Mundi, five Maiden's Blush, six double white, six damask, five 'Virgin', four 'York and Lancaster' and eighty 'roses of sorts'.

Perhaps the grandeur and scale of Stowe gave Brown confidence from the start, because if anything marks his work it is boldness and cost. At Longleat he demolished the grand formal garden and turned the canal into a rushing stream; at Chatsworth he scooped away hills to glimpse the river; at Blenheim he grassed over Henry Wise's great parterres and, notoriously, dammed the river to flood the valley and make two great lakes, drowning Vanbrugh's canal and lapping higher and higher around the arches of his beautiful bridge. People, as well as bridges, were disposable: at Sledmere in Yorkshire and Milton Abbas in Dorset, Brown persuaded his patrons to move whole villages out of sight, regardless of resentment. At Milton, where the Earl of Dorchester built his new house on the site of the old monastery and wanted the unsightly cottages out of his view, the villagers dug in their heels until he ordered that the dam holding back Brown's new lake should be breached: the flood swamped their houses and swept away their resistance. They moved into their new model dwellings, designed by Brown himself. (Now, ironically, Milton Abbas looks like a rural idyll.)

Heveningham Hall, showing Capability Brown's landscaping of 1781.

Brown's influence was enormous and not only in the countryside. He touched a quite different milieu when the actor Garrick asked him to design the garden for his villa at Hampton. Garrick's undulating velvet lawns were laboriously smoothed by a man with a horse-drawn roller, with specimen trees in the shrubbery at one side and a new weeping willow on the bank.

Later experts and architects followed Brown's lead, like William Emes and Robert Adam. (One of Adam's houses, his restoration of the fourteenth-century Culzean Castle in Ayrshire, has an amazing garden, with a viaduct, orangery, pagoda as well as lakes and woodland walks.) And soon after Brown died in 1783 a fresh designer, Humphry Repton – who coined the phrase 'landscape gardening' – looked set to take this style to a new level. Like Brown, Repton was a peripatetic consultant but he had a far wider clientele, ranging from Whig grandees to Bristol sugar merchants, Lancashire cloth manufacturers, Norfolk neighbours, London lawyers and Quaker bankers. From his first project in 1788, at the age of thirty-six, Repton spent much of his life on the road. In 1790, writing from his post-chaise, 'my usual desk', he estimated that he travelled between 500 or 600 miles a month. In three decades he undertook over 400 commissions, many requiring numerous visits over several years. He was a realist, who saw convenience – like placing the kitchen garden near the house – as just as important as 'beauty'. After an accident in 1813 he was confined to a bath-chair, and turned his mind energetically to the best kinds of gardening for people like himself. He wanted his gardens and parks to be linked to the wider world, and when he suggested a prospect from a terrace he often included a lively scene of motion – 'a busy scene of shipping', a turnpike with its carts, a view across a city like Leeds, with the smoke rising from its mills (euphemistically described as 'softened by its misty vapour').

Repton presented his ideas in atmospheric watercolours where a scene of the estate as it was could be covered by a hinged flap displaying the 'improved' scene, complete with stylish figures, grazing cows and drifting boats. When the client turned back the overlay – hey presto! Nature was

How to enjoy your flower beds from a bath-chair: Humphry Repton's 'The Luxury of Gardens', 1816.

transformed. He and his patrons inherited the lordly approach of Vanbrugh, Kent and Brown, where the landscape can be ordered and 'revealed' at the whim of its owner. But there was something cheery and comfortable and very 'English' about most of the scene he created. Among his best commissions were Brandsbury in Hampstead, Uppark in Sussex and Sheringham in Norfolk, and the many specialist gardens at Woburn Abbey, which included hothouses and terraced winter gardens, arboretum and rosary, American and Chinese gardens, 'a taxonomic garden and a menagerie'. He could be exotic, as well as plain English: at Sezincote in Gloucestershire, for Charles Cockerell, he planned a Thornery, skirting a stream that dashes downhill for the Temple of the Hindu Goddess Souriya to the Indian bridge with its Brahmin bulls – a grand, grotesque, Regency garden. And at the end of his life he produced plans that looked forward to the leisurely Victorians, with parterre and conservatory, aviary and orangery, to match the billiard rooms and music rooms and libraries within.

On a far smaller scale, every country squire now aimed to have his manor house set in a landscaped park, planting 'belts' and making walks. Parsons and doctors ordered trees and shrubs galore. New manufacturers

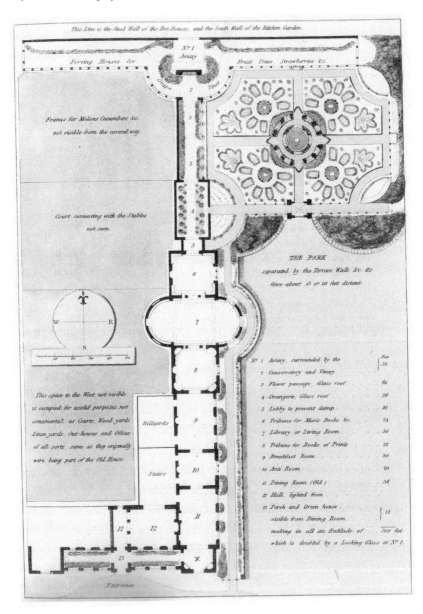

A ground plan from Repton's *Fragments on the Theory and Practice of Landscape Gardening* (1816).

made industrial sites into 'landscapes', like Josiah Wedgwood, who tried desperately to ensure that the Trent-Mersey flowing past Etruria looked like a serpentine river. His friend Matthew Boulton laid out sweeping lawns down from his house to the factory near Birmingham, made his millpond into an ornamental lake, and built a hermitage and a temple by a little 'shell-pond'.

Brown's influence was so dominant that it was bound to provoke a reaction. Sometimes this was simply a shocked response to the plight of the rural poor, whose common rights were so often sacrificed to 'improvements'. Between 1760 and 1800 over 21 million acres of open fields and common lands were enclosed; in some areas parks now marched boundary to boundary across counties. To the owners landscaping made perfect economic sense: the woodland and copses provided cover for game, the grass could be let for grazing, the trees coppiced for timber; but to the poor it meant loss of livelihood and even eviction. Goldsmith's poem, 'The Deserted Village' of 1770, was prompted by such 'improvements', and Gainsborough's landscapes with ragged children and cottagers were also a poignant lament.

The large-scale overhauling of nature also seemed to many to be wasteful and arrogant, the antithesis of true horticulture. In 1786 Cowper published his long poem *The Task*, with its section on 'The Garden':

> Improvement too, the idol of the age,
> Is fed with many a victim. Lo, he comes!
> Th'omnipotent magician, Brown appears! . . .
> . . . He speaks. The lake in front becomes a lawn;
> Woods vanish, hills subside, and vallies rise:
> And streams, as if created for his use,
> Pursue the track of his directing wand.

The end result leaves the poor client 'Drain'd to the last poor item of his wealth', selling his estate to an even wealthier fool. The real gardener, by contrast, laboriously builds his cold frame, plants his seeds, manures the ground, chases away pests – unsung and unacknowledged labours – and takes pleasure in his greenhouse, glowing with greenery and flowers even 'while the winds whistle and the snows descend'.

A generation later Thomas Love Peacock had wonderful fun in *Headlong Hall* when Mr Milestone (Humphry Repton) offers to wave 'the wand of enchantment' over Squire Headlong's thistle-choked estate: 'The rocks shall be blown up, the trees shall be cut down, the wilderness and all its goats shall vanish like mist. Pagodas and Chinese bridges, gravel walks and shrubberies, bowling greens, canals, and clumps of larch shall rise upon its ruins.' Jane Austen (a keen gardener herself) was also merciless, especially in *Mansfield Park*, where the dim Mr Rushworth is badgered by Henry Crawford to improve his estate, chopping down its ancient avenues. As Henry sees, when he sets out to 'examine the capabilities', the layout is positively Jacobean, with a lawn bounded by a high wall, a parterre and bowling green: 'a good place for fault-finding'. In Austen's eyes improvement spells dubious morals: always mistrust a man who sneers at your shrubbery. In *Pride and Prejudice* Elizabeth approves of Pemberley because she had never seen a place, she thought, 'where natural beauty had been so little counteracted by an awkward taste'.

But in Brown's own time, and immediately after his death, the reactions provoked interesting new ideas on the relationship between nature and the garden. Brown's rival, Sir William Chambers, attacked him as boring and cold, offering nothing to excite the curiosity, 'little to flatter the senses and less to touch the passions or gratify the understanding'. 'In England, where no appearance of art is tolerated,' he fumed, 'a stranger is often at a loss to know whether he is walking in a meadow, or in a pleasure ground, made and kept at very considerable expence. At his first entrance, he is treated with the sight of a large green field, scattered over with a few straggling trees . . .' Instead, in his *Dissertation on Oriental Gardening* of 1772 Chambers held up for admiration the Chinese gardens (Chinoiserie was also a current vogue), recommending their diversity, their range of tone from the pleasing and surprising to the terrible and 'horrid'. Unfortunately his Chinese 'Surprises' included sudden explosions, electric shocks and fearful sounds, while his 'Terrible' scenes contained bats and birds of prey, and distant views of gibbets and 'the whole apparatus of torture'. The 'horrid' garden was altogether too alarming for an astonished public.

A more lasting reaction was the return of the old painterly mood. The second Earl Harcourt (whose father had been one of the fiercest improvers) was a devoted fan of Rousseau and created an elaborate flower garden, based on the heroine's garden in *Julie, ou La Nouvelle Héloïse* of 1761, designed for him by the Oxford Professor of Poetry, William Mason, who described it in his poem *The English Garden* (1771–79). Mason even specified the different tints that should shade into the background: warm brown, then 'sober olive', then a softer blue or fainter purple. Ruined trees could 'frame' a view, like a picture or the scenery at the playhouse.

To prove their artistic sensibilities polite society took up garden visiting, following particular circuits: Stourhead, Wilton, Longleat in Wiltshire; Chatsworth, Kedleston and Hardwick; and old favourites like the Leasowes, Stowe and Painshill, Blenheim and Moor Park. On application you could get a free ticket, or send in your card and the housekeeper or gardener would do the honours. In 1781 Boswell was triumphant at getting into Lord Bute's garden at Luton Hoo, 'for which I had obtained a ticket'. Many of these visitors, though, were looking for something novel, something different. Brown's bare landscapes failed to satisfy the new mood of 'sensibility'. In the 1780s the Revd William Gilpin's *Picturesque Tours* appeared, describing journeys through Wales, the Lake District, Scotland and the New Forest, and showing eager travellers scenery that 'could be formed into a picture', not in Italy but in their own native land. Tourists flocked to Westmoreland to see this Picturesque boldness. And one of the favourite gardens among visitors well into the next century was Mount Edgcumbe in Cornwall, the ultimate romantic garden with its mock ruins, its Italian staircases and views of 'the irregular summits of Dartmoor', and stone seat 'at the edge of an almost perpendicular precipice', overlooking Plymouth Sound.

The Picturesque taste was crystallised in 1794 by polemics from two Herefordshire landowners, Uvedale Price and Richard Payne Knight. Since Brown was dead, their target was Repton, whom they attacked for a total lack of any 'painterly' appreciation and for impoverishing the nation by demolishing its old, irregular beauties, associated with ancient 'natural' British rights and freedom. While Price's *Essay on the Picturesque* praised the virtues of a more rugged, dramatic landscape (he particularly admired Mount Edgcumbe, which he called 'a wonderful place'), Knight's *The Landscape – A Didactic Poem* longed nostalgically, in heroic couplets, for the old lost gardens of yews and mounts, terraces and statues. On his Foxley estate Uvedale Price ripped out the old parterre and topiary (an act he later bitterly regretted). Not far away, at Downton Castle near Ludlow, where the river rushes and gurgles through a natural gorge, Payne Knight built a grotto and three rustic bridges, harking back to the ideal landscapes of Claude and Salvator Rosa.

It was hard for most gardeners to achieve this, but some did try. 'The Ladies of Llangollen', Eleanor Butler and Sarah Ponsonby (both of whom had run away from family misery in Ireland in 1778), were fans of Gilpin, and tried to turn their two and a half acres into a Picturesque idyll at their home, Plas Newydd. They lived together happily for the next half-century, driving their gardeners hard and filling their patch with rustic ornaments like a balustrade made out of twisted roots. Their white lilac walk was made for moonlight, their laburnum grove for sun. Even their kitchen garden had a Gothic arch and they embraced the wildness with a little 'ravine' by the steep-banked stream at the edge of their land, with views outwards to the mountains and a medieval castle.

On an unimaginably grander scale, Thomas Beckford introduced Picturesque landscaping at Fonthill Abbey near Bath. Landowners who had quarries on their property filled them with ferns and arches, as at Belsay in Northumberland. At Hawkstone in Shropshire Sir Rowland Hill and his son Richard turned the sandstone cliff into romantic theatre. 'The ideas it forces on the mind are the sublime, the dreadful and the vast,' declared Samuel Johnson in 1774. 'He that mounts the precipices at Hawkstone,

A Picturesque view of the Hawkstone precipice.

wonders how he came thither and doubts how he shall return. His walk is an adventure, and his departure an escape . . .'

Few British gardens could find room for precipices and most owners turned back with some relief to the maligned Repton, who was nothing if not practical. Repton could see that Richard Payne Knight's estate lent itself to the Picturesque but in the 'gardens of a villa near the city, or in the more tame yet interesting pleasure ground which I am frequently called upon to decorate', it would be wholly out of place. When the Duke of Bedford asked him to develop a dramatic site at Endsleigh, on the steep wooded bluffs above the Tamar in Devon, Repton created two terraces, on one of which he placed a little 'children's cottage' and a round flower garden – actually bringing back the formality that had been so out of vogue. The gardening circle swung round once again.

16

Victoriana

OH, VICTORIAN GARDENS – so many kinds, such potent images: terraces and steps, croquet hoops, shrubberies, summer houses, kitchen gardens; backyards in industrial cities; gardens along canals; municipal parks with bandstands. When I was thirteen my family moved from the bleak Cumbrian coast to Dorset and I was astounded at its velvety overflowing greens, its almost suffocating lushness. The garden summed up storybook Victoriana. Long windows opened on to a gravel terrace, with rose beds dividing it from a lawn so flat you could hardly cheat at croquet. Around one side of the house crept a shrubbery dense with overgrown laurels and leggy philadelphus. On the other side a gigantic copper beech swept to the ground over a sea of campanula. Across the lawn the Blackmore Vale was framed by a monkey-puzzle, which my mother hated for its spiky leaves, and a sycamore whose whirling seeds were almost worse, and behind a belt of trees, including a tall Scots pine where someone had once built a rickety tree house, ran a forget-me-not-choked herbaceous border, marking the edge of the kitchen garden where sweet peas as well as runner beans climbed their rows of poles.

The house had once been a rectory and the Victorian vicar must have been proud of his planting. The first monkey-puzzle seeds from Chile had arrived in 1796, but for half a century, until the nurserymen began collecting seeds themselves, it was very rare. The craze for it really began when the eccentric Lady Rolle planted a complete 500-yard monkey-puzzle avenue at Bicton House near Budleigh-Salterton in Devon. Her gardener, James Barnes, had bought seeds from the adventurous local nursery, Loddiges, and had raised the seedlings himself, keeping them in pots in a cold pit in winter and bringing them out into the sun each spring. Within five years the avenue had grown so fast that the branches grazed the Rolles' carriages and they had to be moved back again. The effect was extra-ordinary and orders poured in for the dramatic new trees.

In gardening, as so much else, this was the century of the new. The Horticultural Society was founded in 1804 at a convivial meeting in Hatchard's bookshop, London, with Josiah Wedgwood's son John as one of the founders – it became 'Royal' when Prince Albert obtained a charter for it in 1861. New trees and plants and seeds flooded in from the Caucasus and Siberia, from South and North America, South Africa, India, China and Japan and New Zealand. There were great ranges of new tools, for cutting and pruning, digging and weeding – not least the lawnmower, invented in 1831 by Edward Budding, an engineer in a textile factory who adapted a cloth-shearing machine to provide the perfect smooth lawn; the mower was easy to push in small gardens and on great estates larger versions were pulled by a horse wearing leather shoes, to protect the close-cut sward. Less obvious, but just as important, were the new journals, which flourished after the growth in cheap printing methods and especially after the tax on paper was repealed in 1861, appealing to readers of all classes, including many people who had never gardened seriously before.

The nineteenth century often presents us with a strange tension

Budding's mower, 1832.

between the drama of progress, industry, widening horizons and empire, and an anxious reinstatement of the traditional, whether it be in buildings or rituals or manners. And an obsession with the past – the taste for historical novels and ancient ballads, the medievalism of the Pre-Raphaelites, the baronial-style halls and mock-Gothic churches – also found its way into how people thought about gardens and how they planned them, used them, worked in them.

Gardening styles, as we have seen, move in waves of reaction, and at the start of the century pundits and designers were reacting against three things: the classical Arcadian landscapes with their temples and poetic inscriptions; the bare 'natural', grass-up-to-the-house style of Capability Brown; and the overly Picturesque mode with its hermitages and wild defiles – difficult to find space for in an urban villa. Jane Austen mocked the Picturesque just as much as Brown's improvements. In *Sense and Sensibility* Marianne Dashwood is open-mouthed at Edward Ferrar's teasing confession that he prefers tall, straight trees to crooked, blasted ones and does not like ruined cottages, or 'nettles, or thistles, or heath blossoms'. Like many of her Regency contemporaries, Austen's taste was simply for keeping what was beautiful, productive and well-loved, like Donwell Abbey in *Emma* or Colonel Brandon's 'nice old-fashioned place' in *Sense and Sensibility* that Mrs Jennings so admires: 'great garden walls that are covered with the very best fruit trees in the country: and such a mulberry tree in one corner! Then there is a dovecote, some delightful stewponds and a very pretty canal; and everything, in short, that one could wish for.' Here you can 'sit up in the old yew-arbour behind the house' and watch the carriages roll by.

At the start of the century, in the backlash from the French Revolution, wild nature begins to seem less attractive. Formality enters, order, control: in Repton's later plans the house is often separated from the garden by terraces. The hinged plates for the White Lodge, Richmond Park, from his *Fragments . . . of Landscape Gardening* are a clear instruction to banish nature, keeping it at bay by trellis-work and balustrades. Repton hauled back pattern and geometry in plants such as his flower garden for Beaudesert in Staffordshire, now vanished with the house, which returned, so he claimed, to the original Tudor plans. At Ashridge Park in Hertfordshire, which he called 'the child of my age and declining powers', Repton created fifteen specialist gardens: a terrace and 'Embroidered Parterre', a shrub-sprinkled lawn leading to the deer park, a conservatory and a cloister walk, a sanctuary with vases and a Gothic conduit. A walk led to 'The Monk's Garden Restored' and on to the 'Arboretum of Exotic Trees'. The features were familiar from the eighteenth century, but the many different gardens looked forward to the profusion – and confusion – that lay ahead.

The justification for the terraces and parterres was 'history'. Not classical history, or romantic Picturesque, but 'plain English'. In the years of the Napoleonic Wars and the Regency patriotic passion spread like fever. Owners of country houses scoured the attics for armour to hang on their walls, and the demand for antique swords and guns led to a boom in fakes and reproductions. In gardening, too, the impulse was to look to the past. One of the most surprising examples of this comes in two detailed letters from William Wordsworth to his friend Lady Beaumont in December 1806 and February 1807, where he offers suggestions for her 'winter garden' at Coleorton Hall in Leicestershire. His guiding notion is the retreat: he quotes Thomson's 'Hymn on Solitude', rejecting the city noise: 'Then shield me in the woods again', but although he suggests groves and winding walks he had recently been reading Chaucer and he also recommends a central bower based on the fifteenth-century poem 'The Flower and the Leaf' (quoted in the 'Pleasure' chapter here). The bower would be enclosed in trellis-work, with flower borders 'edged with boxwood, its paths paved with different coloured pebbles, with a mossed seat and stone table and a hedge of eglantine and bay'. Elsewhere his plan contains a simple stone fountain. Sounding rather embarrassed about his outmoded taste, he adds, 'Shall I venture to say here, bye the bye, that I am old-fashioned enough to like in certain places even jettes d'eau', with the 'diamond drops of light that they scatter around them'. Elsewhere 'an ivied cottage' would be surrounded by English shrubs and flowers: the quarry, too, he 'would have in all its ornaments entirely English'. 'I am sensible I have written a very pretty romance in this letter,' he ends, 'I am afraid you will call me an enthusiast and a visionary.'

Other literary gardeners also looked back to the nation's past. Sir Walter Scott's Abbotsford, near Melrose in the Scottish borders, into which he poured all his money from 1811, had formal 'Tudor' areas between the house and the park, with geometrical flower beds and clipped yew pillars. Scott built, too, a small Gothic conservatory on the lines of an old-style orangery, and attacked the 'bare' false naturalism of Kent and Brown. In the next generation, when Bulwer Lytton inherited Knebworth House in Hertfordshire in 1843, he restored the faded grandeur that his mother had obliterated with Tudor-style wings, ornamental turrets and façades spattered with crazy heraldic designs. In front he laid out gardens, 'in the style favoured by James I, with the stone balustrades, straight walks, statues and elaborate parterres'. (As it happened, his Jacobean grassed courtyard was laid out crooked, since he was away and was sending his instructions by post.)

Lytton was definitely in fashion. The Reformation and Elizabethan age summed up 'Merry England' and the greatness of Britain – Drake playing bowls as the Armada approached, the nobility *in extremis* of Philip Sidney, the mixed genius of Shakespeare. Many people saw Capability Brown and his fellow landscapists as vandals, and argued that people should treasure the old gardens that remained, such as Knole. Old seventeenth-century parterres were revived, like the one at Bodysgallen Hall, with its views towards Conwy and Snowdonia. Topiary came back into vogue yet again, avenues were replanted, ruins preserved. When Edward Hussey built a new mansion in the 1830s at Scotney Castle in Kent, the landscape gardener William Sawrey Gilpin (nephew of the Gilpin who inspired the Picturesque) persuaded him to keep the old fourteenth-century castle as part of the view from the terraced bastion by the house, while the quarry was transformed into a 'woodland dell'.

The 'past' was pretty loosely defined as Elizabethan, Jacobean, Italian, French or Dutch. Eventually 'Italian' became the favoured

Trentham Park, Staffordshire, from E. Adveno Brooke, *Gardens of England*, 1858.

description, but far from evoking the romance of Salvator Rosa, this was now a kaleidoscope of neo-Renaissance clichés: massive steps and flashy fountains; hefty terraces with urns; Portugal laurels in tubs to replace orange trees. In 1833 Sir Charles Barry remodelled the gardens at Trentham Park in Staffordshire for the Duke of Sutherland (who had become a millionaire from his canal investments), building two great terraces with elaborate balustrades and statues, and importing a gondola to row on the lake below. Barry's designs are also found at Bowood, Cliveden and Harewood, at Shrublands in Suffolk, with its descending terraces, stairs and wide views, and at Dunrobin Castle in Sutherland in the far north of Scotland, where formal terraced parterres march down to the North Sea.

Elsewhere, Barry's fellow designer, William Andrews Nesfield, adapted plans directly from Dézallier d'Argenville's 1709 work, the *Theory and Practice of Gardening*. Nesfield liked elaborate constructions and well-drilled shapes (he had been trained as an army engineer), and he followed seventeenth-century precedent in using coloured gravels, crushed brick, and shards of glass to line his patterns within their box edging. From the 1840s he provided plans for a host of schemes, including Holkham Hall in Norfolk, the remodelled parterre at Castle Howard, the Royal Botanic Gardens at Kew and the new gardens for the Royal Horticultural Society at Kensington, opened in 1861 (where his coloured gravels caused many raised eyebrows). But perhaps the grandest Italian terrace garden of all was built not by Nesfield, but by Lewis Kennedy and his son George at Drummond Castle in Perthshire, supposedly a tribute to an earlier seventeenth-century garden there, designed in the form of a St Andrew's cross, filled with heathers and rhododendrons, like a brilliant carpet.

Another area where love of tradition meshed happily with excitement over new introductions was in the development of the best-loved flower of all, the rose. For centuries the chief garden beauties had been the five old forms, the *gallica* and *alba*, the musk and the damask, and the densely petalled, headily-scented moss or cabbage rose, but in the early nineteenth century new rivals appeared, and a complex history of crossing and rose breeding began. To oversimplify, in 1792 Britain opened its embassy in Peking and two new plants were sent back to London, 'Parson's Pink China' and 'Slater's Crimon' (this produced the small, perfumed Portland roses, like the deep pink 'Comte de Chambord'. Other Chinese newcomers were the scented 'Alba Plena' (*Rosa banksiae*), named after the wife of Sir Joseph Banks, and the 'Yellow Tea-scented China', brought back in 1824. The tea roses were then developed, with a musky scent of newly opened tea chests, many of them with the prized yellow shades, although they proved tender and often hard to grow.

Meanwhile, a new form had appeared, by chance, in 1817 on the Ile de Bourbon off Madagascar, a stopping point for sailing ships on the Far East route, where the director of the botanic garden spotted a complete novelty, a cross between 'Parson's Pink China' and his old 'Autumn Damask'. He sent seeds to Paris, where the Duc d'Orléans's gardener raised the first shrubs of what became known as the Bourbon rose. The Empress Josephine was enthralled and one of the most beautiful Bourbons is called 'Souvenir de Malmaison' after her famous garden. Heavily scented and long-flowering, these were the favourite roses in Victorian gardens, aristocratic blooms often named after duchesses and princesses, or millionaires' wives, like 'Madame Isaac Perrière'.

An illustration from *The Rose Book*, 1903.

In the 1830s the passion for crossing the new China roses with the damask roses produced the hybrid perpetuals, with their strong, unruly shoots, and in the late 1860s, when these in turn were crossed with the delicately scented tea roses, we had the first hybrid teas. Finally, at the end of the century came the marvellous, soft, free-flowering *rugosa* roses with prickly stems, open flowers and delicate scent, like 'Blanc Double de Couvert' in 1897 and 'Roserai de la Hay' in 1901. Even then, that would not be the end of the story.

When Victoria came to the throne in 1837, the man who was trying to find an approach that would make new plants and designs accessible to ordinary gardens was John Claudius Loudon. He spoke not to the great but to the middle classes, creating a style that would become the essence of Victoriana, the oddly named 'gardenesque'. Loudon was a ferociously energetic Scotsman, a farmer's son born in 1783, filled with a burning drive for self-improvement, studying botany and science, and later teaching himself French and Italian. After being apprenticed to an Edinburgh nurseryman he came to England in 1803 when he was twenty. A keen botanist, he arrived in London with introductions to the Joseph Banks circle, but severe rheumatic fever three years later set back his career. He then ventured into 'scientific' farming, before travelling to Russia and across Europe, meeting botanists and visiting gardens. On his return he turned to writing and from 1830 his wife Jane – who has her own place later in this history – often acted as his amanuensis.

Loudon's books were the bibles of nineteenth-century gardeners. They began with his massive *Encyclopaedia of Gardening* (1822), full of information from his Continental travels. In 1826 he started *The Gardener's Magazine*, which he edited until his death in 1843, after which Jane continued the work. This gave him space to write on all his interests, from fruit growing (a particular passion) to cottages and gardening libraries, public parks where 'the exhausted factory operative might inhale the freshening breeze and find some portion of recovered health' and 'garden cemeteries'.

(He himself was buried in the new Kensal Green.) Above all, he helped to raise the status of professional gardeners, welcoming the lawnmower because it saved back-breaking work, fighting for better conditions, wages and educations, and encouraging gardeners to write in his journal.

In the 1830s Loudon wrote an impressive study of native trees and shrubs, and in 1838 published his most influential book, *The Suburban Gardener and Villa Companion*. Loudon classified gardens in four types, following the standards laid down in the Building Act of 1774: First Rate were the gardens of grand mansions with over ten acres; Second Rate belonged to wealthy tradesmen and professionals, with bay windows and big gardens of two to ten acres; Third Raters, like those in the new suburbs of Chelsea, were about seventeen feet wide, with long gardens and perhaps a separate wash-house or stable. At the bottom of the scale, Fourth Raters were the terraced houses of mechanics – usually with a meagre fourteen-foot frontage, two rooms per floor and a small back garden – and the slightly larger cottages of artisans and junior clerks. He had something to say to them all.

Loudon's dream garden is still a romantic, picturesque place. The house is covered with climbers and has a conservatory. Long windows open on to a terrace with shrubs, urns or statues, and from there a winding path leads across a lawn encircled with trees and scattered with flower beds, towards a particular feature – perhaps a rockery, or a summer house or a pool. Behind lay the kitchen garden and glasshouses. The important point was that each plant should have space so that it could be seen separately and could flourish in the best conditions – although often the actual effect was rather thin and spotty.

But could the 'gardenesque' be adapted to the suburbs? Apparently so. Loudon was full of praise, for example, for the prizewinning villa gardens of Mrs Lawrence, at Drayton Green and then at Ealing Park in Middlesex. At Drayton Green every possible fashion was crammed into a few acres: a French parterre, a rustic arch (with Cupid), urns and pollarded walks; at Ealing Park she grew over 3000 species of plants, including 500 roses, 227

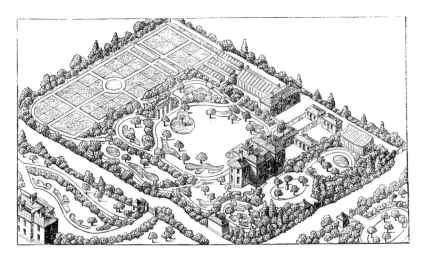

J.C. Loudon, plan for a large suburban villa, with curvy 'island beds' on the lawn, from *The Suburban Gardener and Villa Companion*, 1838.

orchids and 140 alpines. The grandest eclectic garden, however, was Biddulph Grange, created from scratch on bleak Staffordshire moors from 1842 onwards by James Bateman and his wife Maria. It had a formal terrace and a rhododendron garden, a Chinese garden, an Egyptian court, an arboretum and a pinetum, a Cheshire cottage, a ferny dell, mighty avenues of wellingtonias and Bateman's speciality, a vast collection of orchids.

Bateman was also patron of the new vogue for rock gardening. These were not like modern rockeries, but huge constructions based on real rock formations – one garden even had a scale model of the Chamonix valley – planted with alpines and with genuine mountain plants, like bilberries and junipers. And although a rockery was often just a pile of broken plates and pots, half-bricks and odd pebbles, the *Garden Book* of 1853 suggested it be made of something grander, like stones, or

the fused masses of brick procured from brick kilns, or indeed any coarse material most convenient to be got. These are built up in the most rugged and misshapen forms imaginable and afterward covered with Roman cement, and formed into recesses, projections, and overhanging crags . . . when the whole is perfectly dry and set, it is painted with oil paint to represent veined or stratified granite.

From the 1850s on the Backhouse nursery in York was known for supplying a 'complete rock garden', installation and all. The firm of James Pulham went one better, creating massive structures out of clinker set in cement, used in Battersea Park and at Sandringham. Holes were left for soil, into which the poor rock plants were crammed. We can still see some magnificent Victorian rock gardens, like the giant rocks at Chatsworth, or Europe's largest rockery, at Cragside, in Northumberland. (At this millionaire's palace nothing was on a small scale – 7 million trees and bushes were planted on the bare hillsides.)

There is a coda. A newcomer arrived to decorate the rockery. Around 1867 Sir Charles Isham of Lamport Hall in Northamptonshire brought some fashionable porcelain *Gnomen-figuren* from Germany. (One lone survivor from the original collection of twenty-one was discovered in a crevice in 1997, and reputedly insured for a million pounds.) Isham thought his gnomes were rather smart. So did many others: in 1906 Sir Frank Crisp – best known for his collection of illustrations of medieval gardens – had around a hundred in the 'subterranean passages and grottoes' of his stupendous alpine garden at Friar Park in Henley. Later, needless to say, the horticultural establishment turned up its nose: in the mid-1990s the writer James Bartholomew noted that they were banned from Chelsea Flower Show and quoted the RHS Article 15, which forbade 'highly coloured gnomes, fairies or any similar creatures, actual or mythical for use as garden ornaments'. It makes no difference: toadstools, red hats and all, the gnomes are here to stay.

17

Brightness is all

VICTORIAN GARDENING DISPLAY, in great mansions, public parks and private gardens, was intimately related to plant hunting and collecting. There was nothing subtle about mid-Victorian flower beds: even the fine new mock seventeenth-century parterres at great houses, like those at Chatsworth where Joseph Paxton was head gardener, were a riot of colour. In the 'bedding system', which began in the 1830s, low-growing plants were laid out in blocks of single colours, all of the same height, in contrasting patterns. British gardeners already had bright-red pelargoniums, golden marigolds, purple heliotrope and blue lobelias to hand, but now these were joined by brilliant half-hardy perennials from South America, raised in the new glasshouses and planted out in the spring: yellow calceolaria from Chile, scarlet salvias from Mexico, scented white petunias, begonias and verbena from Brazil, clarkia and eschscholtzia from California. This massed colour was not only enjoyed by the rich: on bank holidays like Whit

Monday, Chatsworth was open to all, and in 1867 *The Gardener* reported it as swarming with holidaymakers, pale-faced workers from Manchester cotton mills and Staffordshire potteries, mechanics from Leeds, Bradford and Halifax, all brought on special trains 'admiring the conservatories, rockeries and fountains . . .'

Victorian England, with its leaning towards philanthropy and public health, encouraged the creation of new gardens around schools and hospitals, and the opening of great public parks in many cities. London had always had its squares and many more were built in this century, ringed round with fences, where nannies wheeled babies, and children played beneath planes and sycamores, flowering lilac and laburnum, the trees that survived the soot best. But these were neighbourhood gardens, often private. The first truly public park was Regent's Park in London, opened to subscribers in 1820 and to the general public in 1835. Soon the capital also had Battersea and Victoria Park, Hackney (which, it was argued, would diminish the annual deaths in east London 'by several thousand'). There was another Victoria Park in Bath. In the north, Birkenhead Park on Merseyside, designed by Joseph Paxton, was the first local authority park to grant free entry, in 1843. There were sports grounds and boating lakes, but no alcohol was permitted, no gambling and no swearing. And in every one of these neat, well-ordered public spaces bedding took pride of place. In 1877 no one thought it odd when Nathan Cole devoted almost half his book on *The Royal Parks and Gardens of London* to designs for flower borders and bedding.

The dazzle of carpet bedding (a term initially coined by the *Gardener's Chronicle* for a low, packed mass of succulents) would not have been possible without the flood of new plants from every continent. Many were introduced by 'amateurs', including missionaries, colonial officials and employees of the East India Company, but collecting was soon put on a more organised footing. The driving force in the past had been Kew, but the Royal Botanic Gardens slumped rather sadly between Joseph Banks's death in 1820 and the 1840s. In the interim the Horticultural Society took the lead, sending collectors worldwide, and the new species were often reared, as before, by

devoted individual plantsmen and nurserymen. A great stir was created at
the Society by new arrivals like the 'Peach of the Negroes' (modern *Nauclea
latifolia*), included in a report on 'The Edible Fruits of Sierra Leone' in 1823,
or the Strawberry Tree from the Himalayas. 'It is hoped', the 1834 report
read, 'that when the navigation of the Indus is freely opened, great facilities
will exist for transporting the productions of the Himalaya to the shores of

Hoya pottsii, by Mrs Augusta Withers. Illustrating 'Description of the Plants
belonging to the Genus Hoya', by James Traill, 1826.

Europe . . .' These dry, formal letters and reports are dusted with excitement. In 1826 James Traill, under-gardener at the Society's garden, described the *Hoya pottsii*, telling how on his return from China four years earlier Mr John Potts had given the Secretary, Joseph Sabine, 'a single leaf of this hoya, which he had gathered in one of his excursions near Macao; it was carefully planted and anxiously attended to, until it sent forth a shoot from its base in the spring of 1824.' Illustrated by the botanical artist Augusta Withers, the hoya curls and writhes its glossy leaves, displaying its globe of starry flowers and pyramids of seeds.

One of the Society's chief roles was in distributing seed, plants and cuttings among its members. It was also responsible for giving the correct names to cultivated varieties, a continuing problem, and not just for newly introduced species. Many native or long-established trees and flowers, vegetables and fruit had different local names but were really the same variety. The confusion was such that the Society even ran special conferences on naming in the 1880s, including a Daffodil Conference and an Orchid Conference.

Kew began to flourish again from the mid-1840s, when the Crown handed it over to Parliament and William Jackson Hooker came down from Glasgow Botanic Gardens as director. Soon Hooker was joined by his son, Joseph, a friend of Charles Darwin and himself a famous botanist and plant collector, who ran Kew for another twenty years after his father died. Kew had close links with other botanic gardens founded in this century: in Liverpool, Dublin, Hull, Glasgow, Belfast, Birmingham, Regent's Park. For trees, there were new arboreta, from Westonbirt in Gloucestershire, founded in 1829, to Castelwellan in County Down, or the one at Derby, designed by Loudon in 1840, where visitors could bring picnics and listen to the band – and occasionally read the labels carefully attached to the trees for their greater education. The most northerly arboretum was at Leckmelm, near Ullapool in the north-west of Scotland on the shores of Loch Broom, and many of the trees here – wellingtonias, monkey-puzzles and cedars, some of them of record-breaking heights – date from the 1870s when the garden was first made.

Special gardens for tender plants from the Orient – and the Americas and Australasia – magnolias, camellias, agaves and proteas, and the tree ferns of New Zealand – sprang into being. Many flourished in the damp, mild valleys of the West Country, like Glendurgan, Cotehele, Heligan, Lanhydrock, Trengwainton in Cornwall and Tresco Abbey in the Scilly Isles. A later garden was Caerhays, created in the 1890s by John Charles Wilson, who supported the plant hunters E. H. Wilson and George Forrest. Elsewhere, keen landowners specialised in American trees, or Japanese plants, including the new maples, bamboos and cherries. (At the end of the century, in the 1890s, there was a brief craze for Japanese-style gardens complete with tea houses.)

The Horticultural Society and the Botanic Gardens were not the only specialists: the nurserymen were also flourishing. Some were long established, like Loddiges of Hackney, founded in the 1770s by the German Conrad Loddiges, who specialised in American plants: they had a huge eight-acre arboretum and their catalogue, the *Botanical Cabinet*, was published in twenty volumes: in 1826 it included 8000 species. There were newcomers, too, especially the famous Veitch family. This was founded by one of many 'Scotch gardeners' who came south in the late eighteenth century, including three of the seven founders of the Horticultural Society: William Aiton, head gardener at Kew; William Forsyth and the nurseryman James Dickson (after whom *dicksonia*, the tree fern, is named). The Scottish gardeners were acknowledged powers ('a gardener is Scotch as a French teacher is Parisian,' wrote George Eliot in *Adam Bede*). They inspired many jokes and much terror in employers – a mood that lived on in fictional descendants like Beatrix Potter's Mr McGregor, with the 'scritch, scritch' of his hoe, or P. G. Wodehouse's Angus McAllister, who blazed fury if a single flower was picked at Blandings Castle.

John Veitch worked at Killerton in Devon, where his grateful employer helped him to start his own nursery. His ambitious son, the austere, evangelical James, and his grandson James Junior – 'a curious combination of scientist and showman' – raised prize-winning rhododendrons, camellias, dahlias and fuchsias, and orchids. But the masterstroke was James's visionary insistence on sending his own plant hunters abroad, instead of relying, as Loddiges did, on obtaining seeds through exchange with botanical societies overseas. The Veitches kept close links with Kew and the Horticultural Society, who gave their new introductions official names and instant authority, and they made sure that their stunning plants appeared in the sumptuous new *Curtis's Botanical Magazine*. The Veitches soon had glasshouses in Chelsea and their influence spread nationwide as Veitch-trained gardeners took up all the top positions in the country.

Their first collectors were the West Country brothers, William and Thomas Lobb. In 1840 William – clutching a copy of *Daily Food for Christians* thrust on him by James Veitch – went to South America to find monkey-puzzle seeds, and within three years they were selling this once rare tree at £10 per hundred seedlings. Later William also brought back the mighty sequoia 'Wellingtonia' from California, while Thomas collected rhododendrons and orchids in Indonesia, India and Malaya: the first orchid hybrid, developed by John Dominy, flowered in 1856. Over the next forty years the hunting continued, the names of collectors and plants too numerous to list. High in the mountains of Chile Edward Pearce found the glorious tree *Euchryphia glutinosa*, with its glossy leaves and creamy late-summer blossoms. After Japan's ports were finally opened to the West in 1858 John Gould Veitch raided the islands for plants, including the stunning golden-ray lily. In 1900, aged twenty-three, Ernest Wilson set off for China at the height of the Boxer Rebellion, to find *Davidia involucrata*, the Handkerchief or Dove Tree, its white bracts fluttering like 'huge butterflies or small doves'. Over the years Wilson introduced innumerable species including acers, viburnum and *Magnolia delavayai*. He conducted much of his later collecting for the Arnold Arboretum in Boston. But although he was a hero, Wilson's wholesale looting sends a chill down the spine today. One hoard of 18,000 bulbs of *Lilium regale* was lost on the voyage home; next year, to make good the loss, his team cleared entire valleys, scooping 25,000 bulbs, carefully packing them in wet clay.

The legacy of the collectors is with us today, not only in the plants but in their names, like the kerria, named after William Kerr, who introduced it in 1804, or *Pieris forrestii*, after George Forrest (both plants came from China, where Fortune, despite its name, also found the Japanese anemone). Fashion followed fashion, craze followed craze. One or two specimens of dahlias, from Mexico, reached Britain in the 1790s but it was first grown successfully in 1804, when Lady Holland sent some tubers home from Madrid. In the fever that followed, over 1500 varieties were developed and in 1836 the *Floricultural Cabinet* even carried correspondence on how to pronounce it: since it was called after the Swedish botanist Dahl, wrote a certain F. R. Horner crossly, it should therefore be '*ah*': 'nothing but ignorant conceit could have inflicted upon it the pronunciation as if written *Daylia*; – it is at best a piece of affected Cockneyism'. Next came the vogue for chrysanthemums, then orchids and then rhododendrons. We already had the European and American rhododendrons, pale-pink and mauve, but in the 1820s came a new sensation when a brilliant scarlet tree rhododendron brought back from India flowered for the first time. The hunt was on, and the eager collectors included Joseph Hooker, who brought back a range of fine specimens from his Himalayan expeditions.

Collecting wasn't all romance. David Douglas travelled for the Horticultural Society to North America in the 1820s and brought us the giant fir and many other conifers. He also found the flowering currant, penstemons from the Cascade mountains and an invaluable lupin (*Lupinus polyphyllus*) from British Columbia. This was different from the old European form, or the scented yellow tree lupin discovered in California in 1792, and with its huge, heavy spikes of flowers it would eventually foster our familiar garden species. But Douglas seems to have had a miserable time despite his finds: he suffered from rheumatism, bad feet, fever, hostile Indians and countless accidents, with hunger driving him to eat his finds and torrential rapids overturning his canoe ('Melancholy to relate, I lost the whole of my insects, a few seeds, and my pistols'). Finally, at thirty-five, he was killed by a raging bull when he fell into an animal trap in Hawaii. Later in the century George Forrest lost sixteen men, all but one of his team, when attacked by Tibetans.

No one can skim over this hard-won wealth of new arrivals without mentioning the 'Wardian case', which transformed collecting after the 1830s. Dr Nathaniel Ward, an amateur naturalist, had noticed that a tiny fern grew perfectly in one of the glass jars he used to pupate caterpillars: it was sealed, and the moisture condensed by day and returned to the plant by night. He developed larger cases to transport plants, providing a sealed environment protected from the salt and winds and extremes of temperature that had ruined so many specimens in the past. (Wardian cases found their place in the parlour, too, especially for the Victorians' favourite ferns, little forests under glass, glowing green among the antimacassars.) The conditions at sea were not the only problem. Priceless collections were lost in shipwrecks, gnawed by rats or left mouldering at the docks. And the adventure of collecting was followed by slow, patient work of germinating the new seeds and raising the tender plants, with nurserymen and their assistants often working in difficult conditions, bending over their benches, gasping in the humid steam of hothouse and orchid house.

All this was in sharp contrast to the public face, the supplying of smart Londoners with glamorous exotics. Staff in Veitch's Chelsea nursery

The Wardian case.

wore frock-coats and white gloves – hardly gardening apparel. 'Their manners were supposed to be exemplary, their horticultural knowledge without question and their patience endless . . . As the ladies swept through the displays and narrow places in the glasshouses their crinolines snapped off flowers and damaged plants. Gentlemen brushed glowing cigars in the foliage, grabbed delicate orchids and nepenthes to sniff and peer at . . .' The staff had to stand by stoically and smile – the customer was always right.

Gardening was enriched by new nurseries, too, including Lawsons in Edinburgh, Backhouse of York (of rock garden fame), or Jackmans in Woking, who won a prize for their large-flowered purple *Clematis x jackmanii* in 1863. And other familiar names now appear: Sutton and Sons began to flourish in the 1850s, William Thompson of Ipswich (now Thompson and Morgan) sent out his first catalogue in 1855. The penny post, introduced in 1840, sped the catalogues to their customers and brought back their orders. Nurserymen became known for creating hybrids and innumerable new species of popular flowers: chrysanthemums, gladioli, delphiniums, peonies.

Few of those new exotics could have been raised here were it not for the new technologies of iron and glass and greenhouse heating. At the start of Victoria's reign John Loudon invented 'bell-houses' for tender trees, and patented a wrought-iron glazing bar: his collaborator, the firm of W. & D. Bailey, built ravishing glasshouses, like the sixty-foot-high conservatory at Bretton Hall in Yorkshire. But the great breakthrough was the development of 'cylinder glass' (or plate-glass) by Lucas Chance in Birmingham in 1832. After the Glass Tax was repealed in 1845, and the taxes on brick and timber were reduced, the installation of garden buildings boomed. The technology was brought to perfection on a huge scale by Joseph Paxton, first in his 'Great Stove' at Chatsworth, whose iron frame was famously inspired by the ribs of the giant water-lily, *Victoria amazonica*.

Paxton's Great Stove took 500 people four years to build and was visited in 1843 by Queen Victoria, who drove through the great glasshouse in a carriage. It was like a fairyland, 'filled with the rarest Exotics from all parts of the globe . . . the feathery cocoa palm, with its head peering almost to the lofty arched roof; the far-famed silk-cotton tree, supplying a sheet of cream coloured blossoms . . . the singular milk-tree of the Caraccas'. Yet although it provided a protective zone for the plants, the Great Stove created its own pollution: eight boilers consumed hundred of tons of coal brought in by special tramway, their smoke issuing through a tunnel to billow out from a great chimney higher up on the hillside behind. Another supreme glasshouse was the new Palm House at Kew, designed by Decimus Burton, as Christopher Thacker puts it, 'with the purity of form and singleness of purpose of an igloo and the size of a cathedral' and still a fascinating place to visit. And the greatest of all, of course, was Paxton's Crystal Palace, built for the Great Exhibition of 1851.

By the 1880s, however, many people were beginning to question the need for huge glasshouses and acres of bedding, by now the chief feature of the age. And many of the old landowners were finding it hard to afford such massive expenditure on their gardens. During a series of terrible wheat harvests in the 1870s Britain began to import cheap American wheat and because the price was so low the imports continued even when the harvests improved. For landowners this spelt disaster: the price of wheat halved; tenant farmers could not afford their rents and the price of agricultural land tumbled. In addition, from now until the First World War successive governments increased land taxes. All this meant that the landed classes cut back their spending on their country estates and many were sold to the new tycoons of industry or the City. A whole cluster of Sussex estates, for example, passed to City men, one of which was Nymans, which the investment banker, Ludwig Messel, bought in 1890. Messel soon became one of Veitch's most lavish customers, supporting many plant-hunting expeditions and building a conservatory for his orchids, a pinetum and arboretum, a rock garden and an unusual heather garden, and a Japanese garden.

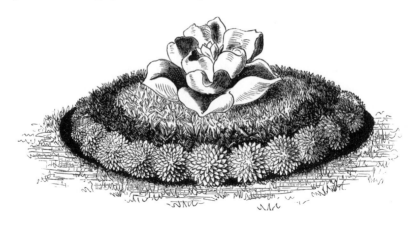

'Bed of succulents and coloured-leaved plants', from William Robinson, *The English Flower Garden*, 1895 edition.

Messel loved plants, but other owners were perhaps more concerned with luxury and status. And since they were emulating the highest style of the old rich – country house parties and all – they continued to go for colour and bedding. Alfred de Rothschild had fifty glasshouses in his kitchen garden at Halton in Buckinghamshire and his gardener, Ernest Field, remembered hearing as a young man that the rich displayed their wealth by their bedding plant list: '10,000 plants for a squire, 20,000 for a baronet, 30,000 for an earl and 40,000 for a duke'. In 1903 Rothschild had 40,418. For some people, well into the twentieth century, brightness remained all.

18

Cottagers, florists and shows

THE ROMANCE OF THE cottage garden began in the late eighteenth century, when landowners created ornamental cottages, often because they had swept away the old ones to make their new landscapes. Some built model villages with neat rectangular gardens, while the advocates of the Picturesque pressed for village greens and thatch and rambling roses.

In the 1790s the model cottage garden, approved for its neatness and productivity, had fruit and vegetables but no flowers (although many actually did). One drawing is often reproduced, but the book for which it was produced rarely seems to be read. It is the frontispiece to Thomas Bernard's *An Account of a Cottage Garden near Tadcaster* (1798). The cottage belonged to sixty-seven-year-old Britton Abbott, a farm labourer with seven children (five survived) who had obtained his roadside plot from the squire and planted a quick-set hedge around it. His garden had fifteen apple trees, a greengage and three plums, gooseberry and currant bushes, vegetables and beehives: he sold his fruit, making about £3 a year, and got forty bushels of potatoes from his ground.

A generation later Cobbett's advice to the cottager was firmly technical: he, too, like old Britton Abbott, liked things *'neatly kept and productive'*. Cobbett was one of the most powerful voices fighting the effects of enclosures, which had caused misery during the Napoleonic Wars. He wrote fiercely, for example, against the enclosure of Horton Heath in Dorset:

> The cottagers produced from their little bits, in food, for themselves and for things to be sold at market, more than any neighbouring farm of 200 acres . . . I learnt to hate a system that could induce them to tear up 'wastes' and sweep away occupiers like those I have described! Wastes indeed! Give a dog an ill name. Was Horton Heath waste? Was it a waste when a hundred, perhaps, of healthy boys and girls were playing there on a Sunday, instead of creeping about covered with filth in the alleys of a town?

For years past, coming ever thicker and faster, acts had allowed landlords to take over the 'wastes' and common land – where the rural poor kept their cow or geese, gathered fuel, picked berries and mushrooms for sustenance – often taking in the old common fields. It was evident, even to many in the upper and middling classes, that something must be done to compensate them and ease their suffering, and from the 1760s articles had appeared in the *Gentleman's Magazine*, proposing 'cow and cot' schemes. Occasionally landowners set aside some land for common fields, but it was not until 1819 that Parliament gave parish wardens the power to set aside twenty acres of parish land to let, a limit extended to fifty acres after the rural 'Captain Swing' riots of 1830. Throughout this decade the Young England movement argued for allotments as a revival of 'ancient' practice and finally, in 1845, against a barrage of hostility from landowners, the

AN

ACCOUNT

OF A

COTTAGE AND GARDEN

NEAR TADCASTER.

WITH

OBSERVATIONS

UPON LABOURERS HAVING FREEHOLD COTTAGES
AND GARDENS,

AND UPON A PLAN FOR SUPPLYING COTTAGERS
WITH COWS.

PRINTED AT THE DESIRE OF THE SOCIETY
FOR BETTERING THE CONDITION, AND
INCREASING THE COMFORTS OF THE POOR

LONDON:

PRINTED FOR T. BECKET, BOOKSELLER, PALL-MALL

1797.

PRICE ONE SHILLING A DOZEN.

' *The great specific of the age for the sorrows of the poor was charity* '

General Inclosure Act specified that in all cases the Commissioners must appropriate 'such an allotment for the labouring poor as they thought necessary'.

Everyone was full of advice. Loudon, who published *The Manual of Cottage Gardening and Husbandry* in 1830, thought that an eighth of an acre was an ideal size, and suggested it be divided between onions and leeks, carrots, parsnips, beans and cabbages, with the bulk given over to potatoes: soft fruit could be trained against the house and hedges could be thickened with fruit trees grafted on to their wild relatives: apples on to crab apples, plums on to sloes. *The Annals of Horticulture* published a 'Field Gardening for the English Labourer' in 1847 and a year later the barrister and garden historian George William Johnson founded *The Cottage Gardener*, the first cheap magazine for the small gardener, appearing every Thursday. By 1854 it claimed to sell 6000 copies a week. It was packed with articles and advertisements for manure and seeds and garden nets, and its opening edition declared that it would deliberately not cover 'grand' plants, like orchids or pineapples, but would concentrate instead on the cabbage, the apple and the mignonette. In fact, it soon spread its remit to include conservatories and the like, and for the rest of its short life it became, like so many others, a 'gentleman's magazine', changing its name to the *Journal of Horticulture* in 1861.

Meanwhile, allotment clubs and benevolent societies tried in practical ways to improve the variety in a cottager's garden by providing free seeds, despite arousing the wrath of the commercial seedsmen. Campaigning clergymen took to the field, like John Stevens Henslow, Professor of Botany at Cambridge and rector of the miserably poor parish of Hitcham. In 1849 Henslow obtained sixteen acres of charity land, which was divided into quarter-acre allotments let at a small annual rent. This became a model, not least because Henslow had powerful friends, like Charles Darwin and John Lindley of the Horticultural Society, whom he persuaded to come down to judge the lively shows of the 'Hitcham Labourers and Mechanics Society'.

Henslow and his peers were supported by the firm belief that gardening was the cure for all ills ('Contact with the brown earth cures all diseases,' wrote the kindly gardening expert Shirley Hibberd in 1877). It brought one closer to God – who, after all, had created Eden. It was a cure for depression, political agitation, drunkenness and ambition, keeping men off the streets and out of the pubs. All in all, gardening was a healthy, hard-working, wholesome, democratic art. Many vicars – often keen gardeners themselves – encouraged their parishioners by giving cuttings and supervising garden schemes, like the Revd William Wilks, later an efficient Secretary of the RHS, the popular vicar of Shirley, in Surrey, where he found and developed the 'Shirley poppy'. And Mary Keen quotes Samuel Reynolds Hole, Dean of Rochester, writing in the 1880s: 'Our curate is not only a lover of flowers himself, but a zealous missionary florist. He was instrumental in founding our Cottage-Gardening Society, which has reclaimed many a waste place from sterility, many a sot from the beerhouse, and brought comfort to many a house.'

If rural villages had good landlords or concerned vicars and 'improved cottages', their gardens could be models of productivity, however patronising the system. Their vegetable plots produced a hefty crop. Half the space was given over to potatoes but as the years rolled by many cottagers and allotment gardeners became daring experimenters, growing celery, shallots, broccoli, artichokes, and endives, and raising the long-despised tomato in cold frames or sunny beds. In *Lark Rise to Candleford*, looking back to the 1880s, Flora Thompson remembered how the men took great pride in their gardens, digging in manure from their pigsties, hoeing and watering, and competing to have the earliest and best vegetables: 'Fat green peas, broad beans as big as a halfpenny, cauliflowers a child could make an armchair of, runner beans and cabbages and kale.'

In Thompson's village the women never worked in the vegetable garden, but 'all grew the old-fashioned cottage garden flowers, pinks and sweet Williams and love in a mist', and cultivated a herb garden for cooking, scenting the clothes, making tonics and camomile tea. As far as flowers went, from the start of the century the cottage garden had a pretty invariable list: hawthorn hedges, honeysuckle and climbing roses, everlasting sweet peas; crocuses, primroses, tulips and crown imperials in spring, and in summer hollyhocks, carnations, marguerites, sweet williams, marigolds, peonies, foxgloves and monkshood, violas and pansies, campanulas, mignonette and Solomon's seal, scented stock and lily of the valley. Almost everyone had a window box, full of geraniums, fuchsias, cacti – cottage exotics. In the 1820s Mary Mitford, the author of *Our Village*, grew geraniums and trained them round a wire pyramid making the display 'the great object from the greenhouse' in summer. She was very pleased with herself: 'Such geraniums! It does not become us poor mortals to be vain – but really, my geraniums!'

But these were the special plants. A different tone is set in John Clare's journal of 1825, where he patiently watches the bluetit feeding caterpillars to her young in the orchard, or notes down his own tasks: 'Thurs. 26 May. Took up my hyacinth bulbs & laid them in ridges of earth to dry – made a new frame for my auriculas – found a large white orchis in Oxney wood of a curious species and very rare.' Clare's cottage poems, like Mitford's *Our Village*, helped to promote the rural idyll: a white paling fence, with pansies and woodbine and

> The tall-topped larkheels, feather'd thick with flowers
> The woodbine, climbing o'er the door in bowers
> The London tufts, of many a mottled hue,
> The pale pink pea, and monkshood darkly blue . . .

Almost because of their neglect, or lack of fashion consciousness, cottages became a repository of plants that had vanished from smart gardens, including special double primroses and pinks. A farmer's wife near Mary Mitford was a 'florist', a specialist in pinks, tulips and auriculas and 'black ranunculuses', who knew all their Latin names. But Loudon, a great promoter and designer of tied cottages, noted that while most did have gardens, at least to provide salads and vegetables, it was not the rural families but 'Tradesmen and operative manufacturers, who have a permanent interest in their cottages,' who 'have generally the best cottage-gardens; and many of them, especially at Norwich, Manchester and Paisley, excel in the culture of florists' flowers'.

Florists' clubs seem to have begun among the cloth makers of Norwich in the sixteenth century, spreading to London and then to the other provinces, as workers like the Huguenot Spitalfields silk weavers moved to new areas. The florists aimed to breed new varieties and perfect specimens from a narrow range of hardy plants, all of which could be grown from seed in a small area and germinated under glass or in frames, and although they had now fallen out of favour in smart society the favourites in the nineteenth century were still the auricula, pink, carnation, tulip, ranunculus, hyacinth and polyanthus. But some traditional cottage flowers were disdained. The hollyhock, declared *The Gardener and Practical Florist* in disgust:

> is not and never can be a florist's flower, any more than a
> horse can be a lap-dog. It is essentially an outdoor plant . . .
> A lady would as soon think of having a pig in a parlour as
> a ramping spike of Hollyhock in a bouquet; and even a
> coachman, who on state days is expected to wear a nosegay
> as large as a cauliflower, would look awkward, with six feet
> of Hollyhock stuck in his buttonhole.

Factory workers and artisans across the country organised clubs, meetings in the local inn and paying a subscription to fund the annual feast – a show and a dinner, often patronised by a local bigwig who donated the cups. By the 1830s Loudon claimed there was a florists' club in every town and village in the northern manufacturing districts. Allotments were as vital to these urban flower growers as they were to the rural poor. In some towns these were a traditional provision. By the 1780s the centre of Birmingham

'Single Hollyhock in Cottage Garden', from
William Robinson, *The English Flower
Garden*, 1895 edition.

was ringed with gardens let at 10s or so a year, but in the 1830s the rent had
escalated to 'guinea gardens', let out to the metalworkers and the rising
middle classes, mostly for vegetables. Local factories like Boulton and
Watt's Soho works provided workers with irrigated plots, in the hope, it is
said, of encouraging sobriety and self-sufficiency. In Nottingham, land on
Hunger Hills had been rented to freemen since the mid-seventeenth
century, but in 1842, after a successful petition from the Nottingham
Independent Cottage Garden Society, this was divided into 400 plots,
rented for £1 a year to local workers in the hosiery trade. There were said
to be 5000 plots let out to 'mechanics'. A little later, Dean Hole put this
estimate up to about 20,000.

Experts abounded. Paisley weavers were famous for their 'laced
pinks', developed from seeds obtained before the French Revolution,
which they later sold to other parts of the country: in all, they raised 300
new varieties. Auriculas were prized in Lancashire, and pansies and violas

were favoured in Scotland and the Midlands, where the recent railway companies took up the craze, encouraging stationmasters to grow violas in the company colours and running competitions for the best station. Men tended their plants obsessively, dashing out to save them if a storm hit in the night and spending all their savings on special covers, and frames, and carrying boxes. All through the spring and summer they took their blooms to shows across the country and the personal glory meant just as much as the silver cup, especially as they were reported in the gardening magazines. (Extra money could be gained by placing bets on who would win, irresistible in the eighteenth century, when people gambled on almost anything, from a horse race to the time of the next shower of rain.)

Semi-official books like *The Florist's Director* of 1792, laid down strict rules about display, to prevent cheating, and clear rules for judging flowers, insisting, for example, on a regular shape, preferably circular. The complexity and competitiveness of it all can be felt in their records. I found one, meticulously entitled *An Account of the Different Flower Shows in 1826, of Auriculas, Tulips, Ranunculuses, Star Pinks and Carnations, held in Lancashire, Cheshire, Yorkshire and other Parts of the Kingdom*. This isn't an

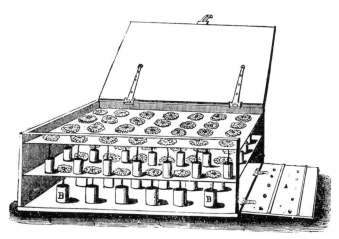

A deal box made to carry flowers to shows, with tin cylinders filled with damp sand to hold them firmly, illustrated in *The Floricultural Cabinet*, 1836.

'account', but a careful listing of prize-winners and varieties at shows in different places, from the King's Arms in Woodstock to the Wheatsheaf in Hulme (both showing pinks) and the Green Dragon Inn at Derby (auriculas). To give a taste, at the Carnation Show at the Angel Inn, Rotherham, there were prizes for classes such as 'Bizards', 'Pink Flakes', Crimson Bizards', 'Scarlet Flakes', 'Purple Flakes', 'Scarlet Picotees' and 'Purple Picotees'. Under each of these headings come the named varieties 'Perfection', 'Sir Isaac Newton', 'Lord Bago', 'Smalley's Foxhunter', 'Royal Sovereign', 'Lord Byron' – plus several unknowns. Each class had twelve entries and at Rotherham, in every class, Miss Walker battled for glory with Mr Barnes and Mr Needham. Pulses must have been racing.

After the 1830s, as the flower-growing plots around the manu-facturing cities were swallowed up by streets, the local clubs declined, while later in the century other clubs were founded for particular flowers that did not fall within the florists' strict range. But the competition remained intense and specialist journals were founded, like *The Floricultural Cabinet* (1833–59) and *The Florist* (1848–84). The shows continued, too, some started for particular reasons, like the Nailsea Show, which began in 1854 to raise money for the war wounded from the Crimea. Others raised funds for local charities. Many were for vegetables and fruit rather than flowers, like the show run by the Ipswich Cucumber Society (judged by length) or the gooseberry shows in the north (judged by weight). The Lancashire gooseberry shows were very old-established: they had begun in the 1740s and within fifty years there were so many that a register was needed to keep track of the varieties and classes. Leek growing was the favourite speciality of miners, both as an individual and a community project, and here, more than anywhere, size mattered. In fact, in almost all vegetable shows, substance not quality won the prize. In an old copy of Shirley Hibberd's *The Kitchen Garden* I came across a yellowing cutting from the *The Standard* of 26 May 1886. The long strip was filled with acrimonious correspondence about 'The Big Mushroom', reported by a Revd F. B. Meadows. Everyone who wrote in had found a bigger one. Mr J. Barton had apparently gathered one thirty-one inches in diameter, 'from his outdoor ridges, near Westbourne Park Station'. It was stupid to buy French mushrooms when we could raise superb ones at home, declared one correspondent, signing off with a flourish, 'I am, Sir, your obedient servant, J. Wright (Author of "Mushrooms for the Million")'.

By 1910, so Charles Curtis claimed in *The Book of the Flower Show*, there were easily 1000 societies, holding one or more shows each year. Some were still held in the upper room of an inn, but most had moved out of the pub into tents in 'a park, garden or meadow, kindly lent by a local celebrity or enthusiast'. Some were nationally famous, like the Shrewsbury fête, where there were sideshows, horse jumping, and 'enormous sums of money are taken at the gate'. Organisers were advised to spice things up by introducing new classes, but still to remember that the aim was educational: correct labelling was all-important. Running a society then looks a complicated business, with all the rules, election of officers, duties, accounts and meetings, let alone the tact required in dealing with protests and disputes ('the gardener is only human,' wrote Curtis generously), and the vital importance of tidying up:

> 9. All Plants, Flowers etc, brought to the Exhibition in dirty pots or boxes or *in any way* that might appear to the Tent Committee to be discreditable to the Society, shall at once be removed from the stages.

Respectable Victorian virtues ruled – hard work, enthusiasm, self-help and discipline – but it was the plants themselves that shone glory on their owners, as they still do in the shows of today.

19

Town mouse

IRONICALLY, JUST AS THE fashionable gardeners were beginning to fall in love with old cottage plants, so cottagers and small-town gardeners fell victim to the bedding craze, crammed with calceolarias, dahlias, lobelias, verbena and begonias. In the towns a clerk's terraced house could be as bright as a banker's, with beds cut into the lawn, glowing orange, purple, scarlet, yellow and blue. The owners planned their flower beds with regimental precision, using edging plants, then filling in with 'carpet plants' and adding bold accents by taller 'dot plants', like standard fuchsias and roses. In London there was a huge demand for standard roses, which were often sold potted, imported from France, although sadly the city was so polluted that many had to be grown under special umbrellas to protect them from the soot.

Loudon's 'fourth-rate' houses were everywhere, 'part of a street or a row' in the heart of the city. Most terraces were meanly built by speculative developers and were rented or leased and often shared with other families or lodgers. Their little court at the front had railings or low walls, sometimes with a small grass plot and trim borders, elsewhere with just a single rose, or a window box, or a mass of shrubs: laurestinus and laurel, holly and rhododendron and broom. Behind lay long narrow plots, with little room for trees or shade, usually with a privy against the back wall but sometimes with a tool shed or summer house. And although Loudon imagined these laid out with grass intersected by paths, he wisely insisted that the occupier should settle his priorities before planning: was he keenest on saving expense, on recreation, on growing fruit and vegetables or florists' flowers, or even 'forming a botanical collection'? Once sure, he could decide what to go for: bedding for colour, or 'showy Perennials, which are common and cheap', or jazzy vases, urns and little statues.

Even at this level, some gardeners hired a jobbing gardener to help at odd intervals. But city gardening was a dispiriting task. The smoke made life hard for the plants and the soil was often poor and shallow, covering builder's rubble, gas pipes, sewers. Yet almost everyone tried, constructing rockeries and grottoes, as well as beds of flowers. Some grew alpines in pots in small backyards, and filled their balconies and rooftops and window boxes. They bought plants from the new nurseries or from a barrow in the market, or raised them from seeds in a small greenhouse or in the glazed porch by the front door, or even on the windowsill. One suggestion was that you could extend the ordinary window by adding a bay and using the space in between as a greenhouse: if the panes were kept clean 'the view into this plant cabinet' could 'create an allusion to the green-house of the villa, or the conservatory of the mansion'.

A grand estate could thus exist in miniature. And the elaborate nationalistic small garden has one supreme fictional example. This is the tiny house of Mr Wemmick in Dickens's *Great Expectations* of 1861, set among the lanes of Walworth, with its Gothic windows, drawbridge and gun. At the back 'so as not to impede the idea of fortifications . . . there's a pig and there are fowls and rabbits; then I knock together my own little frame, you see, and grow cucumbers . . .' Wemmick conducts Pip onwards to a bower about a dozen yards off, but which was approached by such ingenious twists of path that it took quite a long time to get at. Our punch was cooling in an ornamental lake, on whose margin the bower was raised. This piece of water (with an island in the middle that might have been our salad for supper) was of a circular form, and he had constructed a fountain in it, which, when you set a little mill going and took a cork out of a pipe, played to that powerful extent that it made the back of your hand quite wet.

Dickens pokes affectionate fun at Wemmick, the Englishman in his castle: he himself was very proud of his garden at Gadshill. He had his urns, and grottoesque tunnel and shrubbery, and was vice-president of the Rochester Chatham and Strood Horticultural and Floricultural Society from its foundation until 1866. From the beginning, he was a realist, too, as we guess from the scene where Mr Tupman lures the maiden aunt into the summer house in *Pickwick Papers*: 'There was a bower at the further end, with honeysuckle, jessamine and creeping plants – one of those sweet retreats which humane men erect for the accommodation of spiders.'

It was for men and women like Wemmick and the spinster aunt, with a little patch of thirty feet by sixty, that Shirley Hibberd wrote. The most delightful and sensible of Victorian experts, Hibberd edited the *Floral World* from 1858 and his articles formed the basis of his books, like *The Town Garden: A Manual for the Management of City and Suburban Gardens* (1855). He wrote fifteen others including one on ferns, a great Victorian passion, and *The Amateur's Flower Garden* and *The Amateur's Kitchen Garden*. Hibberd lived in Stoke Newington, where he had a long narrow garden, and he tried hard to persuade urban readers to come to terms with where they lived: not to pile rockeries before their hall door as if they were perched on the face of a cliff instead of a terraced street and to avoid 'winding paths, to make butchers boys giddy and perplex the stranger' when all the visitor wanted

Mr Tupman and the spinster aunt startled by the fat boy, illustrated by 'Phiz' in *The Pickwick Papers*, 1836. Dickens tells us that she is 'blushing as red as the watering-pot itself'.

was to get inside and sit down to dinner. He made gardening sound easy, spoke against garishness and advocated hardy plants amid a harmony of green. Yet even Hibberd could not resist the glorious profusion of new flowers, including the 'pelargonium pyramid'. Indeed, his followers might have been guilty of the great Victorian sin, identified by his fellow writer Edward Kemp (who had been Paxton's assistant at Birkenhead Park) in *How to Lay out a Small Garden*. The thing to avoid, Kemp declared – though no one listened – was '*attempting too much*'.

Soon the owners of small gardens would multiply: between 1800 and 1900 Britain's population rose from 10 to 40 million and the desire to escape the urban crush increased year by year. From the 1870s to the end of the century builders and philanthropic industrialists planned leafy new housing estates, at Bedford Park in Chiswick, London, at Lever's soap factory Port Sunlight in Liverpool, at the Cadbury chocolate kingdom of Bournville in Birmingham. In 1898, the visionary Ebenezer Howard proposed a new utopia in *Garden Cities of Tomorrow*, combining the best of town and country: 'Low Rents, High Wages; Low Prices, No Sweating; Bright Homes and Gardens, No Smoke, No Slums'. Letchworth, the first embodiment of this ideal, was marked out in 1903: it was designed for about 30,000 people, with about five houses to an acre, plenty of room for gardens. Four years later Hampstead Garden Suburb followed this lead. On the long narrow plots hundreds of new householders laid down square lawns, long paths and pergolas, and placed a little rose garden around a sundial. Each was slightly different: someone with a passion for bedding plants might live between a fruit grower and a lover of Japanese maples; one garden might be given over to sandpits and swings; another might boast an 'Arts and Crafts' style with little stepped terraces and herbaceous borders; another could be devoted to topiary.

In all their variations, from now on for most people these would be the British gardens they knew best. But thinking of the clerk in the 1890s, catching the 9 a.m. to the City, how can we omit Mr Pooter in *The Diary of a Nobody* by George and Weedon Grossmith? One of the chief delights of his new house, The Laurels, Brickfield Terrace, Holloway, is the 'nice little back garden which runs down to the railway'. Pooter is galvanised into action: on Sunday, 8 April, he discovers 'a beautiful spot for growing mustard and cress and radishes' and although unduly hopeful – 'April 12: Mustard-and-cress and radishes not come up yet' – he is not daunted:

> April 14: Spent the whole of the afternoon in the garden,
> having this morning picked up at a bookstall for fivepence
> a capital book, in good condition, on *Gardening*. I procured
> and sowed some half-hardy annuals in what I fancy will be

a warm, sunny border. I thought of a joke and called out Carrie. Carrie came out rather testy, I thought. I said, 'I have just discovered we have got a lodging house.' She replied: 'How do you mean?' I said: 'Look at the boarders.' Carrie said: 'Is that all you wanted me for?'

Alas, poor Pooter: the garden goes the way of all his pretensions, from the Amateur Dramatic club to the plaster-of-Paris stag's head that he hangs in his hall. And although he sets to work in the garden 'after business' with baffled zeal, historians now tell us that in those days, in smoky Holloway, very few flowers would grow.

An advertisement for short-handled clippers with multiple blades, to keep your topiary under control.

Don't sneer at Mrs Lawrence

M RS L AWRENCE'S VILLA GARDEN at Drayton Green might seem a nightmare
jumble of styles, crammed to the brim with fashionable species. But she
deserves our respect, not our scoffing: she was indomitable and knowledgeable; she won over fifty prizes at the Horticultural Society. She takes her
place in a powerful line of plantswomen. When Mr Nathaniel Wallich, head of
the Botanic Gardens in Calcutta, discovered an unknown tree covered in
glowing vermilion flowers in a ruined monastery in Burma, for example, it was
named *Amherstia nobilis*, in honour of Lady Amherst, wife of the governor-
general of India, a notable and intrepid botanist. The Duke of Devonshire sent
for specimens of this tree at Chatsworth, but his refused to flower – it was Mrs
Lawrence who achieved the first blooms in her garden at Ealing Park. She was
also the first to grow the stunning purple-blue climbing nasturtium,
Tropaeolum aʒureum, from Chile, having the plant rushed to her by James
Veitch in a hansom cab as soon as Dr Lindley had identified and named it.

Mrs Lawrence did not do the hard work herself. She employed six gardeners and a couple of women for collecting 'insects and dead leaves'. But although she was exceptional, she was also typical. An interest in plants, especially flowers, was expected of middle-and upper-class women. As they had done since the days of Queen Anne, rich women built up unrivalled plant collections, like Lady Dorothy Nevill at Dangstein in Hampshire, who was known for her insectivorous plants, or Maria Bateman at Biddulph Grange, who specialised in lilies and had her own private garden, with a secret door, full of bulbs and herbaceous plants.

But this was not exactly 'gardening' in a down-to-earth, physical sense, of the kind recommended by Jane Loudon in her *Instructions on Gardening for Ladies* (1840). She begins quite bluntly with digging: 'a lady, with a small, light spade may, by taking time, succeed in doing all the digging that can be required in a small garden.' Her advice takes into account the position of the body and spade: dig when the ground is dry, she adds, to avoid both 'the danger of taking cold by standing on damp earth' and the sticky soil clogging on the spade. She advised wearing clogs and gaiters, and although she was worried at first that women might not be strong enough to use the new mowing machines, she soon decided they offered 'excellent exercise to the arms and every part of the body'.

Jane Loudon had spent years helpings the volatile John Claudius produce his books and magazines: she had been a novelist before she married and it was her futuristic *The Mummy! A Tale of the Twenty-second Century*, with technological fantasies from coffee machines to air travel, that first attracted Loudon's attention. They married in 1830 and worked as a team, a suburban industry, writing and publishing, travelling the country to different gardens, supervising Loudon's own schemes, like the Derby arboretum, and enjoying London's literary life – their friends included Dickens and Thackeray. But money troubles pursued them. When John Claudius died in 1843 the Royal Horticultural Society immediately offered to mount an appeal to pay his debts.

Jane continued to support herself by her pen. In *Gardening for*

Ladies she had admitted it might be impractical for a woman to look after fruit trees and vegetables, but insisted that no doubts 'can exist regarding her management of the flower garden. That is pre-eminently a woman's kind of garden labour; only, indeed, to give an interest in its effects.' Her flower gardens were formal, with an occasional detour into picturesque 'rock-work'. Her plans for beds were intricate, including dozens of single beds, each with one type of plant, changed three times a season to give colour all year. The justification was aesthetic and feminine but her new journal, *The Lady's Magazine of Gardening* (complete with correspondence column), also covered tools and techniques. Her other books included the *Lady's*

Companion to the Flower Garden and *The Lady's Country Companion* (or 'How to Enjoy a Country Life Rationally') of 1845, written as letters of advice to a young wife battling with a cross old head gardener.

The shelves groaned with books directed at women. Louisa Johnson's *Every Lady Her Own Flower Gardener* (1843) soared through a new edition every year and was soon followed by *Every Lady's Guide to her own Greenhouse, Hothouse and Conservatory*. This was a daring idea, since entering the greenhouse was really stepping on the head gardener's territory, and it also meant getting to grips with the practical problems of plumbing and heating and dung spreading (with the help of a manservant, who would do what he was told and had no horticultural pretensions).

Louisa addressed herself not to the leisured rich but to 'the Industrious and Economical', and she tackled their needs head on. She felt, she said, that women needed a short, sensible guide, to become 'our own gardener; we wish to know about everything *ourselves*, without expense, without being deluged in Latin words and technical terms . . . Some of us have gardens, but we cannot afford a gardener; we like flowers, but we cannot attempt to take more than common pains to raise them.' Other writers, like 'Rosa' in the magazine *The Cottage Gardener* in 1849, spurred women on to be independent of men, especially professional gardeners. 'To enjoy your garden thoroughly,' she wrote, 'you must say with Queen Elizabeth "I will have but one mistress here and no master".'

More and more women took up their spades. Victorian dress could make this difficult: you should avoid leaving bare ground between shrubs and bushes, 'Rosa' suggested, for weeds sprang perpetually and it was difficult to get at them: 'The rose and the sweet-briar tear our bonnets and collars to pieces, and we tread most vexatiously on our raiment when stopping to avoid them.' Louisa Johnson suggested that they kit themselves out properly, in a stout Holland gardener's apron, with big pockets for pruning knife, 'small stout hammer', nails and a ball of string. Preconceptions about delicate Victorian females fall away as we watch them. When Elizabeth Gaskell, novelist and Manchester minister's wife, moved to a new house in early 1851, the garden was her great excitement. In March she tells her daughter Marianne, 'we have got peas, Jerusalem Artichokes, cabbages, mignonette etc down, pinks, carnations, campions, Canterbury bells': next come 'Thunbergias' and 'gladioli' and news that robins are building a nest in their new greenhouse. Soon she is fretting about what seeds to get, then deciding to sow 'very few annuals this year; striking plants in the frames, & relying on putting out the greenhouse things for a summer show'. When Frank the gardener is away and she is in the house by herself, she proudly plants cabbages, writing happily about dibbling and declaring, 'the correct length is two feet apart!'

But flowers, not vegetables, were really still the female province. Flowers filled the house as well as the garden: Mrs Beeton was adamant that a table for dinner for six to twelve people must hold two to four bowls of flowers, in simple colours, set off by asparagus ferns. And that was modest. From the 1860s the fashion was for two shallow bowls, small above, large below, supported by a glass stem, with cascading arrangements: delicate flowers like forget-me-nots and rosebuds at lunchtime, more luscious ones like scarlet pelargoniums and roses at night. At grand parties arches were covered with climbers, exotic plants stood in pots, palms and ferns formed banks behind. On a simpler level the enjoyment of flowers and its link to the sentiment of 'home' is felt in Shirley Hibberd's *Rustic Adornments for Homes of Taste* (1856) – not so different from the flower-arranging tips in women's magazines of the 1950s

> So many are the social qualities of flowers that it would be a difficult task to enumerate them. We always feel welcome when, on entering a room, we find a display of flowers on the table. Where there are flowers about, the hostess appears glad, the children pleased, the very dog and cat grateful for our arrival, the whole scene and all the personages seem more hearty, homely and beautiful, because of the bewitching roses, and orchids, and lilies, and mignonette.

Women wore flowers in their hair and corsages on their bosoms – camellias, stephanotis and gardenias from the hothouse. Girls were encouraged to paint flowers; there were games of flower fortune telling and sombre devotional works like the *Chapters on Flowers*, by Charlotte Elizabeth Tonna, of 1836. There were lists of 'birthday' flowers for each day of the year, and friends gave each other private flower names. As a young woman of twenty, the future George Eliot called her friends Maria Lewis and Martha Jackson 'Veronica' and 'Ivy', signifying respectively constancy and fidelity, and signed herself by the name Martha gave her, 'Clematis' – it meant mental beauty, but Eliot used it to suggest she was a feeble climber, needing the support of her stronger friends.

The language of flowers soon grew more tangled. *Le Langage des Fleurs* by 'Charlotte de la Tour' (1818) was translated into English in 1834, and in the next forty years, in both Britain and America, books poured forth, often with ravishing illustrations. Here are only a few out of hundreds of definitions.

Angelica   inspiration
Bluebell   constancy
Carnation   pure love
Daisy   innocence
Hollyhock   ambition
Marigold (French)   jealousy – or despair
Nasturtium   patriotism
Orange blossom   chastity
Rose (white)   innocent love; (pink)   romantic love;
(red)   passion
Wallflower   fidelity in misfortune
Weeping willow   forsaken
Zinnia   thoughts of absent friends

You had to take care exactly which specimen you chose: while a single pink meant 'perfection', a variegated pink spelt 'rejection'. The books must have

The frontispiece, by Gordon Browne, from Maud Maryon's *How the Garden Grew*, 1900, showing Mary watching her gardener, old Griggs, and an illustration of her garden in bloom.

made pretty presents and spurred flirtatious conversation, but I doubt if Britain was really full of speaking bouquets. Yet perhaps the craze tells us something about the need to express emotion in a period when the rules of decorum became oppressively strict.

Jane Loudon had set a precedent, however, for digging and planting rather than sentimental sighing over bouquets. And when a new, more natural style of gardening became popular towards the end of the century, instead of complex, expensive arrangements of bedding, women found it much easier to look after the flower beds themselves. The new sporty women took to gardening too, and the suggestion was that it made them far more feminine. Gardening became a central part of middle-class life, celebrated by writers like Mrs C. W. Earle (Maria Theresa Villiers), whose *Pot-Pourri from a Surrey Garden* of 1896 combines advice on rearing children with tips on rearing plants, and opinions on education, art and household management. Theresa was sixty-one when she published this book (in defiance of her husband, who allegedly offered her £100 not to) and it was such a success that three sequels followed. She was splendidly practical, acknowledging that nothing could be perfect, that her own garden was often 'crowded, spotty and untidy', and that 'wild gardening' could be just as demanding as formal gardening, if you weren't to lose your primroses under nettles. Also, she wrote, it must be admitted that one of the great drawbacks 'is the state into which the hands and fingers get'. Unfortunately, she adds, one's hands belong not only to oneself, but to the family, who do not scruple to tell the gardening amateur that her appearance is 'revolting'. Constant washing and keeping them smooth with Vaseline, or a mixture of starch and glycerine, helped. And 'Old dog-skin or old kid gloves are better for weeding than the so-called gardening gloves; and for many purposes the wash-leather housemaids glove, sold at any village shop, is invaluable'. Mrs Earle's later books included the helpful *Gardening for the Ignorant*.

Two other gardeners from this era are touchingly evoked by Jane Brown in *The Pursuit of Pleasure*. The first is the Scotswoman, Frances Hope, who joined the better-known Gertrude Jekyll (whose place is in a later chapter), in writing for *The Garden* in the 1880s, suggesting plans for borders and beds and woodland areas. Hope linked her gardening to her social and philanthropic beliefs, taking herbs to the women in Edinburgh tenements, supplying posies to the Royal Infirmary and Asylum for the Blind, and starting 'Flower Missions' – encouraging blind women to cultivate their own scented flowers, hyacinths and stocks and mint. We see her regretfully admiring the rock garden in Edinburgh Botanic Garden, 'but one cannot have everything and we are well content with our borders on the flat, and make the best of it'. Her borders at Wardie Lodge near Edinburgh were indeed magnificent: one was eighty-six feet long and nearly six feet wide, edged with grey houseleeks and filled with bulbs in spring, annuals in summer, purple kale for colour in winter.

Frances Hope's younger contemporary, Ellen Willmott, had no need to hanker for a rock garden: her fabulously rich father simply ordered one from Backhouse's nursery. Travelling across Europe, she bought plants in every country to send back home to the family garden at Warley Place in Essex, a house she eventually inherited. She made a garden in France and another in Italy, and employed 103 gardeners in three countries. Eventually, she was said to have over 100,000 varieties of plants and gardeners across the world sent for her seed lists since she grew so many rarities. She won four RHS gold medals for her daffodils – her great love. With Gertrude Jekyll she was awarded the Society's Victoria Medal in 1897 and in 1904 became the first woman elected to the Linnaean Society. But finally, inevitably, her money ran out – lost through falling investments, lavished on her gardens and on a disastrously ambitious publishing project, *The Genus Rosa*, with illustrations by the painter Alfred Parsons. During the First World War, when the army took over Warley Place, her rose collection was devastated and she had no funds to restore it – the brambles and weeds took their revenge. She was a difficult, confrontational character but her name, Jane Brown reminds us, 'is remembered in all the *willmottiae* and *warleyensis* hybrids that still fill our gardens: *Narcissus* 'Ellen Willmott', *Primula willmottiae*, *Rosa willmottiae* . . . And one plant perhaps more aptly named than any other, *Eryngium giganteum*, 'Miss Willmott's Ghost'.

During these years, women had slowly been joining the ranks of professional gardeners. In 1895 Kew took on women for the first time: they had a special uniform of bloomers, drawing gaping crowds:

> From the roofs of the buses they had a fine view
> Of the ladies in bloomers who gardened at Kew.
> The orchids were slighted, the lilies were scorned,
> The dahlias were flouted, till botanists mourned,
> But the Londoners shouted, 'What ho there, Go to;
> Who wants to see blooms now you've bloomers at Kew.

Without such public fuss Daisy Warwick, the Prince of Wales's mistress and by now a startling convert to socialism, founded an agricultural college for women in Reading in 1898, which moved to Studley Castle (with Edward VII's patronage) five years later. Around the same time Lady Frances Wolseley started the College for Lady Gardeners at Glynde, with Gertrude Jekyll, Theresa Earle and Ellen Willmott as its patrons. The girls from Glynde were expected to be fit: they had to eat stout breakfasts of porridge and bacon and egg, and don a khaki coat, short skirt, leggings and boots, and silk corded ties, throwing on oilskins when they dug in the rain.

By 1910 women gardeners could choose from seven colleges and when the Great War came their skills were in huge demand. Yet for radical women, gardening could represent everything domineering in the British establishment. The Royal Botanic Garden at Kew was an irresistible, publicity-ripe target for the suffragettes, with its acres of glazing. They attacked the Orchid House and burnt down the Tea Pavilion, and one can imagine the gardeners past and present – Mrs Lawrence, Jane Loudon and Louisa Johnson – exclaiming in horror at the report in the *Journal of Horticulture and Home Farmer* of 13 February 1913:

> Kew has been marked out by the suffragettes as one of the scenes of their exploits. They smashed a quantity of glass in the orchid house, and in a manner that one can scarcely accredit to sane adults, wantonly tried to destroy the plants. Rare and delicate plants, under bell-glasses, attracted the special venom of these feminists.

Women, far from delicate, would not be kept under glass any more.

Rebellion

As the nineteenth century drew to a close, more and more people became tired of the 'Crystal Palace style', with its parterres full of bedding and glasshouses stuffed with exotics. Some people, indeed, had loathed bedding since it first came into fashion: even in 1839 a writer to the *Gardener's Magazine* objected that 'scores of unmeaning flower beds in the shape of kidneys and tadpoles and sausages and leeches and commas now disfigure the lawn'.

At the end of the century Dean Hole, once an addict of 'bedding out', came to see it as a disease of the eye, a delirium of simultaneous 'scarlet and yellow fever', which could only be restored by a return to nature: 'then gradually my temperature went down to normal. My reason was restored, and my aching eyes turned away from their kaleidoscope.' A little later E. A. Bowles declared that 'the modern millionaire's made-by-contract, opulent style of gardening' gave him 'a sort of gardening bilious attack and a feeling of pity for the plants and contempt for the gardening skill that relies upon Bank of England notes for manure'.

The jibe about 'Bank of England notes' was part of a wider revulsion against material greed and the spread of the city. In reaction, garden lovers turned back to the country and the cottage garden. Old-fashioned borders of mixed shrubs, hardy perennials and herbs had never really disappeared in many rectories, manor houses and farms: in 1829 Cobbett made a distinction between '*beds*' which were a 'mass of one sort of flower', and '*borders*', where a variety were mingled together, blending in colour, 'so disposed as to form a regular series higher and higher as they approach the back part, or the middle, of the border; and so selected as to insure a succession of blossom from the earliest months of spring until the coming of the frosts'. Mixed borders found their way into grander gardens, like the double herbaceous borders, said to be the earliest recorded in England, at Arley Hall in Cheshire, where plans date from 1846.

Nostalgic myth making grew in parallel to the outward spread of the towns, and over the century gardening taste was slowly affected by writers and artists, all looking back to some 'old-fashioned', pre-industrial idyll – to orchards, cobbled paths, muted colours, old plants. The Pre-Raphaelites loathed parterres: the gardens in their paintings are starred with wild flowers, climbing roses and lilies. Tennyson's poetic gardens were heavy with scent and his *Rural Idylls* embodied a dream of changeless country life: 'no dwelling of men', he wrote, 'has ever been sweeter or pleasanter than an ancient English house.'

Often the lost farm or cottage garden glowed with memory of a lost childhood. Elizabeth Gaskell could accurately describe the limitations of a cottage garden in the north of England with its spare fruit bushes, potatoes, onions, cabbage bed and herbs, and perhaps a rose tree and 'some marigolds, the petals of which flavoured the salt-beef broth'. But when she remembered her grandparents' garden at Sandlebridge she became lyrical, just as George Eliot did when she described an old country garden in *Scenes of Clerical Life* as a charming paradisical mingling of all that was pleasant to the eye and good for food. The rich flower-border running along every walk, with its endless succession of spring flowers, anemones, auriculas, wall-flowers, sweet-williams, campanulas, snap-dragons, and tiger-lilies, had taller beauties such as moss and Provence roses, varied with espalier apple trees; the crimson of a carnation was carried on in the lurking crimson of the neighbouring strawberry beds; you gathered a moss rose one moment and a bunch of currants the next; you were in a delicious fluctuation between the scent of jasmine and the juice of gooseberries.

From the 1860s on, people talked more and more about preserving the past. The craze for collecting antiques began to flourish, the interest in folklore and folk songs developed, and new houses were built in the style of old Tudor granges. In 1877 William Morris (who thought carpet bedding 'an aberration of the human mind') was one of the founders of the Society for the Protection of Ancient Buildings, promoting vernacular architecture and simple native styles; five years later the Ancient Monuments Act was passed and 1895 saw the foundation of the National Trust.

Morris had long been an advocate of old gardens. In 1859 he had moved into the medieval-inspired Red House, designed by his friend Philip Webb, near Bexleyheath in Kent. The four-acre garden was an integral part of the plan, with jasmine, roses, honeysuckle and passion flowers trained up the red-brick walls, and flower beds bordered with lavender and rosemary. There were lilies in summer and sunflowers in autumn. Proud that his house was on the pilgrim's route to Canterbury, Morris created 'a Chaucerian pleasaunce', with trellises of wattle, smothered in roses, for the women of the house (in theory at least) to embroider and make music. Similarly, the ideal June garden at the end of *News from Nowhere*, with overflowing roses, cooing doves, cawing rooks and wheeling swifts, was based on his later garden at Kelmscott Manor, the old Elizabethan farmhouse on the upper Thames at Lechlade where he spent his summers from 1871. Georgie Burne-Jones, visiting him here at the end of his life, noted that 'the garden is enchanting with flowers, one mass of them, and all kept in beautiful order'. In a lecture of 1879 on 'Making the Best of It', Morris set out his guiding rules for a garden: 'Large and small, it should look both orderly and rich. It should be well fenced from the outside world. It should by no means imitate either the wilfulness or wildness of nature, but should look like a thing never to be seen except near a house. It should in fact look like part of a house.' Like Wordsworth's 1806 bower, above all it is to be 'well fenced from the outside world'. This, then, is a retreat, an architectural garden – an extension of domesticity.

More and more gardeners began to search for plants grown in medieval or Elizabethan times, to turn back to old authorities like Bacon's 'On Gardens' for ideas, to hunt out places like Montacute and Haddon Hall, which had escaped the landscaping rage. Pictorially the cottage garden blossomed in watercolours like those of Arthur Claude Strachan and reached its peak in Helen Allingham's paintings in the 1880s of the countryside round her home at Witley in Surrey, now disappearing beneath new villa developments. In the same era, in 1883, the novelist Mrs Ewing wrote the children's story *Mary's Meadow*, in which Mary finds an old 'hose-in-hose' cowslip in a cottage garden and plants it in a local meadow to make 'an earthly paradise': eventually the curmudgeonly squire who owns the land falls under its spell and gives the field to Mary. Mrs Ewing herself founded the Parkinson Society, 'to search out and cultivate old flowers that have become scarce.'

One garden art blessed by this nostalgia was topiary. In the late eighteenth century it had summed up old-fashioned gardening and bad taste, was revived in the 'Merry England' phase at the start of Victoria's reign, then dismissed again, but now it was valued in contrast to the dazzling flower beds. An extraordinary topiary garden was laid out by William Barron at Elvaston in Derbyshire in the 1830 and 1840s, and gardens like Levens Hall, unmentioned for centuries, began to be admired.

Levens Hall, nostalgically evoked by John Nash in *The Mansions of England in Olden Times*, 1849.

The eager hunt often led to mistakes: several admired 'period' gardens like Castle Bromwich or Packwood House in Warwickshire were revered as much older than they were: the 'old' maze at Hatfield had been planted as recently as 1841.

The most powerful voice of rebellion against formal bedding was that of the Irishman William Robinson. He had come to England in 1862 to work at the Royal Botanic Society's gardens at Regent's Park, where he took charge of the native plants collection. As he travelled the countryside for his work he was entranced by the wild flowers and the village gardens, but from his stays on the Continent he also learnt to admire the bold, statuesque exotic planting and the 'natural' areas of hardy plants in the parks of Paris, and the rock-clinging plants of the high Alps. He wrote both on French gardens and on Alpines before he turned his attention to Britain. For years, Robinson fulminated about the evils of bedding, mock-Italian styles and sentimental statues and standard roses. Almost single-handedly he began a movement that would fatally undermine the high Victorian style.

Robinson's book, *The Wild Garden*, appeared in 1870, illustrated with vignettes by Alfred Parsons. His 'wild garden', he explained, was not the old 'Wilderness' or the Picturesque glade, or even a restriction to native plants, but placing plants, old or exotic, in areas where they would thrive:

> What it does mean is best explained by the winter Aconite flowering under a grove of naked trees in February; by the Snowflake, tall and numerous in meadows by the Thames side; by the blue Lupin dyeing an islet with its purple in a Scotch river; and by the blue Apennine Anemone staining an English wood blue before the coming of our bluebells. Multiply these instances a thousandfold, given by many types of plants, from countries colder than ours, and one may get a just idea of the 'Wild Garden'.

These ideas were spread by his popular weekly magazine, *Gardening* (later *Garden Illustrated*), which he edited from 1871, and by the epoch-making book, *The English Flower Garden*, 1883. This had contributions from men like Canon Ellacombe and Samuel Reynolds Hole, the genial, fox-hunting Dean of Rochester, first president of the Rose Society and author of the extremely popular *Book about Roses* of 1869. Both these dedicated clergymen were talented amateur gardeners whose wisdom was drawn from a lifetime's experience. Canon Ellacombe lived almost all his ninety-six years in the same rectory at Bitton in Gloucestershire, where he followed his father as rector, occasionally taking Continental holidays and collecting Alpines tied in his handkerchief. It was a peaceful, busy life: the canon had ten children, composed Latin verses before supper and was an expert on Shakespeare's flowers. In his garden he cherished the traditional florists' flowers (but disliked spiky zinnias and tulips) and he loved the old perennials, writing

'A Cottage at Mattingley, near Winchfield, Hampshire', in *The English Flower Garden*, 1895 edition.

about them passionately for *The Garden*. He was also a plant collector, cramming as much as he could into his small patch: in five years in the 1870s botanists at home and abroad sent him nearly 5000 plants and 1000 packets of seeds. Many of his plants had their own stories, like the black pansies his father brought back from Italy, or the *Limonum cosirensis* given him by a sailor who had sung in Bitton choir as a boy. He threw out ones he didn't like and many others he gave away: all treasures should be shared, he believed. He was tough and his delight never aged. In his eighties he set off up a remote Alpine pass with a friend, riding through deep snow, negotiating torrents between boulders, amid thunder and rain. 'The Canon was quite placid,' remembered his friend Baker, 'sitting on his horse as if he were part of it (it was often as not on its head or its knees!), a huge cotton umbrella over his head, and continually shouting, "Baker! Baker! What's that flower?"'

Canon Ellacombe and Dean Hole both wrote memoirs. Dean Hole also touched the nostalgic public heart with *Our Gardens*, published in 1899. 'I asked a schoolboy, in the sweet summertide,' he wrote, 'what he thought a garden was for?'

> And he said *Strawberries*. His younger sister suggested *Croquet* and the elder *Garden-parties*. The brother from Oxford made a prompt declaration in favour of *Lawn Tennis and Cigarettes*, but was rebuked by a solemn senior, who wore spectacles, and more back hair than is usual with males, and was told that 'a garden was designed for botanical research and for the classification of plants'.

The Dean then asks a middle-aged nymph in a feather hat, who declares it is 'for the soul, sir, the soul of a poet!' and a stout gentleman who admits that what moves him most in horticulture are green peas and new potatoes. In the end he does, however, find some fellow creatures, who were 'devoted to the culture of flowers, and enjoyed from this occupation a large portion of the happiness, which is the purest and surest we can know on earth, the happiness of Home'.

J.D. Sedding, design for a formal garden in *Garden Craft Old and New*, 1891.

Despite this gentle clerical ethos of 'Home, Sweet Home!' *The English Flower Garden* set off a storm. In the book Robinson had damned architects for bringing charmless sterility to the English countryside with their terraces and geometrical borders. Swift as a die, two architects leapt to their pens: John Dando Sedding in *Garden Craft Old and New* (1891) and Reginald Blomfield in *The Formal Garden in England* (1892). Both were colleagues of William Morris and both passionately reasserted the role of 'art' and planning in gardens as well as nature. Sedding, an ecclesiastical architect and a founder of the Art Workers' Guild, commended the charm of old styles while Blomfield wrote a hymn of praise to the history of formality in England. The 'new landscape gardeners' like Robinson, they both complained, had no sense of design at all, or any understanding of the relation of the house to the garden. Robinson was furious and stormed head-first into a heated debate, in person and in print.

The fuss and bitterness masked the odd fact that both sides had so much in common. Both hated bedding, both loved Elizabethan gardens. And ironically, the garden that Robinson himself made, helped by his gardener Ernest Markham (remembered for the clematis named after him), at his own house, the Tudor manor of Gravetye, sheltering in the Sussex downs, was very similar to Blomfield's formal ideal, with terraces and pergolas and long borders. The argument about 'nature and art', 'formality and freedom' had been unduly distracting. A new voice was needed, offering a style that could combine nature with artifice, structure with informality, lushness with decorum. That voice was already beginning to make itself heard, in the writing of Gertrude Jekyll.

IV

FRUIT

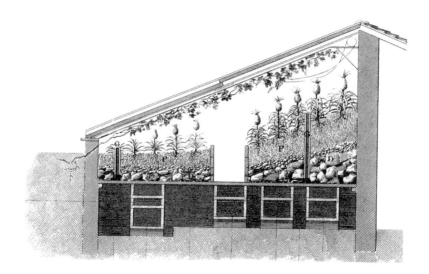

22

The big kitchen garden

AN OLD KITCHEN GARDEN, with the mellow brick walls, gnarled trees and greenhouses with their peeling white paint, can look as if it has been there for ever. In fact, the plot has probably shifted quite a lot. In Tudor and Jacobean times it was next to the house, within easy reach of the kitchen, but landscapers like Capability Brown often moved the whole unsightly rectangle, with its water butts and sheds, half a mile or so away, screening it with trees and laying a gravelled 'service road' to take the produce to the house in carts and wheelbarrows. William Cobbett's *The English Gardener* of 1829 begins with a lament for the garden he knew as a boy, where 'the peaches, nectarines, apricots, fine plums never failed'. It had belonged to Waverley Abbey before the Dissolution and had been preserved until Sir Robert Rich 'tore everything to atoms' when he built a new mansion 'little better than the vulgar box of a cockney'. The old garden reverted to sedgy marsh and Sir Robert built another, 'but he stuck the walls up in a field, unsheltered by hills and trees; and though it was twice the size of the monks' garden, I dare say it has never yielded a tenth part of the produce'.

Cobbett felt that admiring vegetables was just as delightful as looking at flowers. He was right and, whether they were near the house or not, Victorian kitchen gardens were a glory. The high-walled plot was encircled with a 'slip', a wide strip of land, which could be used as an overflow for crops like potatoes, or for soft fruit and flowers. In the slip stood stacks of turf to provide potting loam, piles of garden waste and the pyramids of dung from the cowsheds and stables, sometimes diluted with water as liquid feed. Here, too, were the big wooden compost bins, where garden boys were encouraged to pee (urine gives added nitrogen), and a cluster of outhouses and frames. In the potting shed, its walls painted blue to deter flies, were smooth wooden benches with bins for potting compost beneath and shelves of pots ranked according to size. Nearby stood the tool shed with neatly hung spades and forks, raffia and string, mousetraps and wasp traps, shears and pruning hooks, watering cans, sulphur sprays and smoke guns. Built along the walls of the garden itself was the bothy where the journeymen and garden boys slept, so that they could stoke the boiler on cold nights.

Most big kitchen gardens covered an acre and a half, while grand people might need as much as four acres to provide for their large families, servants, weekend and summer guests. They were ruled by the proud (and invariably Scottish) head gardener, whose house stood nearby, ringed with a neat fence. A good gardener, like a good cook, was a 'treasure'. In Cobbett's day he earned £40 a year (£10 less than the butler) but by the end of the century his pay might reach £100. Wages for all the garden staff rose steadily as the years went by, but still they were often meagre, supplemented by money made on the side from selling vegetables or precious plants to the markets. The head gardener's role was to supervise: he rarely put his hands on a spade, but took all the glory of the prizes and local shows, especially if his garden was 'visited' in the gardening magazines. Head gardeners wrote articles for the journals, sat on RHS bodies like the Fruit

Leek.

(Allium ; porrum.) FRENCH, *Poireau.* ☞ For Cultivation, see page 53.

Webbs' New Colossal Leek.

The best Leek. 1s. 6d. per packet. (SEE ILLUSTRATION.)

A new and very choice variety of this useful vegetable ; rapid in growth, and extremely hardy. It is of splendid quality, and being of immense size and superior shape is specially suitable for exhibition purposes.

From R. RATCLIFFE, Esq., The Poplars.
" *Your Colossal Leeks were the finest I ever had, and the admiration of all who saw them.*"

From Mr. HENRY RAMSDALE, Chew Moor.
" *Please forward two packets of your New Colossal Leek Seed, as the last I had gave great satisfaction.*"

From Mr. THOMAS MINKS, Victoria Garesfield.
" *Please send one packet of your Colossal Leek. I had one last year from which I grew splendid specimens ; they are the best I ever had—they do not belie their name.*"

From Mr. HENRY WILLS, Bedworth.
" *I was very successful with your Seeds, and had some splendid produce. I took your First Prizes with your Celery, and two with your Leeks. I also had the pleasure of winning your First Prize at Nuneaton.*"

		Per ounce.	s.	d.
Henry's Prize.—A large and splendid variety, .	.	6d. per packet,	1	3
Musselburgh.—A very hardy variety of large size, 6d. and 1s. per packet,			1	6
The Lyon.—A fine variety for exhibition, .	.	1s. per packet.		
Ayton Castle Giant.—Very large, .	. . .	6d. per packet,	1	0
Large Rouen.—Leaves broad ; stem very thick, .	.	6d. per packet,	1	0
London Flag.—A well-known sort, .	. . . .			6

WEBBS' NEW COLOSSAL LEEK.

Advertisement, *Webbs' Garden Catalogue*, 1888.

and Vegetable Committee, set up in 1858, and gave their names to commercial growers to endorse new varieties of vegetables, fruit and seeds. Although these men might have started as a twelve-year-old clearing the paths, they clung to their status. Reputation was all: James Barnes of Bicton in Devon successfully sued his employer, Lady Rolle, for defamation when she casually wrote to a friend that her gardens had been neglected.

Beneath this lordly personage there were separate gardeners for flower beds and lawn, trees and shrubberies, and kitchen garden. The glasshouses had their own staff, 'the inside men', who never mixed with the humbler men on the outside beds. At the bottom of the heap came the apprentice boy, who was taken on when he was twelve to fourteen for around 2s 6d a week. If he was ambitious he would study and move on fast, training at one of the famous gardens, but meanwhile he had to clean the hundreds of flowerpots, wash and tie the beans for the cook, stoke the boilers, spread ashes on the paths, lug boxes of apples into the fruit room, bury the potatoes, turnips and carrots in the root cellar for the winter and help with the endless task of watering. This was easier after the gutta-percha hose was invented in 1845, replacing the heavy old leather or canvas hoses, but the garden boys still pushed an old bowser (a cyclindrical iron tank on metal wheels) along the narrow paths, stopping to fill their watering can when needed. The diary of William Cresswell, a twenty-two-year-old under-gardener at Audley End in Essex in the 1870s, written every night in the bothy after a hard day's work, gives us just a tiny glimpse of this life:

> 2 June 1874
> Wind S. Very close and warm, and bright. Thunder in afternoon with heavy showers of rain. Potting off Tazetes singnata primula.[sic] Mr Claydon stung by bees whilst swarming. Stung on eye, swelled very much. Mr B. [Mr Bryan, the head gardener] went to London by mail train (midday). Catching Bats in evening with net, as flew out from corner of room. Sat up late writing letters to Aunts Mary and May and Mr Kennedy.

The gardening staff, like William, also had to deal with the birds and animals and insects that threatened their work. They netted fruit against the bird, put down traps for mice (who loved the hotbeds), caught the cabbage whites in great butterfly nets and sprinkled slugs with quicklime or laid ashes and sawdust to deter them from munching the lettuce. Worst of all, in Cobbett's view, were the ants, 'A very pretty subject for poets, but a most dismal one for gardeners'. The big ones could invade a melon bed and ravage the wall fruit and were impossible to get rid of:

> I know nothing but fire or boiling water, or squeezing to death, that will destroy ants; and if you pour boiling water on their nest in the grass, you destroy the grass; set fire to a nest of the great ants and you burn up the hedge or the trees . . . As to squeezing them to death, they are amongst

the twigs and roots of your trees and plants: they are in the blossoms, and creeping all about the fruit . . .

In busy times the gardeners worked in the evening till the light faded and even went on potting by candlelight. The regime was strict: swearing and negligence – like not washing the glasshouses – were punished by fines, while flirting with the housemaid meant instant dismissal. In some houses this went on well into the twentieth century. In *Akenfield*, Ronald Blythe interviewed a man who had been taken on at fourteen, who remembered how his team wore green baize aprons and collars and ties, no matter how hot it was, were sacked if caught smoking and must never be seen from the house, 'And if people were sitting on the terrace or the lawn, and you had a great barrow-load of weeds, you might have to push it as much as a mile to keep out of view.'

Their work did not go altogether unsung: Kipling, for one, pointed out that the labour behind the 'borders, beds and shrubberies and lawns and avenues' is 'more than meets the eye':

From where the old thick laurels grow, along the thin red wall,
You find the tool- and potting-sheds which are the heart of all;
The cold-frames and the hot-houses, the dungpits and the tanks,
The rollers, carts and drain-pipes, with the barrows and the planks.

And there you'll see the gardeners, the men and 'prentice boys
Told off to do as they are bid and do it without noise;
For, except when seeds are planted and we shout to scare the birds
The Glory of the Garden it abideth not in words . . .

. . . Our England is a garden, and such gardens are not made
By singing:- 'O how beautiful!' and sitting in the shade,
While better men than we go out and start their working lives
At grubbing weeds from gravel paths with broken dinner knives.

Throughout Victoria's reign 'science' increasingly entered the garden, complicating simple tasks like grubbing weeds. Heated debates took place about improving the soil, and the best methods of digging and manuring and fertilising. Phosphates came into use and since these came from pulverised bones there was a gruesome rush to find them: tons of bones were imported, many supposedly from foreign battlefields. Guano was the next wonder fertiliser, a super-rich source of nitrogen: by the mid-1840s Britain was importing over 280,000 tons a year from Peru.

Pests were everywhere, and the head gardener would make up dangerous concoctions in the form of powders and sprays and washes. The deadly Paris Green, copper aceto-arsenite, was developed in the 1860s in the war against chewing insects; Bordeaux mixture, copper sulphate and lime, began to be used against mildew and blight two decades later. Paris Green was largely promoted in England by a woman scientist, Eleanor Ormerod, who wrote twenty-four annual reports on *Observations of Injurious Insects* and was celebrated by Virginia Woolf in her 'Lives of the Obscure': she was as fierce about sparrows as she was about bugs, provoking loud animosity among sparrow lovers. In their battle against pests gardeners were keen on fumigation with sulphurous smoke and their weapons included arsenic, cyanide and nicotine, all banned by modern

Advertisement for 'Mr Vermond's Knapsack Pump'.

regulations, but some of the simpler organic methods they used are still good today, like hosing plants to wash off aphids, or boiling elder leaves for liquid sprays to ward off mildew.

Within the garden the herbs and heat-loving plants were grown in the borders alongside the walls. (Herbs were vital, especially parsley, which the Victorians sprinkled over almost everything, except puddings. At Nuneham Court in Oxfordshire the head gardener, Mr Stewart, never forgot the terrible day he was 'caught napping in the matter of Parsley': after 'the wiggings I had from the cook', he said, he vowed he would 'never more remain minus that indispensable herb for a single hour'.) Paths still divided the main garden into quarters, where the vegetables grew in long rows. Usually one quarter would contain soft fruit – blackcurrants, goose-berries, strawberries, Japanese wine berries – and permanent crops, like asparagus and globe artichokes, rhubarb and seakale, a Victorian favourite, forced under special pots or baskets. The other three beds saw a three-year rotation. Thus the bed that held root crops would be used the next year for surface crops like peas and salads, which leave nitrogen behind them in the soil, and after them this patch would be manured for the greedy brassicas.

Almost all gardens had their mushroom shed, since the cook called for mushrooms constantly. In winter especially, wrote William Taylor, the gardener at Longleat, 'the Mushroom is amongst choice vegetables what the Grape is amongst choice fruits – it is indispensable . . . If I were asked what it is which causes the greatest number of sleepless nights to the professional gardener I should say, Mushrooms.' If supply failed, his peace of mind was gone. Another cause of insomnia was celery – vital for eating with cheese, but wretchedly prone to rain and frost and rabbits. The head gardener made an elaborate cropping plan and obtained most of his seeds from the specialist nurserymen's catalogues, keeping a record of what he ordered each year, what did well and what failed. Even on a small country estate, like Normanby Hall near Scunthorpe in Lincolnshire, where the kitchen garden covered only an acre, the family expected to eat fresh garden peas from May to November and cabbages from April to December, when they were replaced by broccoli and sprouts. When they were in London, hampers of fresh produce were sent to them by train once or twice a week.

The Victorians had far more varieties than we do of almost any vegetable you care to name, for every season. Many old varieties of vegetables have vanished, although the tiny English lettuce 'Stoke', the climbing French bean 'Caseknife', the dwarf early French bean 'Early Warwick' have now all been saved and are available from the Henry Doubleday Research Association's Heritage Seed Library. In 1847, the worst year of the Irish potato famine, *The Annals of Horticulture* listed forty-nine varieties of potatoes: sixteen early, twenty-seven late and five rare varieties including 'Golden Potato of Peru, Pied Golden Potato, Mouse Potato, Pine Apple or Cone Potato, Spanish Dwarf Potato'.

The demand for fruit was particularly high and the subject crops up constantly in the early archives of the Horticultural Society. One letter describes the virtues of the Queen of Sheba gooseberry, another the Shropshire damson, a third notes how cross-pollination has given rise to an improved strawberry. (In 1824 James Barrett claimed he had measured one that was 'six inches and a half in circumference'!) And since the large old standard fruit trees took up so much room, as the century wore on a new interest arose in dwarf trees arranged in cordons or espaliers or trained around wire pyramids. In the 1870s new techniques of dwarfing and root training were developed by the Suffolk nurseryman Thomas Rivers: plums and greengages were grafted on to sloes, pears on to quince, apples on to new small American stock. Growers developed new apples in every part of the country and many now familiar names were heard for the first time: Cox's Orange Pippin, Worcester Pearmain, the crisp, pink 'Beauty of Bath'. When the RHS held their National Apple Conference in 1883 they discovered they had over 1500 cultivars, called by over 2000 local names. (The best cooker was judged to be 'King of the Pippins' and the best dessert apple 'Lord Suffield'.)

'Harvesting the pear wall', from the *Journal of Horticulture*.

The Victorians also had early Mediterranean fruit, like the fragrant apricot 'Moorpark', grown on trellises in front of the extra-thick 'hot wall', heated by gentle fires in little fireplaces built into the back. Thomas Rivers was active here, too, developing new peaches and luscious larger nectarines, spaced across the season. In the 1870s one Sussex gardener grew all Rivers's varieties and sent fresh peaches to the table from mid-July to late September.

Then there were the frames and pits. The frames were a wooden skeleton covered with straw mats or glass, which covered a deep trench, where layers of beaten-down horse manure and oak leaves steamed beneath the loam. A century before, gardeners had used these chiefly for melons but they now adapted them for forcing early salads, tomatoes, strawberries and cucumbers (trained along poles and hanging down straight as a rule beneath narrow glass bells). There were also larger brick-built pits, sometimes heated by an extra layer of manure outside, although by mid-century go-ahead gardeners found that warm pipes could do the trick better and without the messy work of heaving dung. In these long, low pits – until British growers in the Azores began supplying them in the 1870s – gardeners still raised their precious pineapples, like the one weighing ten and a half pounds, presented to George IV for his coronation banquet in 1821, golden, juicy fruits emerging from the dung, like the sun out of darkness.

The increased use of glass, seen in the glamorous conservatories and palm houses, had a huge impact on the kitchen garden. New tall greenhouses now leaned against the walls, often proliferating into a mass of special buildings: a fig house, an orangery, a vinery or a tall, narrow peach house, seventy feet long; a camellia house, or a cool heath house for winter-flowering heathers from Africa; an Australian house; a geranium house to raise the summer bedding. John Abercrombie had coined the words 'hothouse' and 'vinery' in the late eighteenth century and had already listed 105 tropical plants that could be grown under glass, and had used them for forcing early fruit and vegetables: new potatoes in March, strawberries in winter. The specialities now grew ever more exotic. The tireless Thomas Rivers grew oranges, pomegranates, lychees, guavas and mangoes. Lord Egremont's grandson remembered how his Victorian grandfather built a greenhouse to grow bananas. But when he tasted the first home-grown one, peeling it with a golden knife and impaling a sliver with a golden fork, he flung 'dish, plate, knife, fork and banana on the floor and shouted, "Oh God, it tastes just like any other damn banana!"' The offending tree was summarily destroyed and it was estimated that that single banana cost some £3000.

If lychees and bananas were excessive luxuries, grapes were an absolute staple of the Victorian table. The vines were planted outside, entering the glazed vinery through holes in the wall and trained on rods below the sloping roof. From Christmas, when the vine was pruned and the panes cleaned, to early summer, when light filtered through the canopy of leaves, other plants could also be forced on the floor. As the grapes ripened, the heat was increased up to 80°F (27°C), and the vinery was full of a heavy, dusty scent. Over a hundred varieties were grown – the Golden Chasselas, the rich Muscats of Alexandria, the Alicantes for the winter months – displayed at table arranged on their own leaves, glinting gold beneath the ever popular Black Hamburghs or streaked with fiery scarlet under the Barbarossa.

The huge glasshouses also provided palms for the conservatory, flowers for the ballroom, gardenias for the ladies' hair, orchids for the corsage, carnations for the buttonhole. These glass palaces, as some called them, were hideously expensive to run but they were a badge of prestige. At Rangemore in Burton-on-Trent, which belonged to the brewer Bass, there were forty glasshouses, with three and a half miles of pipes, and three huge boilers. Inside, the work was hot and long and hard, a perpetual anxiety. The boilers called for hefty-armed stoking, and the complicated systems of pipes needed delicate regulation with stopcocks and valves. Too hot and the plants would fry; too cold and they would shrivel; too humid and they would rot. Without wind or bees, there were problems of pollination and the gardeners had to run with brushes from one flower to the next. But the glasshouse staff took great pride in displaying their wondrous produce. At Audley End in Essex William Cresswell got into trouble when he showed 'Mr Ward, noted Pine and Grape grower, Bishops Stortford' around the house himself, 'their time being limited. Mr Bryan angry for not sending for him.'

The glory days of the kitchen garden stretched from the Regency to around 1910. Hints of trouble came with the agricultural depression of the 1880s, when many landowners had to tighten their belts. And habits were changing: the long summer in the country was giving way to villas in Italy or yachts in Monte Carlo; in London the market gardens could supply fruit and vegetables and grapes, while peaches and apricots now arrived from the Mediterranean in perfect condition. And after the 1914–18 war, when so many gardeners joined the doomed ranks in the trenches, it was hard, if not impossible, to recapture the vanished past.

23

Country Life

In late-Victorian and Edwardian photographs the country house gardens shimmer with a dream of sunlit ease. Some continued the grand Italianate style of the century before, but the best-loved Edwardian gardens were places to enjoy, to relax in , not a showcase for display like their Victorian forebears. They could encompass a tennis court and croquet lawn, a lily pond and a wood, all carefully composed yet lyrically 'natural'. All the effort that went into them remained invisible – and it could be considerable, as a stalwart designer and plantswoman like Gertrude Jekyll knew.

Born into a well-off family in 1843, Gertrude was a painter and craftswoman, whose early acquaintances included Ruskin and William Morris and artists such as G. F. Watts, Leighton and Burne-Jones. She turned to gardening when her eyesight became too weak for painting and in 1883 she bought her own land across the road from her mother's house at Munstead Wood, near Godalming in Surrey. Now she had a luxurious

Pl. 21

1. *Tropæolum majus* ———— 2. *Tropæolum majus var. atrosanguineum*
3. *Tropæolum minus* ——— 4. *Tropæolum minus fl. pl.* ——— 5. *Tropæolum peregrinum*

Day & Haghe Lith.ᵗ to the Queen

32. Nasturtium from Jane Loudon's *The Ladies' Flower Garden*, 1842.

33. (*top left*) *Golding Constable's Flower Garden*, 1815 by John Constable.

34. (*above*) *Golding Constable's Kitchen Garden*, 1815 by John Constable.

35. (*top right*) Carrots and turnips from the *Album Benary* by G. Severeyns, published 1876-93.

36. (*right*) Detail from a portrait of a gardener from Bramham Park, Yorkshire, c.1822 by George Gerrard.

37. (*above*) *A Devon Cottage*
by Arthur Claude Strachan.
38. (*right*) *In Munstead Wood
Garden*, by Helen
Allingham, c.1900.

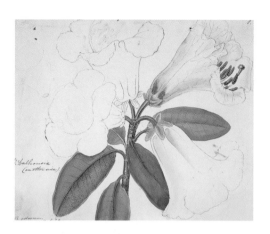

39. (*top left*) *Rhododendron Dalhousiae*, c.1849 by J. D. Hooker.

40. (*top right*) Earthenware plate with a brown and gilt version of the so-called *Darwin Water Lily* pattern, c.1807/8.

41. (*above*) Working on the 'Great Stove', Chatsworth, Derbyshire, c.1900.

42. (*top*) Studley Castle Horticultural College for Women, Warwickshire, c.1910.

43. (*left*) Women gardeners at Kew, 1896.

44. (*right*) Vegetable allotments in Hyde Park during World War II.

45. (*top left*) *Gardens in the Pound, Cookham*, c.1936 by Stanley Spencer.

46. (*top right*) Christopher Lloyd's Great Dixter, East Sussex.

47. (*above*) Heligan, Cornwall.

48. (*top*) Dutch Garden, Lyme Park, Cheshire.

49. (*above*) Little Sparta, Lanarkshire, created by Ian Hamilton Finlay.

50. Derek Jarman's garden, Dungeness.

fifteen acres to experiment with, as she described in her articles for *The Garden*. In her twenties and thirties, she had been fascinated by the Renaissance gardens of Italy and the Moorish gardens of Spain, but she also loved old British gardens. 'Some of the most delightful gardens', she wrote, were 'the little strips in front of roadside cottages . . . where else can one see Wallflowers, or Double Daisies, or White Rose bushes; such clustering masses of perennial Peas, or such well-kept flowery edgings of Pink, or Thrift, or London Pride?'

Gertrude was stubby and unglamorous, and awkward in company, but she was absolutely sure of herself when it came to plants. In 1889, when she was forty-five, she met the twenty-year-old Edwin Lutyens, a fellow admirer of the Arts and Crafts movement with its fondness for traditional natural materials. They would work together for the next thirty years, planning over a hundred gardens from Surrey to Scotland; Lutyens's 'hard elements' gave the gardens they designed a geometric structure, often based around a pool, or flight of steps, while Jekyll's planting softened them. Many of their gardens have vanished (most of the acres of Munstead Wood were built over), but the layout is still clear at places like Folly Farm in Berkshire and some have been restored, including the Manor House at Upton Grey in Hampshire and Barrington Court in Somerset.

In their best gardens, as at Hestercombe in Somerset, the dream of the formal past found a new, harmonious, flower-filled present. Hestercombe was restored in the 1970s after years of neglect, when it became the headquarters of the Somerset Fire Brigade, and some of Jekyll's planting plans were found in a shed. Today it feels an enchanted place, a Queen Anne-style garden with a sunken 'Great Plat', orangery and walled Dutch garden, and massive pergola with spreading views across the Somerset countryside. To double the pleasure of a visit, in recent years the eighteenth-century woodland garden made by Shenstone's friend, Coplestone Warre Bamfylde, has been discovered and restored behind the house, bringing to light a magic valley with rills and lake and temple among the trees.

Gertrude knew her plants well, and understood their preferences and habits, growing them in the wide borders at Munstead Wood before she recommended them in a design. But although she was practical, she kept her artist's touch: she had studied Turner's paintings and was inspired by Monet's garden at Giverny, and saw plants as 'a box of paints'. She planted in drifts of colour, in masses rather than blocks, and created long rectangular borders for all seasons: Grey Borders, September Borders, White Borders, and Blue Borders thrown into contrast by sudden splashes of tall yellow verbascums, or white lilies. Throughout the twentieth century this pattern remained popular, but after so many pale imitations it is refreshing to turn back to Jekyll's own writing and hear that strong, clear voice, which addressed British gardeners for fifty years from 1880 to 1930.

She relished things flowing into each other, like a tree peony with *Clematis montana* behind 'on a wall low enough to let its wreaths of bloom show near the peony'. Sometimes she was fierce: 'Azaleas should never be planted among or even within sight of Rhododendrons . . . they are incongruous in appearance, and impossible to group together for colour.' But more often her enjoyment shines through. She sees how a garden could melt into nature with Alpines overflowing a stone wall or bulbs at the edge

Sir Edwin Lutyens's sketch of Gertrude Jekyll digging a sunflower, 6 August, 1897.

of a wood. She notes the colour of green moss in February, or the tiny gold flowers of *Ranunculus montanus* in the rock garden in April, the petals 'curiously brilliant, glistening and flashing like glass'. Jekyll was as interested in scent as in colour: she liked the aromatic herbs of the south, rosemary and lavender and thyme. But she also appreciated scents one might overlook, like the smell of bracken which, she wrote in *Home and Garden*, seemed like that of the sea when you come across it after a long time, or the odd fragrance around clumps of brambles, 'a little like the waft of a Fir Wood; it occurs again (quite naturally) in the first taste of blackberry jam, and then turns up again in Sweet Sultan. It is allied to the smell of the dying Strawberry Leaves.'

Lutyens, too, responded with emotion to plants, never more so than to those that scattered the graveyards of Flanders in 1917: 'the poppies and wild-flowers that are as friendly to the unexploded shell as they are to the leg of a garden seat in Surrey'. He and Jekyll designed the war cemeteries to evoke dignity and peace, with green hedges, simple trees like oaks and poplars, gentle borders of flowers familiar from their English gardens, hellebores, forget-me-nots, columbines. Gertrude became more and more solitary in her old age, writing her books and tending her garden, which she proudly (or very grumpily, according to Edith Wharton) showed off to visitors. When she died in 1932, Lutyens carved this inscription on her tombstone: *Gertrude Jekyll: Artist, Gardener, Craftswoman.* He might have added 'poet'.

Lutyens designed several gardens without her collaboration, among them the brilliant Italianate 'rooms', with massive yew hedges, that link the house with the orangery at Ammerdown House near Bath. One famous example is at Great Dixter, on a ridge of the downs in east Sussex. Here, in 1910, he worked with Nathaniel Lloyd (who later wrote a book on topiary), laying out an irregular pattern of varied spaces, marked by walls and steps and topiary hedges. Lloyd added the sunken garden by the barn with its octagonal pool, and after nearly a century – thanks to Christopher Lloyd, who has gardened there since he 'helped' his plantswoman mother

Daisy as a small boy – this is still one of the most vivid and dynamic gardens, an exuberant, joyful tapestry of colour and shape. Some of the loveliest effects stem from the original design – like the fan-shaped fig, spreading its fingered leaves against the black weather-boarded barn, or the contrast between the formality and the meadows, genuine wild planting, William Robinson style.

The meadows are not recent experiments nor, as Christopher Lloyd writes, 'just plots of grass that we gave up mowing for lack of labour'. This kind of planting was a passion of Daisy Lloyd, who ran Great Dixter from Nathaniel's death in 1933 until 1972. The meadows rush up to the front door and sweep down from the terrace behind. In spring there are wild daffodils and snakeshead fritillaries; in summer, hundreds of the small orchids native to the weald: early purples, green-winged, twayblade and spotted. I can't think of anywhere else where you walk along a path, admiring a vast, complicated herbaceous border on one side, then glance the other way on to a rustling meadow: formal and wild are just a few feet apart, so close they almost laugh at each other.

This style of gardening suited a particular class: Nathaniel Lloyd came from 'a comfortably off middle-class family in Manchester' and had run his own colour printing firm, while Daisy was the daughter of a London solicitor. They were typical owners of a Lutyens and Jekyll house and garden – people of moderate wealth, attracted by the Arts and Crafts emphasis on conservation and native plants and styles and by the easy, charming designs of great garden makers like Thomas Mawson at the start of the century. Before the First World War and into the 1930s Gertrude Jekyll's books and *Country Life* made gardening even more popular among the upper middle classes. The plantsman E. A. Bowles also inspired them: his garden at Myddleton House in Enfield became famous for its swaths of irises, brilliant tulips and unique rock garden, crowning the slope of his 'Alpine Meadow'.

It was in vogue to be healthy and fit and out of doors, and fashionable for the women of the house to work in the garden. Growing

Terrace walk and herb garden, from Thomas Mawson, *The Art and Craft of Garden Making* (1900).

flowers and arranging them became the favourite pastime of the unmarried daughters, and Jekyll catered for this too with *Flower Decoration in the House* (1907), which would inspire Constance Spry a generation later. The new enjoyment of the outdoors helped to banish the conservatory, which was seen as an artificial barrier between house and garden but the move towards herbaceous borders and shrubs made it easier for owners to manage the garden themselves.

Perhaps because of its closeness to family life, the Edwardian garden had a special appeal as a place of innocence, as in Mrs Gurney's famously sentimental verse of 1910:

> The kiss of the sun for pardon
> The song of the birds for mirth
> One is nearer God's heart in a garden
> Than anywhere else on earth.

Only a year separates this from Frances Hodgson Burnett's *The Secret Garden* (1911), in which the difficult orphaned Mary is transformed as she brings back to life the tangled garden behind the locked door, which restores her crippled cousin to health. *The Secret Garden* was based on a real place, Great Maytham, at Rolvenden in Kent (later rebuilt and redesigned by Lutyens). But there were some things that the gardens, real or fictional, could not heal, among them the terrible losses of the First World War.

Somehow the *Country Life* ethos survived the war, especially for the very rich. Both before and after 1914–18, another of its stars was Norah Lindsay, thirty years younger than Gertrude Jekyll and totally different. Where Jekyll was stout and retiring, Norah was the glamorous darling of the house parties given by hostesses like Sybil Colefax, Nancy Astor and Emerald Cunard. She, too, liked gradations of delicate colour and tall sculptural plants, but her genius was in using masses of casually grouped plants tumbling over the edge of paved paths, rising behind old-fashioned box hedges, creating dramatic effects, like the four plump, square herbaceous beds that replaced the old parterre at Blickling in Norfolk.

Norah advised a number of this set on their planting. And it was notable how many of its members were American – as was Frances Hodgson Burnett herself, in effect, having emigrated to the States in her youth. American money had already saved great gardens: when Consuelo Vanderbilt married into the Marlborough family, her cash restored the splendour of Blenheim and created Achille Duchêne's shining water garden. The oil heiress Cara Broughton helped fund the avenues and rose gardens of Anglesey Abbey near Cambridge, created largely by her son, Lord Fairhaven. William Waldorf Astor bought Cliveden in 1893, adding even more Italianate features to Charles Barry's grand design (including the balustrade from the Villa Borghese, which Astor 'acquired' when he was ambassador to Rome). Ten years later he bought Hever Castle in Kent, where he not only created an Old English garden, complete with a herb garden and maze, but also commissioned a special five-acre Italian garden to hold his collection of sculpture. Not far away, but on a more modest scale, the revived period garden blended with the Italian style at Godinton Park on the edge of the Kent weald. The garden here, restored by Reginald Blomfield in 1902, curves round three sides of the Jacobean house, with battlemented yew hedges, deep borders of flowers, a sunken water garden beneath weeping willows and a 'wilderness' of fine trees. In Godinton's sheltered Italian 'giardino segreto', with its narrow rectangular canal, the bees buzz among the herbs even in February.

The whole idea of the Italian Renaissance villa enchanted the cultured, leisurely *Country Life* milieu, whose denizens went to Florence in the spring and the Riviera in the summer. In 1904 Edith Wharton published her pioneering *Italian Villas and their Gardens*, and this was soon followed by weightier tomes from other scholars. Part of Wharton's aim was to counter the English and American love of flowers, and to make her readers see that three basic elements – 'marble, water and perennial verdure' – could have their own mysterious charm all year through. But she also insisted that 'a marble sarcophagus and a dozen twisted columns will not make an Italian garden': what was needed was a real understanding of the history and philosophy, the siting of a house within its landscape.

The Italian craze was seen in the garden that the architect Harold Peto built for himself at Ilford in Wiltshire. Peto had worked in the South of France and Italy, and amassed an astounding clutter of objects. Around the start of the century he had terraced the hill behind his house, laying lawns, planting beds with roses, rosemary and lavender, dotting it with shrubs and cypresses, and decorating the steps with urns and pillars and colonnades. But he could work in less flamboyant styles. When the City magnate Alexander Henderson, later Lord Faringdon, hired him in 1904 to work at Buscot Park in Berkshire, he designed an Italianate garden that is a model of restraint with its long canal beneath the beech trees, staircases and statues.

After the war, only a handful of people could afford to take up 'grand gardening'. One was Edith, Marchioness of Londonderry, who laid out the dazzling gardens around Mount Stewart House in Northern Ireland. Another Twenties planner who never counted cost was Philip Sassoon. His garden at Port Lympne was a fantasy unlike any other, containing a fountain pool overlooking Romney Marsh and flights of gleaming, shallow marble steps, descending between box-edged terraces. Sassoon's cousin, Lionel Rothschild, was a complete contrast. An avid horticulturalist inspired by the new rhododendrons arriving from South-East Asia, between the wars he created a wonderful rhododendron garden at Exbury in Hampshire, breeding and hybridising 1000 new varieties, and registering and naming half of them. (Vita Sackville-West refused to countenance rhododendrons at Sissinghurst, since they were like 'fat stockbrokers, whom we do not want to have to dinner'.)

Woodland gardening became the new fashion, and the tall rhododendrons and camellias rose and flowered on hillsides from Trewithen in Cornwall to Bodnant in North Wales, Muncaster Castle in Cumbria and Inverewe in Wester Ross. At Leonardslee in Sussex, Sir Edmund Loder raised the renowned 'Loderi' rhododendron hybrids, with their huge scented flowers; at Cawdor Castle near Nairn, the Auchindoune garden was created in the 1920s for plants Lord Cawdor brought back from his Himalayan expedition with the plant hunter Frank Kingdon Ward. Another continuing craze was for Alpines, spurred by Reginald Farrer, 'the father of rock gardening'. At Mount Stuart on the Isle of Bute Thomas Mawson designed a rockery covering two acres: next to it is the 'wee' garden, eight acres full of exotic plants, and beyond it the pinetum, a rescue ground for endangered conifers.

*

Many of the most original gardens of the first half of the twentieth century were one-offs, created by their owners rather than by professional designers. At Hidcote in Oxfordshire, the American Lawrence Johnston began laying out his garden on windswept fields in 1907 and worked on it for the next forty years: in old age he gave it to the National Trust, the first garden to be accepted on its own merits. To protect it from the wind, Johnston planted trees and laid hedges of holly, hornbeam, yew and copper beech, turning the space into a series of compartments flowing downhill each side of the main path, each leading into another, offering alluring glimpses, or surprises, or sudden distant views. Johnston was a plantsman, too, so all the separate enclosures were a haven for particular plants and at the foot of the slope the woodland garden shades into the countryside beyond, across an invisible ha-ha.

Kiftsgate, next door – birthplace of the Kiftsgate rose, that monstrous, arching beauty – has a similar mood, developed by his friends the Muirs, with Johnston's help. And the Hidcote model also shaped the smaller garden at Tintinhull, hidden behind stone walls at the end of a Somerset village. This was created by another American, Phillis Reiss, who begun her work in 1933 and continued it for the next twenty-eight years. In a late stroke of brilliance she turned the tennis court into a pool garden in a memory of her nephew who was killed in the war, its waters reflecting the Italian pergola and the lush borders on either side. It feels like a garden that has been cherished and so it should: for years it was looked after by Penelope Hobhouse, one of today's best gardeners and writers.

You can feel Johnston's influence, too, in interlinked gardens at Sissinghurst Castle in Kent, where Vita Sackville-West and Harold Nicolson began clearing the neglected, overgrown land in 1930. But the inspiration behind Sissinghurst was the English past, particularly Vita's childhood home at Knole, not far away, which she could not inherit because she was a woman. Harold Nicolson's planning gave structure, while she imposed her dramatic planting. The partnership worked, but not without

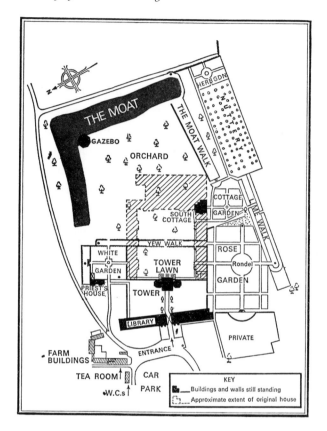

Plan of Sissinghurst, from an early visitors' guide

tension. In the afternoon, wrote Nicolson in his diary in 1946, 'I moon
about with Vita trying to convince her that planning is an element in
gardening.' He wants to persuade her that the moat-walk bank must be
planted with forethought while she 'wishes just to jab in the things she has
left over'.

> The tragedy of the romantic temperament is that it dislikes
> form so much that it ignores the effect of masses. She wants
> to put in stuff which 'will give a lovely red colour in the

autumn'. I wish to put in stuff which will furnish shape to
the perspective. In the end we part, not as friends.

For the dominating, troubled Vita, the interlocking gardens that
Harold designed were, as he put it, 'a series of privacies . . . all a series of escapes
from the world, giving the impression of cumulative escape'. Eventually they
created ten different gardens, the gaps between the hedges and walls luring one
on. In the courtyard, clematis rambles among salvias, spiky thistles, runs of
dark violas; in the huge rose garden the walls are smothered in climbers, and
delphiniums and alliums jostle between bushes. The scent is dizzying. In the
cottage garden you meet a blaze of orange and yellow: day lilies, euphorbias,
bergamot. Then the mood changes: in high summer, in the avenue of pleached
limes the bulbs are over and the azaleas by the moat walk are past, but the herb
garden basks in the heat and the buttercups sway in the meadow.

The white garden was the last to be made. In a January article for
the *Observer* in 1949, Vita Sackville-West wrote about her plans: she
imagined a large square, divided by a short path of grey flagstones, ending
in a rough wooden seat. When you sat there with your back to the yew
hedge, she hoped that your eyes would range over a sea of grey foliage,
southernwood, artemisia and cotton-lavender, pierced with tall lilies:

> There will be white pansies, and white peonies and white
> irises with their grey leaves . . . at least I hope there will be
> all these things. I don't want to boast in advance about my
> grey, green and white garden. It may be a terrible
> failure . . . All the same, I cannot help hoping that the great
> ghostly barn-owl will sweep silently across a pale garden,
> next summer, in the twilight — the pale garden that I am
> now planting, under the first flakes of snow.

Although she opened her garden to the public from time to time, Vita
shuddered at the thought of handing all this over to an 'institution'. Ten

years before she died she wrote furiously: 'Never, never, never. *Au grand jamais, jamais*. Never, never, never. Not that hard little metal plaque at my door. Nigel can do what he likes when I am dead, but as long as I live no Nat. Trust or any other foreign body shall have my darling. No, no.' But among her papers her son Nigel Nicolson found a note saying that she would understand if this had to happen – Sissinghurst was eventually handed over in 1967.

"Grand planting weather."

24

From war to war

VERY SOON AFTER WAR began in 1914 the government started to look at gardening with new eyes. Within days of its outbreak, the Board of Agriculture and Fisheries appealed to private gardeners to keep seed stocks to give to allotment holders. To begin with there was no great panic, but as the war, supposed to be over by Christmas, dragged on and on, the tone changed. In December 1916 local authorities were given powers to take over land and early the next year, when the German U-boat campaign really began, there was general alarm. As one gardening writer, William Rowles, put it in 1917, 'English homes would lose a great part of their charm without the flower garden, but the hard times of today and the possibly harder times we may expect in the near future, urge on us the importance of giving food a preference.' George V duly replaced the geraniums in the flower beds outside Buckingham Palace with potatoes.

There was no great leap forward – if you blow the dust off a copy of Tom Jerrold's *Our War-Time Kitchen Garden* of 1917, you find it is simply his standard work, *The Kitchen Garden*, reissued with hardly a comma altered. But thousands of gardeners saw growing vegetables, especially potatoes, as their own small defiant answer to German U-boats. The number of allotments almost trebled. City parks produced tomatoes in their glasshouses, and cabbages and cauliflowers instead of geraniums, selling them cheaply to the public. At Lady Wolseley's college at Glynde, where she could hear the boom of guns across the Channel, her trainee women gardeners took cartfuls of vegetables to the nearby village. In 1917 the Women's Land Army was formed. And some gardens were given over to medicinal plants, since Britain had been so dependent on Germany for drugs: now, suddenly, dandelions, marigolds and foxgloves were valued for their healing power, as they had been in the past.

Peace – and grief – made gardens more precious. The gaze turned inwards, away from the world. A retired friend of mine remembers her father-in-law's garden, so vital to him and to the family. He had been badly wounded on the Somme, but seemed completely at peace in his garden, which was tremendously long but very narrow, the width of their little terraced house. He grew practically all their vegetables and fruit, and his wife celebrated Whit Sunday each year with a lunch off the first season's crop. He saved his own seeds, sorting out and sowing them in soil that was rich and black from the compost and manure dug in over many years. He had a small shed with a folding chair and outside it a patch of lawn circled with snapdragons. The other flowers – Japanese anemones, gladioli, roses, chrysanths, stocks, sweet peas, sweet williams – grew in rows, like the vegetables. They were poor, since he could not work for a long time after the war, and the garden was their lifeline, as it must have been for many people. It used to give him huge pleasure to load his grown-up children with boxes of vegetables when they called. He never went to a garden centre in his life.

For the middle classes, as well as the poorer army veterans, in the 1920s and through the depression of the 1930s the garden was a place for pleasure, for escape from the office, the school, the city streets. Any good-sized garden had to have a terrace for the deckchairs and tea, a double herbaceous border and a rose garden crammed with the new hybrid teas. Often there was a goldfish pond, an abundance of crazy paving and a small rock garden, and even a tennis court. There was also a huge new class of garden owners. Between the wars, over 4 million houses were built and many of them used land far more generously than the Victorian suburban terraces. The guideline, set down in a report of 1918, was twelve houses to an acre and some new houses had gardens as long as 250 or 300 feet. And as the houses were not rented, but bought, literally millions of home owners were free to let their imaginations range. They listened to the radio, another new luxury, where the novelist Marion Cran broadcast the first gardening programmes in 1923. Her talks and idiosyncratic writing made it clear she was speaking to a new audience: her first book was *The Garden of Ignorance* (or *Experiences of a Woman in a Garden*), and her second *The Garden of Experience*. In 1934 C. M. Middleton took over, and 'Mr Middleton's' *In Your Garden* was required listening.

The mock-Tudor houses built in so many suburbs in the 1930s had generous gardens, and I think my own grandmother's in Thames Ditton was typical. It had roses in front, hybrid teas and floribundas, and the back garden was simply a long rectangle. A Victoria plum rained squishy fruit outside the back door and lower down were gnarled apples (Worcester and Bramley), a pear and a cherry. At each side of the long lawn stretched mini-Jekyll borders, far too thin and never quite under control, dominated by Canterbury bells and the multicoloured Russell lupins that caused such a stir when they were introduced in 1937, patiently developed by the Yorkshireman George Russell from the form that Douglas had long ago brought from British Columbia. The bumpy grass, speckled with daisies, ran down to a trellis with an Albertine rose (I now realise this was a fairly 'new' rose, introduced in 1921, though 'Dorothy Perkins' was probably more popular). Behind this grew the vegetables and the fruit bushes, leaving space for the shed, the compost heap and the blackberries straggling in over the back fence.

Fences were low enough to chat over – they are generally much higher today – and there was much keeping up with the Joneses. Suburbanites were proud of their gardens while knowing very little about the plants they grew. A. P. Herbert had their measure in *Punch* in 1932:

> 'The *anaemias* are wonderful,' I said.
>
> My companion gave me a doubtful glance but said nothing. We walked on beside a herbaceous border. 'And those *arthritis*,' I said, pointing to a clutch of scarlet blooms. 'Always so divine at this time of the year.'
>
> Again the dubious glance, and again no utterance except an appreciative 'Um'.

Popular writers like E. F. Benson and P. G. Wodehouse poked merciless fun at pretension. But the new gardeners took their task very seriously and gardening was a favourite weekend occupation. *The Gardener's Companion* of 1938 (source of the A. P. Herbert quote) helpfully includes a weekend calendar. It is written in incomprehensible double-digging prose, from the first general instructions for January: 'Complete and dispatch the seed order. Wheel on manure, and excavate as necessary. End trenches of ground to be worked later – while surface is frosted. Trench or bastard-trench as opportunity offers.' Everything is a potential foe: 'Sparrow. Well known . . . A Destructive bird throughout the year.' And read closely, this household book turns out to be stuffed with poison:

> Drastically thin crowded growth in standard trees, and paint wounds with white-lead paint.
>
> Beware slugs in the rock-garden and elsewhere. Set traps and use deterrents such as Sanitas powder or permanganate of potash crystals.
>
> Spray fruit with a tar-oil preparation.

*

And that's only the first weekend. The gardeners this instructor envisages never collapse into their deckchairs, except briefly in August, when the barked orders give way to a moment of lazy prose: 'When the garden is ablaze with colour, the wise gardener will be considering any garden alterations he may have in mind, and, in other ways, be looking forward to displays and crops of succeeding years.' But if you put your spade down to dream, remember, 'Bulbs for outside planting need to be ordered promptly.' As the months pass, the weekend nearest the Festive Season prompts some alarming questions:

> Hedgerows are great sources of infestation and infection; what about yours?
> Are they free from weeds and rubbish and from dead wood?
> Is the garden a place of delight at Christmas? If not, consider how it may be improved.
> Are all the compost materials available?
> Will the stock of seed trays, pots, labels, etc., be adequate?
> Did your seedlings 'damp off' last year, and if so why?

It paid to do things perfectly. In the Twenties and Thirties the local flower and vegetable show was still in its heyday, becoming ever more complicated, with craft stalls and sideshows and children's races, prizes for pot plants and cacti, jams and cakes and flower arrangements. In country areas these were often combined with local agricultural shows, or with the sequence of 'Queens' – May Queen, Rose Queen, Carnival Queen – throughout the summer. And on a more serious level, lovers of particular plants formed new national societies, a list which can act as an indicator of shifting favourites: Sweet Pea, 1900; Viola and Pansy, 1911; Iris, 1922; Gladiolus, 1926; Herbs, 1927; Delphinium, 1928 and the Alpine Garden, 1929, recognising the popularity of Alpines since Reginald Farrar's book *My Rock Garden* of 1907.

No relaxing on Midsummer's Day, according to *Good Gardening*, 1937.

*

The garden was still a world enclosed. But it could not stay immune from events beyond the fence. Shortly before the war Vita Sackville-West wrote, 'At 3 p.m. I was listening to the first report of Herr Hitler's speech to the Reichstag, but by 3.30 p.m. I had gotten myself with relief out into the very different atmosphere of the open fields, the quietly busy fields, busy with their April life.' During the Munich crisis, like many other gardeners, she and Harold dug an amateurish trench in the orchard: 'This sudden hasty burrowing into the earth struck one as truly horribly uncivilised: man seeking refuge from man under the peacefully ripening apples and pears of September.'

The outbreak of war called all gardeners to attention. The government immediately began a campaign, 'Grow More Food', but the heading of an *Evening Standard* leader in late 1939 gave them a far stronger tag: 'Dig for Victory' (or 'Dig-for-Dear-Life' as the irreverent called it). Half a million more allotments were called for, with the land compulsorily purchased under emergency legislation. Government pamphlets were issued with memorable titles like 'Cloches v. Hitler' and pundits rallied to give information. In 1940 E. Graham declared, 'Green leafy vegetables, green salads, carrots, beans, peas and potatoes – all are particularly important', adding with a flourish 'exit the herbaceous border'. But he did not think people should banish all flowers and recommended edging the plot with low-growing alyssum, aubretia and campanula, and filling the window boxes with annuals. Graham was not alone: many experts saw the importance of 'cheerfulness and colour' in the dark days of war. Indeed, they even gave advice on what plants you could use to screen your air raid shelter – ivy and periwinkle, honeysuckle and climbing nasturtiums.

Before 1939 imports of salads, and onions in particular, had been massive – only 2 per cent of onions were home-grown – but the gradual fall of European countries to the Nazis stopped almost all the supply. Cabbages grew in Kensington Gardens in the shadow of the Albert Memorial; beans ran up their poles in the moat of the Tower of London School gardens, parks and playing fields were turned over to vegetables. 'Every extra row of vegetables in allotments saves shipping,' pronounced Lord Woolton, Minister of Food: digging could save seamen's lives.

The Women's Land Army mobilised again, with as many as 80,000 women turning to back-breaking work on farms and fields, some of them in the great estate gardens with their fertile soil, where both the kitchen and flower gardens became vegetable plots (although the old heated glass-houses fell into neglect because the lack of fuel made keeping the boilers going impossible and many rare plants were lost). Nurserymen now had to give 90 per cent of their ground to food, using the remaining space for saving their stock. (The RHS and Red Cross also organised a much appreciated scheme to send seeds to prisoners of war: in 1943 nearly a hundred parcels were sent to seventy-two different camps.)

The Ministry organised 'Dig for Victory' exhibitions and local councils set up demonstration plots. Makes of fertilisers and cloches geared their advertising to the war effort. County horticulturalists and local nurserymen and growers gave lectures in towns and villages. In 1941 *The Vegetable Grower's Handbook* ('an enthusiast's attempt to aid the Diggers for Victory'), published by Baker Nurseries of Wolverhampton, became a best-seller and was soon reissued by Penguin. In the same year the RHS manual, *The Vegetable Garden Displayed*, sold over a quarter of a million copies. The Society's emphasis was on economy, cutting down on extravagances like forcing early vegetables or hedge trimming, and concentrating on the essentials. Despite the paper shortage, books poured forth on intensive cultivation so that gardeners could get as many as four crops a year. Everything could be stored, preserved, bottled: 'New Potatoes out-of-season are always appreciated,' wrote E. Graham reassuringly, 'and bottled ones are particularly flavoursome.' A special series of handbooks appeared advising on how to keep bees, chickens and rabbits in your backyard, and how to build a pigsty and fatten its occupant on kitchen waste: there were eventually nearly 7000 'Pig Clubs'.

While the government printed its pamphlets so did the press. *Amateur Gardening* produced some handy paperbacks, including *The War-Time Greenhouse*. Our crumbling family copy fell open, inevitably, at 'Tomatoes', with passages heavily underlined in blue pencil: but the atmosphere of war was brought home by a little cutting between the pages. On one side was a report of troops from the Normandy beachheads pressing forward towards Caen, on the other 'Today in the Garden', 7 June – 'Runner Beans: Plant out seedlings in boxes . . . place a ring of soot around each stem to ward off slugs'.

One memorable set of pamphlets, complete with cartoons, was published by the *Daily Express*, edited by Mr Middleton of radio fame. The son of a head gardener from Northamptonshire, his weekly column for the *Express* had a gung-ho, easy style and his broadcasts, and those of Roy Hay, who followed him in 1942, persuaded thousands to take up the spade. Even in the devastated East End of London they kept digging: 'Bethnal Green had made gardening history,' wrote Hay later. 'Hitler could bomb their houses, smash their chicken-runs and rabbit hutches, but he could never kill their enthusiasm for gardening.' Overall, the national effort was enormous: it was estimated that in 1944 British gardeners produced between 2 and 3 million tons of food. But people still found time to sit in the backyard simply for fun.

Londoners in a back garden during the Blitz, 1940.

Not all the advice was deadly earnest. 'Let us now turn our attention to fruit and vegetables,' wrote Peter Ender in *Down the Garden Path*.

> It is impossible to overestimate the importance of these to Britain in time of war.
>
> The Ministry of Agriculture has announced that if every citizen begins cultivating his garden to the fullest possible extent, there will be enough melons alone to keep eleven million garage doors open. In addition to this, the pips available will be sufficient to supply the peashooters of

thirteen Borstal boys, and will realise 33,822,709 gross of peas for police whistles. Think how enormous, then, are the possibilities opened up by the cultivation of the home garden.

With the end of the war the soldiers returned to their gardens. One of them was Brigadier 'Peter' Phillips, better known to gardeners as C. E. Lucas Phillips. In the First World War, a major by the age of twenty, he had fought in France and in Flanders: in the second he was at Dunkirk, in the western Desert and Italy. He won an MC and a Croix de Guerre, and his books included *Cockleshell Heroes*, *The Greatest Raid of All*, *Alamein* and *Springboard to Victory* – but the one that made him famous was *The Small Garden* of 1952. A classic of the first years of peace, it was detailed, affable, forthright and stubbornly sensible, written for gardeners who might have an acre, but probably had a suburban garden of less than half that size. This was a book 'by an amateur for amateurs', based on fifty years of experience and the memory of his own early tribulations, like the attempt to grow sweet peas under an elm tree and the problems of catching the 8.30 daily. 'If you are young, don't overdo it,' he advises, 'though personally I have always found it a happy slavery, overcoming even the lure of golf (after cricket had long been left behind!).' His book spoke to the masses, selling hundreds of thousands of copies over fifty years.

'Adventure forward on your own,' commanded the brigadier. Any victory you dug for now would be your own.

25

Modernists and artists

IF YOU THINK OF style in the 1920s and 1930s – smooth curves of art deco, gleaming chrome, the architecture of the Bauhaus school, Frank Lloyd Wright and Le Corbusier, the abstraction of Cubism and Expressionism – the garden rooms of Sissinghurst and other famous gardens created in those years suddenly feel old-fashioned, out of touch with the time. Perhaps this was part of their charm. But while new gardens of straight lines, concrete, steel and gleaming pools were created for the streamlined constructions of Germany or California, suited to the modern buildings, in Britain they simply didn't appeal.

One imaginative designer of the 1930s was Christopher Tunnard, who planned the bold garden for St Anne's Hill, Chertsey. But it wasn't until the 1950s, and the exuberant gardens of the Festival of Britain with their bold-shaped plants, that any 'modern' movement really took place here. Even then, it was conservative, rather than radical. At first all the attention of the people and the government was on repairing the cities, clearing the bomb-sites, replacing the slums. The first move was to build the new towns – the 'subtopia' of Harlow, Hemel Hempstead, Crawley and elsewhere. After that, with more money and more nerve, the planners took the philosophy of Corbusier and the 1930s to the cities, embarking on their policy of high-rise buildings. Garden designers, working with town planners, had to cope with these new landscapes. But the champions of the Modern movement in Britain were not adherents of straight lines or futuristic brutalism. What distinguished them all was their interest in landscape shapes, in the relationship of humanity to nature: they were striving for simplicity and harmony, and their work makes sense best when we remember they were contemporaries, and in many cases friends, of sculptors like Henry Moore and Barbara Hepworth, and painters like Ben Nicholson.

The key figures, Brenda Colvin and Sylvia Crowe, were graduates of Swanley Horticultural College and both had been among the founders of the Institute of Landscape Architects in 1929. They, too, looked to the past for inspiration, but this time to the open, sweeping style of Capability Brown where they felt nature could be combined with the freedom of modern abstraction. Colvin and Crowe worked on many public sites: power stations, reservoirs, old slag heaps at coal mines, dreaming of unifying the powerful modern forms with the old landscapes. The hallmarks were bare grass, an occasional tree, very simple, very plain: in her own garden Brenda Colvin, an early and influential environmentalist, tried 'to give continuous calm enjoyment at all seasons, rather than dazzle the eye in the height of summer'.

Sylvia Crowe also worked on new towns like Harlow and Basildon, and when she became landscape consultant to the Forestry Commission she advised on nearly half a million acres of woodland, emphasising the preservation of landscape and the importance of public access. But she had a great feeling for private gardens, 'the gloriettas of the individual man' (or woman), and her sternly elegant book, *Garden Design* (1958), really tried to introduce the post-war British public to classic principles. She was dismayed at the chaos of so many modern gardens and their disregard for local settings and soils, seen in the mad lugging of stone from Westmoreland to Surrey to make rockeries. Her underlying principles embraced the old notion of the 'genius of the place', insisting on the vital qualities of 'unity, scale, time, space, division, light and shade, texture, tone and colour and styles'.

Another founder of the Institute of Landscape Architects, Geoffrey Jellicoe, also worked on landscaping power stations and new towns, including Hemel Hempstead. Yet as a young man in 1925, he had published *Italian Gardens of the Renaissance* with J. G. Shepherd, and all his life he was interested in the deep philosophy that infused Renaissance gardens: many people have noticed how his own gardens create particular moods that linger in the mind. Jellicoe gardened as an artist, a sculptor, expressing the intense fears about the atomic age and the Cold War, sometimes remodelling the landscape on a great scale, like the low hills named after Greek gods at the atomic power station at Harwell, or the path through the dark wood leading to the light at the Kennedy Memorial at Runnymede. But all through his career he also showed his love of the old. There is something of the eighteenth century about his work: much later, in the 1970s, at Shute House in Wiltshire, he made the little River Nadder cascade down the hill, falling into pool after pool below green arches, like the Mogul gardens of Kashmir. Classicism and Romanticism meet. And when he was eighty (when, he said encouragingly, he suddenly felt a new 'burst of ideas'), he embarked on a huge plan at Sutton Place in Surrey (formerly the home of J. Paul Getty) for a series of gardens that formed an allegory on all of human life – a garden doomed to remain uncompleted.

All these designers valued plants for their shape and texture, and preferred native plants as more in keeping with the harmony and 'genius' of the place. Sometimes these could seem dull and too 'green', but they brought a new appreciation of texture, variety and serenity. They made a lasting impact on gardening in public places, on the cobbles and shrubs and

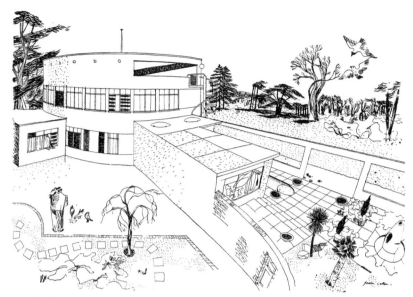

Plan for the garden of St Anne's Hill, Chertsey, drawn by Gordon Cullen, 1938. The house was designed by Raymond McGrath, and the original caption explains that this is 'An architectural garden, part axial, part asymmetrical . . . Screen walls frame the distant views. A sheltered position allows many half-hardy subjects to be grown, including cordylines and the chamaerops palm.'

trees and patterned brick, the curving shapes and open spaces surrounding hospitals, schools, universities, shopping malls. In private gardens, too, the Modernists turned back to the Picturesque, using the straight lines of modern architecture and steel as a frame to make 'pictures' of the garden, in a way reminiscent of eighteenth-century tourists and garden planners.

Some of the most stirring twentieth-century gardens have been made by dreamers, artists and writers – particularly in Scotland, like the exotic tropical paradise on the little Isle of Gigha, across the sound from Kintyre. At Stonypath in Lanarkshire, since 1967 the poet Ian Hamilton Finlay has been creating a nine-acre garden on the edge of the moors, stoutly fighting off all threats of official interference, hence (partly) the name 'Little Sparta'. He has channelled a burn to make ponds, and sculpture-poems and inscriptions are rich with his connections to the old vision of an English Arcadia, or to the life of the sea and the sailor, to warfare and destruction, to the ideals of Rousseau and the French revolution. A temple to Apollo, 'His Music–His Muses–His Missiles', encapsulates the disconcerting blend and on the moorland by the biggest pond carved stones broadcast the words of St Just: 'The present order is the disorder of the future'.

Another Scottish artist who began working with land, and with disorder of a different kind, around the same time, is Joan Hills (now Joan Boyle of the brilliant Boyle family). One of her projects in the early Seventies was called *Seeds for a Random Garden*, in the Boyle family's *Urban Wilderness Series*. This involved selecting patches of ground by throwing darts at a map and gathering seeds, or collecting windblown seeds in a net, or drifting seeds in a river, or mixing them from packets bought at a nursery, and then planting them in portable boxes 'without the slightest consideration for beauty, utility, edibility, scent or horticultural interest', or producing packets for sale, the price chosen by the buyer.

In complete contrast, Charles Jencks has created his swirling mounds and pools, based on the rhythmic patterns of nature, at the Scottish Gallery of Modern Art at Edinburgh. Jencks has also made his own Garden of Cosmic Speculation near Portrack in the Scottish borders, which has been compared with a modern version of Stowe. Full of games and associations, this covers thirty acres, its shapes, earthworks, steel and concrete reflecting the undulating, jagged variety of nature, and offering metaphors to 'explore certain fundamental aspects of the universe', the composition of atoms, the weaving of DNA.

In the south of Britain Derek Jarman used gardening differently. Vibrantly outrageous in his films and books, in his last years, dogged by AIDS-related illness, he made a garden in the most difficult place imaginable, on the pebble ridges by the power station and lighthouses of Dungeness, where the flowers of the coast, sea lavender and grasses, run between buckets on sticks, circles of stones and makeshift statues. There is nothing pretentious or spectacular here: indeed, the patch blends perfectly with the chaos of other shacks and old boats and looping power lines that dot these strange open spaces, washed by light. Yet Jarman's garden speaks to nearly everyone – in her late eighties my mother spent hours there, gazing out across the English Channel, invigorated by this challenge to emptiness and death.

As gardening moves nearer to land art, to the landscape works of Andy Goldsworthy or Richard Long, such endeavours feel far removed from 'ordinary gardening'. But they can be inspiring – they challenge us to be adventurous, to reshape the earth, even if we find it hard to rip out familiar plants, or to bring in steel cubes and metal cones and have fountains that run uphill. The architect-designers did try to make us change. In the 1960s, when tower blocks denied many townspeople a patch of their own and new housing estates were American-style, with grassy frontages, double garages and a few heathers, the truly 'modern' garden was architectural rather than ornamental. The gardens from Britain, Europe, America and Japan that writers of the time chose as models almost all show paving and cobbles; rectangular pools with modern sculpture; flat-roofed, stark-columned porticoes with 'sculptural plants' like fatsias with their shiny, deeply lobed leaves, or the sword-like formiums and yuccas, or a single curly willow or prunus against a wall. Some are stark in the extreme. Concrete was the new garden feature, patterned and cut in discs and squares and honeycombs, used for walls and screens and, of course, the terrace – which was soon labelled the 'patio' and was supposed to merge into the house through the newly fashionable plate-glass sliding doors.

The way that the home was taking over the garden could be measured by the success of John Brooke's *Room Outside* in 1969, subtitled 'A New Approach to Garden Design'. Just opening this book, with its wide margins, square Sixties type and bold diagrams and stark pictures, is like breathing in that era. Brookes had worked with Colvin and Crowe, and he was a functionalist, though a lively one: the garden, he wrote, might be an important place of escape from a hectic world, but it is 'fundamentally *a place for use by people*. It is not a static picture created by plants.' First you had to decide what

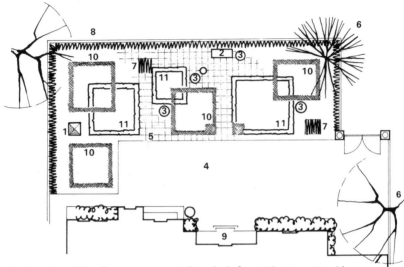

John Brookes, 'Plan for a rose or special garden', from *The Room Outside*, 1966. The structural scheme is designed to be strong and interesting when plants are not in flower: the key is as follows; 1 dovecote, 2 bench seat, 3 tubs for bulbs and annuals, 4 gravel forecourt, 5 brick paving squares, 6 existing tree, 7 clumps of clipped yew, 8 yew hedge, 9 front door, 10 box hedge, 11 santolina hedge.

you wanted to do in it, then create a plan, just as you would for a kitchen. He admired the restful patterns of Japan, the decking and fencing of Scandinavia 'creating an effect of serenity', even the ultra-functional swimming pools, barbecues and minimal maintenance backyards of California.

Brookes has a fine eye for fluid as well as geometric forms, like the flowing lines of trees and sinuous curves of a river, and he sensibly believed in making the best of what you had – focusing on an old tree to provide shade, choosing plants that liked the soil, using a grass mound to create interest. As one can see from the garden that he managed from 1985 at Denmans in Sussex, he likes dramatic foliage and admires plants for form as much as colour, especially when set against different hard textures – thistles and bamboo against a flow of pebbles. It's from here we can date the slow-growing fascination with ornamental grasses, the 'brick-paved suntrap', the grouping of boulders and stones, and copious use of gravel.

Brookes's ideas did catch on, if slowly. The only problem was that if the garden was indeed a room, seen as a single composition, then a key need was privacy: instead of openness, pebbles and pools, the old panelled fences just grew higher and the screens of leylandii began to rise. Over the years the concept of the 'outside room' became a cliché (a mood echoed today in the passion for paving, heaters and outdoor lights). And in the cities, as people converted their Victorian and Edwardian terrace houses and 1930s semis, knocking down walls, clearing away small back kitchens, adding new versions of conservatories, so the garden became always visible. Furniture outside had to be as modern and hip as that within – granite tables, like granite kitchen work surfaces, woven chairs in plastic, metal pots instead of terracotta.

All this looked ahead, but John Brookes had his own sense of history and one of the surprising pleas in *Room Outside* was for the reinstatement of the vegetable plot, too often screened off 'by a decaying rustic pergola'. It should be by the kitchen door, he said sensibly, and we should recognise its charm: 'Certainly the beauty and range of shades of green in some of the allotments and vegetable areas of the Continent has to be seen to be believed.' He wrote nostalgically of the old walled gardens with their espaliers and box hedges, the green freshness of herbs, the splash of colour from gourds in summer. Living with the garden as part of the house had another, perhaps unexpected, result – it was time for the flowers and the vegetables to make a comeback.

26

Eat your greens

WHEN THE WAR WAS over, and the parks and playing fields returned to grass, not everyone gave up their allotment. It was a useful source of vegetables, extra food in time of rationing, with some left over to barter or sell. Allotments now had a venerable history, although they were far from glamorous, usually parcelled out on the land no one else wanted, by the railway or the canal, on the fringes of the cities. The railway companies had matched local councils in providing plots, simply because they had to buy so much land to build their track, and they made it available to their own employees before renting the rest to the public. The same went for the gasworks and the mines. They were linked, too, to the friendly societies and the trade unions; they were part of the effort of workers cooped up in factories, tenements and terraces to help themselves.

Workers relied on their allotments to survive the times when they were laid off, or when factories went on half-time, even to the extent of selling extra produce to neighbours or in the local markets. At the end of the nineteenth century there had been a passionate debate about the 'land issue', including the idea that everyone should have a right to a piece of land to cultivate. From the 1880s on it became a pattern, if the allotment was nearby, for men to spend an hour there before walking to work, tending the ground, feeding the pigs and chickens, then returning again in the evening. At weekends all the family went up, the children being dragged into weeding, the mother bringing the picnic. It was a community venture where men exchanged seed potatoes and dug the pensioners' plots.

After legislation in 1908 a standard local authority plot was ten yards wide by thirty long, and the rent was 10s a year (50p). Dug to feed local people in the First World War, these plots were just as vital for the families of the unemployed during the Depression of the 1930s: some even moved into their sheds and lived there. 'When I was unemployed,' wrote one colliery worker in 1939, quoted in the fact-packed *Practical Gardening and Food Production in Pictures*, 'I purchased some old window frames from a dismantled colliery, a few bags of cement, some sand and glass and with an old iron bedframe and wire netting I built a small glasshouse in which I grow grapes (forty bunches this year), tomatoes (with a surplus which I sell to the neighbours) and plants for planting out in spring.' He had black-currants, loganberries, gooseberries, rhubarb and apples: 'Any man can do what I am doing if he has the ground.'

Faced with the growing threat of fascism, digging the earth came to seem like a symbol of freedom and the vegetable garden a small world where one was in control, working with nature, free from politics. The allotment was often haloed with a rosy light, linked to memories of childhood, just as the Victorian farm gardens had been. 'If I shut my eyes and think of Lower Binfield any time before I was, say, eight, it's always in summer that I remember it,' declared Orwell's hero in *Coming Up for Air* in 1939. He would dream of a hot afternoon in the meadows, 'or it's about dusk in the lane behind the allotments, and there's a smell of pipe tobacco and night stocks floating through the hedge'.

But not all allotments were like this: some were communal, competitive places, seething with envy. And not all children felt like Orwell: a friend who grew up in Watchfield in Berkshire after the war, remembered the humiliation of trundling a wheelbarrow of potatoes back home through the windy streets for his dad, like a badge of poverty. And some allotments, alas, could be lethal. In Cumberland in 1957, the year of the accident at Calder Hall nuclear power station, all gardeners were told to burn their produce for fear it had been contaminated by fallout. My parents and their friends rejected the cabbages and lettuce – they had been rained on, so the concept of 'fallout' made sense – but who could believe that the carrots or the beetroot safely tucked beneath the soil were not safe, were glowing not with health but radiation?

In the Fifties and Sixties the untidy vegetable plots were more than a way of adding to the weekly food basket. But as land prices rose, allotments were looked on with suspicion as eyesores in the modern town. Many were neglected after the frenzied productivity of the war; a number were lost as land was taken over for building houses and flats, and still more went during the years after Beeching 'rationalised' the railway lines and cut thousands of miles of track, and the land surrounding it was sold: in some cities only a tenth of the old plots remained. The men still went up there every weekend, but to the Wilson government, trying to push Britain into the modern world, allotments seemed an anachronism and in 1964 they commissioned an inquiry, chaired by Harry Thorpe, who recommended they be replaced by 'leisure gardens', private plots with little summer houses and community cafés and toilets – a patch of soil for the tower block inhabitants exiled from green earth. Little came of the idea and anyway, by the time planners were considering it seriously, allotments themselves saw a surprising revival. The need for 'green lungs', space for growing things in the cities, suddenly seemed vital again and local authority waiting lists shot up once more.

Since then we've seen bizarre ups and downs. As the standard of living rose and the supermarkets brought cheap vegetables from abroad, growing your own became a pastime rather than a vital resource; leisure

Robert Ball, *Sunday Morning*.

patterns changed and taking your thermos up to the onions and currant bushes came to seem quaintly old-fashioned, more a chore than a pleasure. Then came another upturn in the 1990s, with the growth of interest in ecology, organic gardening and healthy eating. In some London boroughs the waiting lists are up to 15,000 and it can be six or eight years before you get your spade in the soil: in May 2003 an audit of the nation's allotments was ordered by John Prescott, the Deputy Prime Minister, to see if they could be put to better use.

Today there are about 330,000 allotments, almost 90 per cent owned by local authorities. Although some of the older sites have hedges like a patchwork of private gardens, others are open, a slope of squares and rectangles with grassy paths dotted with huts, old bikes, wheelbarrows, rusting baths to hold water. They look lean in winter with a few rows of sprouts, fat in summer with strawberries and peas and the bristly flapping leaves of courgettes. One myth is that allotments are somehow free from hierarchies of race or class. This isn't the case, but they do harbour a cross-section of people: at Uplands in Handsworth, Birmingham, where two big sites were joined after the war, making the largest allotment area in Europe, thirty-eight acres, thirteen different ethnic communities garden, competing fiercely at the September flower show and for the autumn pumpkin prize. Families from the West Indies grow squashes, amaranth and sweet corn; Sikh, Indian and Pakistani owners grow methi (fenugreek) for their curry, scented coriander and hot makoo – a black nightshade for extra hot spice – as well as turnips and potatoes; children from three local schools grow onions, peas and beans and potatoes, taking them home to their families; a long-time allotment owner, Brian Carter, whose father gardened here fifty years ago, helps the children and raises his own prize dahlias. In west London, Nepalese allotments grow karalla, a climbing plant with little gherkin-like fruits, while the Vietnamese grow chop-suey greens.

Another cliché – and this *is* true, and Orwell would probably have approved – is that allotments are bastions of individuality, their chaotic sheds a last defiance against planners and bureaucrats. A few weeks ago our local paper was blazoned with pictures of belligerent allotment holders fighting a road scheme, echoing protests from the days of the Diggers. Maybe it is because of that deep-rooted spirit that allotments have taken to the Internet like weeds to new-dug earth. There are hosts of websites, from directories of associations and tips on organic gardens, to individual diaries recording the (very boring) making of a shed or the rage when vandals burn a scarecrow. Powerful lobby groups weigh in whenever a government white paper on 'Green Spaces' pops up, and 2003 saw a joint 'Allotment Regeneration Project', with half a million allocated for upgrading plots in Newcastle and Sheffield, Solihull, Leicester and Leeds.

The shows have continued, too, with competitors resisting all suggestions that they are anachronistic. In 1989 Ursula Buchan toured the country, getting to know devoted competitors at shows for vegetables, fruit and flowers, and seeing how old traditions die hard. Harry Clarke from Abergavenny, a retired telephone exchange supervisor, was still sowing his onion seeds on Christmas Day, 'a practice developed by gardeners to get them out of the washing up'. Later he would prick them out into pots, then harden them off in the cold greenhouse before planting them out in mid-April, growing them carefully under netting-frames made from the side of his wife's old budgerigar aviary. By the time of the show, on the last Saturday in July, the onions were huge, neatly trimmed, their folded-down tops tied round with raffia.

Meanwhile, at the smart end of the market, growing herbs and vegetables also came back into favour. The interest in herbs came first, born of a romantic reading of the past, a rejection of modern science and medicine. Hilda Leyel started the Culpeper shops and founded the Herbalists (now just Herb) Society in 1927. Many herb gardens in the Thirties and Forties, including that at Sissinghurst, were inspired by Eleanor Sinclair Rohde, who had studied medieval history and wrote fanciful reconstructions of historic gardens. 'I have always wanted to lay out a culinary herb garden in the design of a formal Tudor rose,' she wrote happily, before admitting, 'Rather elaborate and perhaps not very practical, because it would involve considerable labour.' Her nod to wartime difficulties made her modify this into a cartwheel design, which still looks immensely complicated. A generation later herbs leapt back into vogue inspired by the work of Rosemary Verey at Barnsley in Gloucester, where she created a patterned, box-edged herb garden, and a knot garden with interwoven box and fragrant germander, within a border of rosemary.

Soon it became fashionable to design a potager, a modish word which Anna Pavord neatly debunked in *The New Kitchen Garden* in 1996: 'Potager, used in the English sense, means posh vegetables, grown as part of a formal design and mixed with flowers, fruit, or whatever else makes them look decorative as well as useful.' This idea, too, was derived from Rosemary Verey, whose Barnsley plot, much photographed in books in the 1980s, had box-edged squares of ruby chard, pink and yellow cabbages and curly lettuce, with vines and beans trailing over pergolas. She had based it on the famous, if fanciful, garden at Villandry in France designed on 'historical lines' by Dr Joachim Carvallo, and on the plans in William Lawson's *Country House-Wife's Garden* of 1617, and John Evelyn's *The Compleat Gard'ner* of 1693. Some scholars quibble that the modern versions are not true reconstructions, but who cares?

In the 1980s, when money was at last available, the National Trust and other bodies began restoring old Victorian kitchen gardens, complete with their glasshouses. There are now many places to visit, from Glenbervie House on the east coast of Scotland, with its mix of herbaceous flowers, vegetables and fruit, to Titsey Place, sheltering under the North Downs in Surrey, where the old vine house and peach house are packed with tropical plants, and the neat vegetables share space with dripping raspberry canes and forty different kinds of tomatoes. And the biggest adventure, of course, has been the restoring of Heligan in Cornwall and its astounding pineapple pit. And as more of these kitchen gardens came back to life, people began to see the charm of their tidy, traditional aesthetic: rows of onions marching alongside chrysanths or sweet william for cutting. On any allotment a vital tool is string, tightly wound round one peg with the loose end tied to another and slowly unrolled to mark a straight line for a seed drill. And the pleasure of formality goes with a particular mentality, at least as John Carey understood it: vegetable gardeners, he decided, 'harbour, like librarians, a tidy-minded dislike of anyone who actually wants to use the commodities they're in charge of. To have to uproot cabbages, say, from a row, and then hand them over for cooking is always an annoyance. The gaps look unsightly, like snapped-off teeth.'

Carey's tongue-in-cheek articles for the *Sunday Times* in the 1980s were a sure sign that vegetable gardens were chic again. But he knew the hard realities of protecting your plot and offended almost everyone, from cat lovers to Welsh leek growers, by saying so. Faced with bugs and sawfly, 'the only adequate response is to thank God for chemical pesticides and use them liberally':

> Unfortunately the strongest and most effective ones keep being withdrawn form the market on the grounds that they have been found to damage the environment. So when you hit on a really lethal sort it's a good plan to buy it in large quantities, which will allow you to go on using it after it's outlawed. I did this for several seasons with a splendid product, now alas unobtainable, which wiped out everything from snails to flea beetles. It had no adverse effect on the bird population so far as I could see, though the neighbourhood cats did start to look a bit seedy. That, of course, was an advantage from my point of view, for cats are filthy, insanitary beasts and a fearful nuisance to the gardener . . . It has always amazed me that manufacturers of slug bait, and other such garden aids, should proudly announce on the label that their product is 'harmless to pets'. A pesticide that could guarantee to cause pets irreparable damage would, I'd have thought, sell like hot cakes.

The garden sheds of the 1980s were stuffed with even more chemicals than those of the old kitchen gardens or the suburban 1930s. Increasingly, science had seemed the answer to all problems. You could buy nitrates to make everything grow and other products to make everything else die: moss killer to zap the moss in the lawn, pesticides to blast the blackfly, fungicides to obliterate mildew and scab. Every year still sees new products. But one, thank God, has disappeared altogether: DDT, which once seemed the biggest boon of all. This Swiss anti-moth product had been used as an anti-lice barrier for servicemen in the war and an anti-mosquito weapon in the malarial swamps of France, before mutating into a catch-all weapon. Despite warnings, it found its way into countless gardens until it was proved that it poisoned fish, collected in animals, unabsorbed, and probably gave us cancer: it was finally banned in the UK in 1981. Other lethal poisons, dieldrin and aldrin, were banned in 1989. 'Rose-clear', which can blind gardeners as effectively as it cleans up their black spot, was only removed a few years ago and is now back in a less deadly form.

Some people had long been resisting the sway of science. The whole rebellious ethos of the late Sixties set itself against materialism, an impulse seen at its most absurd in urban Laura Ashley smocks and at its most optimistic in rural communes (there was a surge of applications for allotments from women after the Seventies television comedy *The Good Life*). But the campaign for organic gardening is much older than one might think. The Soil Association, with its combination of 'mystical faith in mulch and the practical scientific study of micro-organisms', as Sue Bennett puts it, was founded just after the war in 1946. In Suffolk Lady Eve Balfour, whose book *The Living Soil*, published three years before, had helped to inspire the movement, tried out the new methods, living in harmony with nature, one species among others, using compost and manure instead of fertilisers. Formed by the decomposition of animal and vegetable matter, the soil – humus – 'is far from dead in the sense of having returned to the inorganic world. It is still organic matter, in the transition stage between one form of life and another.'

It is from this that we get the idea of 'organic' gardening and farming, but it was many years before its adherents were considered anything but cranks and weirdos. Brave campaigners like Dr W. E. Shewell-Cooper formed the Good Gardeners' Association and promoted the 'No-Dig' garden. More recently others have joined the fight, notably the Henry Doubleday Research Association, which now has 28,000 members and runs the demonstration organic gardens at Ryton near Coventry, Audley End in Essex and Yalding in Kent. With more awareness of the environment, few of us today would dare to use peat. And thanks to

The 1970s dream of the Good Life, in John and Sally Seymour, *Self-Sufficiency: The Science and Art of Producing and Preserving Your Own Food*, 1973. Another illustration shows a larder with home-cured ham, home-made wine, glowing jars of chutney and jam, and a giant marrow.

jovial evangelists like the late Geoff Hamilton, and Bob Flowerdew and Pippa Greenwood, we're all making compost like crazy again, just as our parents and grandparents and their forebears did. Indeed, a friend suggested to me that compost heaps are somehow particularly British, as rich with history as they are with plant food, taking us back to the old compost yard with its traditional three bins – one for fresh garden rubbish, one for the batch before, now rotting steamily, and one for the good stuff that is ready to use. As Susan Campbell admits, there is 'a certain self-righteousness in making a compost heap', converting garbage into goodness, maintaining the cycle of fertility – returning the nutrients that we have taken out.

But we don't merely have to grow and eat our greens – the call is out for us to rescue them too. The RHS and the HDRA both have Heritage Seed Libraries for old varieties, which seemed doomed to be lost. The HDRA seed guardians are volunteers who grow seed for them and supply over half the 40,000 packets of seed sent out each year. For a tenner you can even Adopt a Vegetable from a touching list of beetroot and celery and more, though I fear that Rat's Tail radish, or Wroxton Brussels sprout won't get as many takers as the Lady Godiva squash or the Jenny Lind melon. Personally I'm going for a climbing French bean: Lazy Housewife.

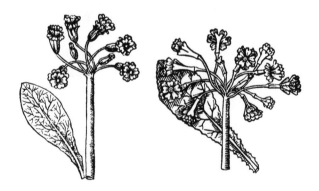

```
┌─────────────────────────────────────────────────────────┐
│  Dahlia    Foxglove    Monarda   Phlox                    │
│            Shirley      Bergamot                          │
│            Hybrids                                        │
│  Iris    Sweet      Erigeron,    Canterbury               │
│  Caprice William    Semiplena    Bell                     │
│  Geum, Fire Opal    Dianthus    Catmint                   │
│            Lobelia                                        │
└─────────────────────────────────────────────────────────┘
```

27

The flowers and the wild

MEANWHILE, WHAT HAD been happening to the flowers? To the great borders, the cottage gardens, the rose beds, the wild-flower meadows, the plants that brought the bees, the damp corners and shrubs that gave homes to toads, small animals and birds? Slowly, in the last half of the twentieth century, all these crept back into favour.

Post-war austerity made people long for glamour and extravagance – the dipping hemline of the New Look, the lush colours of Technicolor movies. Decoration became important, especially to the women who were pushed back into the home after the war when the men reclaimed their jobs. Bizarrely, it now seems, the independent woman who might have been a signals officer in the Wrens, or a worker in a munitions factory, or a driver with the ATS, was now 'simply a housewife' and supposed to be proud of it. It was like the boredom of Victorian and Edwardian days all over again and, as before, one thing you were supposed to do was arrange flowers. No surprise, then, that Constance Spry became a national heroine.

Constance Spry was not what one expects from the 'flower-arranging' label. She was tough and funny and energetic. Her parents in Ireland forbade her to study gardening and she ran away from a terrible marriage to England, where she remarried and began making theatrical, trailing arrangements, opening her first shop, Flower Decoration, in 1928. In 1946 she started a flower-arranging school, catching the nation's eye when she did the flowers for the wedding of Princess Elizabeth and for the Coronation. She liked boldness, old roses, unexpected wild flowers, flashes of lime-green – just what was needed after wartime gloom. Flower-arranging classes spread to Women's Institutes and clubs across the land, and bizarre triangular arrangements, with stiff stems in tangles of netting, graced front halls everywhere. But flower arranging did free women to express themselves, opened people's eyes to the beauty of dramatic foliage and encouraged them to reinstate flowers in the garden.

A very different character, Margery Fish, also, almost inadvertently, showed how flowers could liberate women, in her 1956 book *We Made a Garden*. Mrs Fish had been a secretary on the *Daily Mail* before she married her boss, the news editor, Walter Fish, in her forties. She began gardening when they bought a rambling old house, East Lambrook Manor in Somerset, and was thoroughly under Walter's thumb. He liked straight lines, no weeds, staked delphiniums, brilliant dahlias, concrete paths: she liked creeping plants, tumbling foliage, muted shades. He once slashed to the ground his gardener's chrysanthemums because he thought the man devoted too much time to them. It was only after Walter's death in 1947 that Margery broke free, taking a crowbar to the concrete paths and letting the thyme and daisies run. Like Gertrude Jekyll before her, she visited cottages and collected rare plants, and her books encouraged everyone to let their gardens ramble, be easy and profuse.

People were ready to listen. The houses built after 1946 had far smaller gardens than before, and for a time garden advice books concentrated on cutting down work with ground cover and shrubs. There were little islands of heathers and dwarf conifers in all shades from silver to gold, with the odd azalea, a prunus to give height and blossom, and 'carpeting plants' like the geranium Johnson's Blue (named after A. T. Johnson, an ex-teacher who later wrote a booklet on *Labour-Saving Plants*). But soon the flowers came back.

In the early 1960s the RHS published a series of fifteen illustrated handbooks on annuals and biennials, dahlias, delphiniums, roses and rock and water gardens. At the same time designers like Lanning Roper, whose book *Successful Town Garden* appeared in 1957, showed how cottage plants could bloom in the middle of cities despite the pollution. He suggested tinted walls, trellises, richly coloured flowers and raised beds, and many town gardeners followed him. Three years later he woke people up to the beauties of traditional borders, too, with his *Hardy Herbaceous Plants*. It took only one or two people to show what was missing. When Margery Fish's *Cottage Garden Flowers* and *Ground Cover Plants* appeared in the Sixties they redefined the notion of 'labour-saving'. Now the ground would certainly be covered, but with a mass of varied old-fashioned perennials. In the years to come, many other writers would demonstrate the varied beauty of different planting schemes, especially Rosemary Verey, Penelope Hobhouse and Graham Stuart Thomas – who was equally keen on ground-cover plants, showing his readers how bare corners could be transformed with hostas and ferns, purple-blue pulmonaria in spring, silver lavender and santolina and lime-green *alchemilla mollis* (Lady's Mantle) in summer.

Tastes were changing and one reason was the increase in garden visiting. Graham Stuart Thomas, who was garden adviser to the National Trust from 1956, was a devotee of the golden Arts and Crafts style, and his new designs for the Trust's old gardens helped to bring this back into fashion. With it came a taste for old plants and an interest in their past: in 1956 Alice Coats published her pioneering *Flowers and Their Histories*. Roses, as always, were the focus of interest. Over the past thirty years rose breeders had developed new light-petalled roses to suit the British climate, the most successful of all being 'Peace', which was bred in France in 1939 and arrived here at the close of war in 1945. Crossed with other hybrid teas, 'Peace' produced blooms of all colours and these in turn, crossed with shrub roses, gave us the multi-flowered, brilliantly coloured floribundas. In the 1950s there were over 700 varieties on sale, perfect for the small garden, and growers like Harry Wheatcroft and the Harkness family were famous. But, as with dahlias a century before, the very fact that they were in every garden told against them. In 1955 Graham Stuart Thomas produced his immensely influential *Old Shrub Roses*, praising the delicacy and fragrance of the old gallicas and damask and moss roses. (His rose gardens at Mottisfont Abbey in Romsey, recently replanted, are now the home of the National Collection of nineteenth-century roses.)

After this, suddenly hybrid teas and floribundas appeared vulgar, gaudy, coarse. Taste ruled against them, although in many small front gardens 'Peace', 'Elizabeth of Glamis' and 'Chinatown' still bloom gaily and passers-by lean over and sniff, and sometimes steal the blooms. Then, in the 1960s, the grower David Austin produced the 'English Roses', with the shape and scent of the old and the vigour and repeat flowering of the new. Several of his best-sellers celebrate gardening stars: the rich crimson 'Tradescant'; 'Gertrude Jekyll', a robust, rich pink with a damask perfume; 'Constance Spry', a clear pink, scented like myrrh; and the lovely 'Graham Thomas' itself with its soft yellow, perfumed blooms.

The echoes of Arts and Crafts thinking continue, and the spirit still haunts places like Christopher Lloyd's garden at Great Dixter. This sometimes shocks visitors by its jovial profusion and wilful defiance of fashion – a heap of succulents and a banana plant at the front door, or begonias and marigolds in the little courtyard. Lloyd's exuberant philosophy, set out in his books and articles over many years, has let British gardeners relax, encouraged them to be daring. 'I have no suggested colour schemes,' he says in his guidebook leaflet. 'In fact, I take it as a challenge to combine every sort of colour effectively . . . if I think a yellow candelabra of mullein will look good rising from the middle of a quilt of pink phlox I'll put it there – or let it put itself there.' He rather likes to shock, causing gasps of dismay when he dug up the ailing roses in Lutyens's formal rose beds and replaced them with a tropical extravaganza, a late-summer, blinding, spiky wash of cannas, dahlias and sword-like foliage. 'This has been a lot of fun,' he writes.

If Lloyd has taught us to be bold and have fun, so, in a more restrained way, has Beth Chatto. Both these great gardeners are now in their eighties and their often comic exchanges over the years are found in *Dear Friend and Gardener: Letters on Life and Gardening* (1998). Chatto has the vision of an artist, helped, she says, by her long friendship with the painter and plant collector Cedric Morris. When she and her husband built a house on their fruit farm in Essex (with the least rainfall of anywhere in Britain), the growing conditions varied from a boggy hollow with a spring to dry, heat-slaked gravel, and they took up the challenge by making quite different areas, a woodland, a bog garden and a Mediterranean garden – never watered except in 'local emergencies'. We all think we have problem gardens and Beth Chatto helped us face them.

Today we can all experiment. And if we have the cash, and the patience, we can find every plant we desire. It wasn't always so easy. Until the 1950s gardeners bought plants from nurseries, where they were grown from seed in beds, lifted, delivered and planted when they were dormant, to do least damage. Garden centres were born in America in the Fifties, when the supermarket was just taking off, the chief difference being that plants could be sold in containers, so that they could be seen in flower and replanted at virtually any time of the year. From 1961, enterprising British nurseries, like Wyevale in Hereford, Notcutts in Suffolk and Louis Russell in Surrey, opened their own garden centres. This was good for them because if you could plant at any time, there should be a more even flow of customers to ease the cash flow and seasonal staffing problems. And the range of plants would improve, since instead of growing all their own plants from seed or cuttings, retailers could buy in bulk from wholesalers at home and abroad.

A winning design for a small garden at Chelsea Flower Show, 1968, in the *Daily Express* garden design competition.

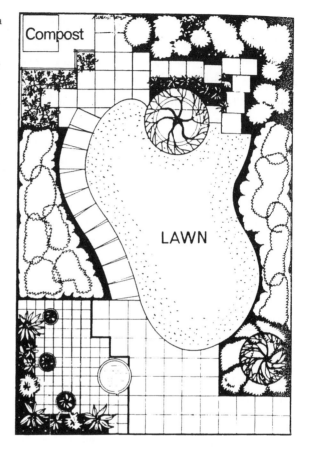

Customers came eagerly, spurred partly by the radio and television. *Gardener's Question Time* had been running on BBC radio since 1947 and Fred Streeter, head gardener at Petworth, had become radio's best-known name with *In Your Garden*, while on television Percy Thrower – a gardener's lad at fourteen – was the star of *Gardening Club*, which began in 1956. As technology improved, gardeners were subjected to a barrage of 'good ideas', new equipment to spike and strim, plastic pots and polythene cloches and windowsill propagators. In 1966 the flymo arrived and the days of strong-armed pushing of the sputtering old petrol mower were past. By the end of the decade the horticultural trade was turning over £100 million a year (it has trebled since). Everyone was out gardening: it was almost a duty. But how many really liked it? In April 1970 the *Daily Express* commissioned a Harris Poll to find out. When asked if gardening was too much hard work for the benefit it gave, 73 per cent disagreed, while 82 per cent thought neglecting your garden was letting the community down. (Not much has changed: the Britain in Bloom competition, which has entries from villages and towns from the Grampians to Jersey, shows how gardening and community pride still go together.)

Not all gardening is harmonious. When C. J. Leyland raised some surprising seedlings on his estate in the 1890s he felt nothing but delight: a few years earlier, quite unexpectedly, the tall Nootka Alaskan cypress had crossed with some Monterey cypresses from California: the seeds took root and literally leapt upwards, growing at a rate of a metre a year, and eventually reaching 30 metres high. For years the new trees were merely the objects of mild admiration in woodland gardens, but with the coming of the garden centres they spread across the land. Phalanxes of leylandii arose, blotting out the sun. Since 1990 there have been over ten thousand disputes between neighbours, some reaching court, or leading to violence and even a murder. As I write, leylandii are the subject of a promising-looking private member's bill. (Rather nicely, the amendment was introduced in the Lords by Lady Gardener of Parkes.)

Luckily, most gardening of the late twentieth century has been benign, however competitive. As money and leisure increased, so garden centres sold fencing and sheds, pools and pots, tables and chairs and sunshades, statues and fountains and gnomes. D. G. Hessayon's 'Expert' planting guides began selling in millions. But like any big chain business, the garden centres all started to look the same, all stocked from the same suppliers. People who liked to feel a bit individual began to hunt for particular plants and turned to local specialists in clematis, or herbs, or cottage flowers, or to smaller nurseries where staff could give genuinely good advice. Paul Kennett, who runs our local garden centre, is one of a generation of owners who grew through the boom but stayed a plantsman.

He started as a Saturday boy at fourteen, went full-time at fifteen and after a spell in the building trade, first rented and then bought the two and a half acres: then he added more land. He still grows 75 per cent of what he sells, although the stock has shifted with the fashions – new patio plants, shrubs, aquatic plants, climbers, long benches of ornamental grasses.

Old-fashioned and 'lost' flowers came back into fashion, too, and sometimes the hedgerows turned out to have hidden treasures. During the war the daffodil growers of Cornwall had to turn their fields over to vegetables, but fearing the loss of old varieties, they planted them along the hedges. John Lanyon, the current gardener at Cotehele in the Tamar valley, found old doubles in corners of the garden, with names like 'Butter and Eggs' and 'Codlins and Cream', and encouraged local people to tell him more: now the meadow and orchard are full of the small, rare flowers. For a long time would-be gardeners were frustrated – they heard of new plants, or rarities, or old varieties, but where could they find them? The answer was at hand – in 1987 the first *Plant Finder* appeared and now, published by the RHS, it shoots annually up the best-seller lists. Mail order has made a comeback, since plants can be sent in little plugs, which travel well and are easily planted. The warmer climate means that more tender plants will grow here and EU regulations have made imports simpler. Growers are constantly developing new varieties, colours, scents: open a catalogue and you see 'New!' 'New!' 'New!' on every page – new delphiniums, new heuchera, new hellebores, new irises, new poppies . . .

The British are learning to enjoy bright colours again, to relish the pom-pom dazzle of dahlias. The pleasure of growing from seed has begun to thrill us. Allotment owners have all the fun in the mid-winter gloom, notes James Fenton, planning their summer crops:

> Why should the flower grower not feel the same? Why should not he or she ask: What do I feel like growing this year? What delights me? What bores me? What is ravishing? What is revolting? Flower fanatic and vegetable

fiend, we are seated at the same kitchen table, leafing through many of the same catalogues. The same gales are howling around the roof-tops. The same frosts are glazing the water-butts. Why should I not feel, this January, the same freedom as my pea-epicurean, my marrow-maniacal friend?

Yet prejudices remain. We are swept by 'favourite plants': *verbena bonariensis*, then alliums, then canna, then grasses – now olive trees, oleanders and agapanthus, perhaps a response to climate change and foreign holidays. Each plant in turn is taken up, then dropped as it goes out of vogue: the swaying purple curtain of verbena, the spiky allium heads, the canna's flash of colour in late summer, the year-long swaying and rustling of the grass. In 2003 the journalist Geraldine Bedell, who spent two weeks researching garden centres, was not surprised to hear that gardens were the new 'room' that had to be made over to sell the house – a good one adding 10 per cent to the value. Her statistics were staggering: she learnt that 56 million trees and shrubs are imported annually out of the 80 million planted. But she also learnt a great deal about snobbery.

Ironically, just as gardening grew into a big industry, so people began to value those aspects that seemed a counter to, or an escape from, the commercial world, setting the exotic garden centre plants against the simplicity and variety of the flowers of the field. In 1962 Rachel Carson's *Silent Spring* woke the world up to the dangers pesticides posed to the environment and by 1970 everyone was talking about ecology and conservation. This anxiety intensified as Britain staggered from the oil crisis of 1973 to the power cuts during the miners' strike and then faced the spread of Dutch elm disease and the drought of two baking summers. And in some regions like East Anglia the countryside of hedges and ditches and trees seemed to be vanishing before the march of the great open fields. Gardeners turned to the meadow again.

Very often, 'new' twentieth-century styles have forebears in earlier eras – as if we were perpetually discovering the wheel. Miriam Rothschild's experiments at Ashton Wold in the 1970s, in planting her meadows with wild-flower seeds, corncockle and scarlet poppies, moon daisies and mayweed and orchids, has been credited with starting the 'wild-flower' movement – yet what about Daisy Lloyd's meadows at Great Dixter? But Lloyd simply ran her own estate, while Rothschild was an eminent scientist, a Fellow of the Royal Society. After her 'Farmer's Nightmare' seed mix, companies began producing wild-flower seeds and garden centres started to sell 'weeds'. Meadow planting is now fashionable and at each Chelsea Flower Show gardeners rediscover 'nature', whether it be Irish fields or Snowdonia's rushing streams.

As we rediscovered the wild flowers, so we began to care about wildlife. In 1986 Chris Baines published the best-selling *How to Make a Wildlife Garden*. His first argument was that the garden helped people to cope with stress: 'Just a few minutes of quiet relaxation amongst trees, with bird song and bumblebees for entertainment, and even the most exhausted

Logs with fungi, hedgehog and thrush, from Fran Hill, *Wildlife Gardening*, 1988

of city workers is ready for anything.' But it was a duty, too: in the past forty years since the war, he warned, Britain had lost 95 per cent of wildlife meadows, and half the lowland woods and fens and mires and heaths. Gardens could be the new conservation sites: people owed it to their grandchildren and to the rest of the world, Baines said, to preserve what they could. Even a tiny plot could have the beginning of a woodland glade, ivy to shelter nesting birds, a pile of decaying logs for lurking toads, a bird box on the wall. Gardeners began buying buddlejas, sedums, marigolds and sages to attract butterflies, and even learnt to welcome nettles. Ponds – a fashion of the Eighties and Nineties – were valued for frogspawn and dragonflies. Families stayed up to watch hedgehogs scuttling across the lawn at night, and urban foxes digging earths under the shed.

Perhaps this is the place to glance sideways, not at nature in the garden, but at the history of what our gardening has done to the wild. Many plants have leapt the fence: think of the great horse chestnuts and the sycamores, or the fuchsia hedges of the West Country and Ireland, the buddlejas that spring from broken rooftops in the city and the blue-toadflax that runs along the pavements, or the wild figs of Sheffield, which grow on the banks of the River Don. But the news is not all good. Japanese knotweed, introduced in the 1820s, has spread across Britain, forming dense thickets that kill all other plants. Loudon thought the giant hogweed was 'magnificent', and Victorians sowed it with passion – but now it stalks along streams and river banks, choking watercourses and blistering passers-by with its toxic hairs, a near ineradicable demon. The flowers and the wild may win our hearts, but we shouldn't be fooled that we can control them.

28

The cherry tree

ONE STORY NEEDS TELLING, that of the smallest gardens of all. Back in the eighteenth century, when the vogue for Rousseau was at its height, Emily, Duchess of Leinster set up a school for her many children on her Irish estate: rote learning was banned, freedom and fresh air and the love of nature were the key. All the children had their own small gardens. Many lovers of liberty followed this lead: in *Practical Education* Maria and Richard Edgeworth recommended gardening as one way of learning through play; William Cobbett gave all his children a flower bed, a small vegetable plot and a grove of trees, and their own spades and hoes.

I'm sure many head gardeners saw children in the same light as cats, or starlings, or other pestiferous vermin. But John Claudius Loudon's father gave him a miniature garden when he was a boy, in which he made 'walks' and flower beds and, said his wife Jane, 'so eager was he to obtain seeds to sow in it, that, when a jar of tamarinds arrived from an uncle in the

West Indies, he gave the other children his share of the fruit, on condition of his having all the seeds.' When Loudon died he was in the middle of dictating a book for young gardeners and Jane herself later wrote *My Own Garden: or The Young Gardener's Year Book*. Few people, she thought, with a family and a garden, 'do not set aside a small part of it for their children'. Queen Victoria took this to heart: at Osborne House on the Isle of Wight she had formal plots laid out for all her children, with beds for vegetables (including asparagus), fruit and flowers, and a quaint thatched tool shed, containing all their wheelbarrows, each with his or her name painted on it. I don't know how much they worked in these, but one of a string of Victorian books for this new market, *The Children's Garden* of 1865, was dedicated to the eleven-year-old Princess Beatrice.

As they grew up, Victorian writers remembered their childhood gardens as a private territory, from which they spied out other worlds, as Robert Louis Stevenson's tree-climbing child does in 'Foreign Lands', full of wonder at what is over the garden wall:

> Up into the cherry tree
> Who should climb but little me?
> I held the trunk with both my hands
> And looked abroad on foreign lands.
>
> I saw the next door garden lie,
> Adorned with flowers before my eye,
> And many pleasant places more
> That I had never seen before.

The garden was a solace against the cruelties of growing up, but it could also, as in *Jane Eyre*, be a reminder of nature's indifference. All the girls at Lowood have their garden, 'scores of little beds', sad and blighted in winter, but in May, when typhus strikes the school, the same beds, edged with thrift and double daisies, are glowing with flowers, hollyhocks, lilies, tulips, 'useless for most of the inmates of Lowood, except to furnish now and then a handful of herbs and blossoms to put in a coffin'.

Many Victorian schools had gardens, or simply window boxes for pupils to manage. But it was their own personal gardens, however tiny, laid out to their heart's desire, that people remembered best: the straggling stocks, the pathetic mustard and cress, the wonderfully reliable nasturtiums, and candy-tuft and marigolds, the sticky poppy seed-heads squeezed and ripped open. Gertrude Jekyll had a little garden with an arbour, all her own, covered with the rose 'Blush Boursault', and she remembered her mother teaching her to separate the weeds from the seedlings by cutting out paper patterns of leaves of all the weeds, one by one, and telling her to pull them up. From that, she said, she 'became an important little helper in the garden. That was my beginning.' In 1908 she wrote *Children and Gardens*, acknowledging the problem of childish impatience and suggesting they be given flowers at once, to cheer them on. Like Jane Loudon before her she insisted that their plots have good soil and sun, and not be a miserable dusty patch in the corner. The children she wrote for were well off, the kind whose parents could afford a play house, or might take them to the Riviera in the winter where they would see the plants she mentions. But by this time the idea had spread to all classes: magazines like *The Garden* had special junior columns and Sutton's Seeds sold collections of brightly coloured flowers especially for children.

Vita Sackville-West also had her patch, struggling to make things grow and despairing when the gardeners 'tidied it up'. On and on went the juvenile books, right up to Enid Blyton's *The Children's Garden*. Countless memoirs begin in the garden, numerous children's books celebrate its mystery. And in early twentieth-century schools, whether they were advanced 'progressive' private schools, still holding to a modified Rousseauian ideal of freedom and nature, or simply the local village primary, gardening, like 'Nature Study', found a key place. This tradition continued up to the 1960s and still does in some schools today, although more often the garden now is a communal bed where everyone helps, designed to bring in the butterflies and bees. Some imaginative teachers run greenhouse clubs after school, and get their pupils interested in propagation, plant genetics and conservation; over 900 schools entered the 'Greenfingers Challenge' competition in 2002 and this year, for the first time, the RHS Seed Department at Wisley is offering free seeds to its school members.

Gardening affects children, and children affect gardens. If a time-stop camera were set to watch an ordinary garden like mine, it would show it changing dramatically over the years: the sandpit replaces the lupins, the swing goes up under the oak tree, the vegetable plot gives way to grass for football, the climbing frame takes over the small lawn, turned into Bedouin camps with old sheets. Then again, they disappear one by one. The climbing frame collapses, the grass returns (though not, so far, the vegetables) and the sandpit between the shrubs becomes a new flower bed where bits of Lego still surface each spring among the bulbs. Some day, I hope, these children will have whole gardens of their own.

Epilogue: All of us

THERE IS SO MUCH history in our gardens, of such different kinds. The grand and formal history of the garden as art and design; the story of plants, and how they arrived here and were cultivated; the tale of the people who worked in the gardens: the professionals, the amateurs, the country housewives, the stationmasters, the suburban weekenders. And the history has itself influenced the innovators. Renaissance gardeners looked back to Pliny and the Romans; the Victorians looked back to baroque parterres; the Arts and Crafts gardeners looked back to medieval meads and Elizabethan herbals. From Loudon onwards, garden writers started to study the past and after 1901, when Alicia Amherst began delving into monastic records, the real research began: now we have a tradition of garden writers who combine scholarship with passionate, hands-on experience, like Roy Strong, Robin Lane Fox, Penelope Hobhouse and Anna Pavord.

Alongside research has gone restoration. This started when the country woke up to the vast number of country houses that lay empty and neglected after 1945, taken over during the war and now too expensive to maintain. Hundreds were pulled down and lost for ever. Once realisation dawned, the National Trust's first drive was to rescue the houses themselves, but then – after Lawrence Johnston gave them Hidcote – they began accepting gardens on their own, like Nymans, Sheffield Park and Trengwainton. From the mid-1950s the list of famous gardens has lengthened: Stourhead, Blickling, Little Moreton, Shugborough, Hardwick Hall, Montacute, Cliveden, Polesden Lacey, Tintinhull, Powis Castle, Studeley Castle, Westbury, Erddig and elsewhere. In 2003 the Trust took over the gem of William Morris's Red House, and the enormous pleasure gardens, woods and lawns, orangery and glasshouses and gardeners' sheds of the Victorian Tyntesfield near Bristol. Seven of their ten most visited sites are gardens.

From the beginning visitors came in droves. In the 1960s there was a huge increase in cars and more disposable income – at least for the middle and professional classes and the retired – and when people looked for places to drive to at the weekend many chose gardens. It was for these leisurely petrol guzzlers that the 'Shell Guides' were published, among them the *Shell Gardens Book* of 1964, with its lovely cloth cover showing a dovecote peeping over roses. (If you see a second-hand copy, grab it.) Contributors included Margery Fish, Christopher Lloyd and Graham Stuart Thomas and historians like Miles Hadfield and Edward Hyams. Succinctly, it educated readers in 'Styles from Monastic to Modern', named the key 'Designers and Inspirers', and explained ferneries and finials and grottoes, wrought-iron work, vineyards and vistas. At the back came the vital section, a thirty-page list by county of gardens to visit.

Work on the *Shell Gardens Book* prompted the founding of the Garden History Society in 1965. Three years later the Countryside Act let local authorities take over abandoned estates as country parks, and the first proper surveys of the National Trust's gardens were undertaken in the 1970s. In 1976, when the church of St Mary on the Lambeth embankment was about to be knocked down, the Tradescant Trust was formed to turn it into the Museum of Garden History. All through this decade there were exhibitions and books and appeals. In 1979 the first survey of historic landscapes and gardens appeared and in 1983, the National Heritage Act paved the way for the county-by-county *Register*. But it took the great storm of 1987 to make people realise how fragile the heritage was: only then did special nurseries begin to grow limes and cedars to replace the giants that might be felled by strong winds or old age.

Conservation is fine, but in planting terms it has its dangers. As Christopher Lloyd noted with typical forthrightness, 'the dead hand of tradition' can stifle inspiration, ruling out quirkiness and individuality, and preventing great gardens from developing. But there is also plenty of daring design and planting around. Garden design, once thought of as arty and highbrow, has become popular as a career. Today gardeners can pick any style, ancient or modern. A television programme explains how to sow a medieval flowery mead; a magazine suggests building an Elizabethan-style turf mound – sculpting in turf is the latest thing – and gives a list of topiary courses and a note on creating the perfect knot garden. An article in *The Times* lists professional designers for all moods: Classic Minimalist (steel and slate), Mystic ('Zen, feng shui, sacred geometry etc.'), New Romantic (meadows and purple grasses), Britain-in-Bloomer (floral clocks and hanging baskets), Exoticist (rainforest or maquis), Advanced Exoticist (Islamic and Japanese), Green and Classy Formalist. Meanwhile, the Westonbirt International Festival shows cutting-edge design and installations. One exhibit in 2003 was 'The Cement Garden' – shades of Ian McEwan – which had, according to Geraldine Bedell, 'instead of boring old trees, a grove of hard hats stuck on metal poles', metal forcing rods bent to make a hedge, and 'a few plants that looked like weeds' and were in fact cow-parsley and dandelions. Another used metal alliums in preference to the real thing. When visitors coming out of the NEC garden show in Birmingham were asked what they thought the garden of the future would be like, some said 'more chrome', others said 'wild flowers'. There is no orthodoxy.

Whether you go for metal plants or box hedging or habitats for wildlife, the mass of information can feel baffling rather than exhilarating. Sometimes we suffer an overdose. But it's worth it: a chance article may suddenly open one's eyes – like Monty Don writing about umbelliferous plants, or James Fenton helping us make a library of gardening writers. The British are greedy for facts. Sensing the impact of television programmes in the 1990s, the Chelsea Physic Garden staff watched the average age of their garden visitors plunge, but they also noticed 'an almost insatiable desire for information': the favourite beds there now are the herb beds for medicine and healing, including the Garden of World Medicine, containing plants used by ancient cultures and indigenous tribal peoples. And big projects can catch the imagination of the whole nation. We have all become aware of the loss of biodiversity – the range of plants and animals living in an area – but the Eden Project in Cornwall, with its amazing biodomes, has brought this home dramatically and has stunned even its promoters by the flood of visitors.

Television has made gardening sexy again, despite the garden make-overs and blue walls. I've heard someone dismiss this with disdain – 'that's not gardening, it's shopping' – but stars like Alan Titchmarsh have taught thousands to tackle a garden for the first time. There is always some small revelation – five different ways of making compost, the mechanisms of insect-eating plants, the tiny species tulips, so delicate and different from the familiar cultivated ones. Television makes crazy ventures seem possible – like wrapping a banana plant in bubble wrap in winter or growing forty kinds of auriculas from seed.

The banana plant made me laugh. It belonged to a man in Norwich, who had fallen in love with tropical plants in Venezuela and was determined to show that chilly East Anglia could have jungles too. And anyone can go tropical, buying spectacular gingers, for example, from nurseries like Kobakoba in Somerset and Mulu in Worcestershire. Our new modern gardens are also just beginning to reflect the rich, mixed cultures of our society. Many people who come to live here from elsewhere are desperately homesick for the landscape and the plants they left behind, which often have spiritual value to them, while their children born here want to discover their own gardening heritage. Planting can foster a sense of belonging and some city groups are now working on this. In Birmingham the 'Concrete and Coriander' project works with local residents, especially Asian women, taking over derelict land and providing raised beds and poly tunnels to grow the herbs and vegetables they know. In Birmingham, too, the nursery garden Akamba Easy Exotics has sprung up like a patch of Africa on a suburban street: many would-be customers, said the owner, couldn't believe these exotics would survive the British frost, so they went away and came again in the spring, just to check that nothing had died – and then they began to buy.

In the cities we crave greenery and at last we are building on the initiatives of groups like the city farms. In May 2003 the British government launched a £30 million scheme to help groups make the most of local open spaces, whether it be a park or a 'quiet area' on a housing estate. After decades of decline, when soaring costs left the parks neglected and only litter and graffiti flowered, funds are being poured back again. In London, Battersea Park is being restored, including most of Russell Page's great Festival of Britain gardens; in Sunderland the Victorian park is revived in all its splendour; in Sheffield city parks have wild-flower meadows; in Glasgow an old tramworks site has been transformed into the Hidden Gardens, influenced by both Christian and Islamic cloister gardens. Many features in Victorian parks, like pavilions and pagodas, are being reborn not as symbols of empire but of inclusion, like the new Mughal gardens in Bradford, where children leap in the canals and fountains, or the Khalsa Wood outside Nottingham, planted by the Sikh community.

Recently, too, the Millennium Commission has splashed out on bringing gardens and glasshouses to life: Cornwall's Eden Project, the Bristol Wildlife Walk, Sheffield's glass Winter Garden. Near Perth, work has begun on Scotland's First National Garden. Although the experience of the National Garden of Wales, only just rescued from a cash crisis, shows that money may be needed to keep them going too. And in November 2003

The new Mughal gardens in Bradford, 2003.

English Heritage reported glumly that billions would be needed to bring our historic parks and gardens up to scratch.

Times have changed. Britain has always drawn in plants and people and ideas from every corner of the map, and although the heroic, piratical plant-hunting ended with the First World War, later heroes like Frank Kingdon Ward explored south-east Asia from 1910 to the 1950s and brought us the Blue Poppy (*Meconopsis betonicfolia*), and more recently Roy Lancaster has travelled from the Caucasus to China seeking new species. An agreement at the Rio Earth Summit in 1992 virtually ended free-lance collecting and now it goes on in a more regulated way, organised by places like Kew and the Botanic Gardens of Edinburgh, which has a Chinese Hillside with plants from the Jade Dragon Snow Mountains in Yunnan growing as if in the wild.

The world is here: in Burgess Park in Camberwell, London, the Chumleigh Gardens have Oriental, Islamic, Mediterranean, African and Caribbean and English gardens, involving elders from communities nearby. Nearby, groups of 'Heart Gardeners', sent by their GPs, raise organic food and medicinal herbs. Gardening is great exercise and therapy, as the charity Thrive has been saying for twenty-five years, finding that it helps stroke patients, for example, to regain speech and mobility and confidence.

And what of the future? The British climate is certainly warming: the number of extremely cold days has dropped from fifteen to twenty per year before 1900 to around ten; Scotland has been 20–30 per cent wetter since 1970 and the south-east of England 25 per cent drier. The leaves on the oak trees are opening earlier; the aphids are coming sooner and there are more of them. All these trends are predicted to increase, with more stormy weather, as well as more heat. The growing seasons will lengthen, but mildew and fungus will increase, and new insects will invade. Olive trees, eucalyptus and cypress will be easier to grow, there will be earlier spring bulbs and sensational autumn colour, but the beeches with their shallow roots will suffer in the drought and high winds may blow them over. We will have earlier vegetable crops, but probably of lower quality; more figs and vines, even olives and bananas, but not such good apples and pears. And the green lawn will brown (it's been suggested that British men may need psychological as well as horticultural advice), and we will struggle to help the delphiniums, lupins and asters, and ferns and mosses and Alpines. So what can we do? Very little, except work even harder at mulching and saving water, and alter our choice of plants to make them more Mediterranean. Some would say this doesn't sound bad – but it would be sad to see our lush green English gardens disappear.

If I took a helicopter today, from Land's End to John o'Groats on this dusty, windy Saturday afternoon in the middle of Wimbledon fortnight, what would I see? The car parks around the great houses and gardens are jammed: people are peering at the pineapple pits at Heligan, walking slowly between the old roses at Mottisfont, admiring the potting shed at Normanby. Toddlers are jumping in the cascade at Chatsworth; children are hiding beneath the topiary at Levens Hall. In the Brecon Beacons a woman is watering her tomatoes; in the Cotswolds a couple are clipping their bay tree, given to bring luck on their marriage. In Hull, the Co-op Greenfinger Garden Club ('a very friendly society') are planning their next meeting. By Loch Ness, holidaymakers walk through the woods of Abriachan Gardens, gazing across to the mountains. In every town and village from south to north, hanging baskets sway outside shops and pubs, dripping with colour. From shore to shore we are out in the garden.

The shape of gardening history here is like a cone balanced on its end. To begin with the circle is narrow, a mere drop, a handful of British and Roman gardeners who cleared a space to grow things for pleasure as well as produce. Up through the centuries the circle widens, like the growth of British society itself – almost on a par with our move to parliamentary democracy, then to the universal franchise and votes for women, and on to the brilliant, difficult, fruitful mixed world of today. And if you filled the cone with plants instead of gardeners, century by century the same would be true – this second cornucopia would gradually be filled, layer by layer, with flowers and shrubs and fruit and trees and vegetables brought here by trade and empire and looting, from Europe, the Americas, the Cape, Australasia and China. Then final layers are added by the leaps forward in plant cultivation and propagation, until the horn of plenty is full to overflowing.

There has never been a book so hard to finish as this, because gardening does not end – it will go on, generation after generation, as long as we don't destroy our green, sea-girt planet. It will change as fashions come and go, and as technology and plant cultivation improve, but in many ways it will stay the same. A hundred, a thousand years from now, people will walk out in the morning, looking at the dew on the leaves, watching to see if the lily has flowered overnight, wondering if the slugs have eaten the new plants – just as Pliny did in ancient Rome, as Friar Henry did in his garden in the fourteenth century, as Gertrude Jekyll did at Munstead Wood, rejoicing in the arrival of June. We may think we are tending our garden, but of course, in many different ways, it is the garden and the plants that are nurturing us.

Postscript, 2017

In the last ten years garden fashions have come and gone. Some have endured, like prairie gardening and ornamental grasses. Some have faded, like the vogue for straight lines and hard angles and architectural plants – now curves are back, and topiary is in flattened balls and clumps, while old-fashioned rural gardens with cow-parsley and mini-meadows have leapt in favour. Leading designers encourage us to rethink old forms: to take a more naturalistic approach; to think of rivers of grass, undulating hedges, 'hot borders' with startling colour contrasts. Each year new trends are announced – as I write, this season apparently marks the comeback of shrubs, as new gardeners have tired of borders and are looking out for 'landmark plants'. I thought shrubs had never gone away, but now we're recommended to buy large, expensive viburnum and magnolias and not wait for them to grow. In reaction, I sense a return to 'slow-gardening', planting trees for the future, visiting small specialist nurseries for the joy of finding new discoveries, raised by people who care.

The great change has been our use of the Internet – for finding and buying plants, for hunting out gardens to visit, for advice on everything from pruning to how to deal with moles (mothballs) or slugs (coffee-grounds and beer). It's become easier, too, to enjoy a small garden now that supermarkets, as well as garden centres and DIY stores, overflow with plants and bulbs – sometimes it feels as if the Victorian age of brightness and bedding is back. But since 2006 many larger garden centres have become malls packed less with plants than with chairs and tables and wicker sofas with luxuriant cushions, as if global warming is changing our lives for good. Perhaps it is. Perhaps we must look forward to more extreme events like droughts and floods and high winds. Perhaps gravel will replace lawns, and tropical flora will fill old herbaceous borders. I doubt it. But I'm sure that when people look back at this time, they will notice that the British have been spending more time outdoors, in gardens as well as street cafés.

It feels as if more people are gardening: at home, in groups, in school schemes and in neighbourhood campaigns like 'Britain in Bloom', over fifty years old now, with 1,600 communities taking part. But the figures tell a different story. In 2015 the Horticultural Trades Association reported that as house sales have fallen and renting has risen, especially for the under-35s, around 1.5 million fewer people claimed to have a garden or allotment than in 2007, with the greatest fall in Greater London. Garden-centre customers are not adventurous purchasers in search of new varieties, but people who began gardening in the 1990s and still stick to their old buying habits. Garden clubs, too, are worried about an ageing membership, being urged to woo younger gardeners with Facebook pages and Twitter accounts, fewer rules and more cocktail parties. (What kind of gardening do the cocktail set do?) It makes me realise yet again how important it is to encourage children to love gardening and to provide gardens for all.

At the same time, however, we've become more concerned for the general environment, urban and rural, and – in theory at least – this has brought a greater linking of horticulture to planning. A few years ago the government took gardens out of the 'Brownfield' category listing, in order to prevent 'garden-grabbing' – the building of new houses on gardens or green spaces – and in 2014 they launched a new initiative to build more 'Garden Cities'. At the moment such cities are more a wish than a reality. But while most new housing estates have tiny gardens, jammed between buildings, this impoverishment is balanced by a better use of open spaces, with areas for flowers and vegetables, or container beds for residents to use. A host of schemes are setting out to bring life to the urban sprawl, like the RHS 'Greening Grey Britain' campaign, which urges everyone 'to turn over some paving or tarmac and plant up a small green area', and especially to find plants that can deal with pollution or difficult conditions. This last reminder, is, perhaps, a response to the continuing fondness for guerrilla gardening on roundabouts or road verges or street corners – which doesn't always work, ending up with sad plants in dusty holes, or a forlorn scattering of seed.

There have been some simple but touching moments, like the planting of 150,000 snowdrop bulbs by local residents, students and passers-by around Manchester in 2015, in memory of the soldiers of the First World War. And some 'unofficial' schemes are impressively ambitious, such as the campaign to save Churchill Way, a disused flyover in Liverpool city centre, and to turn it into a New York High-Line style park, with allotments and plantings. This is just one example of local people taking the initiative to garden on derelict land, or on sites for commercial development, or around housing that is boarded up and left unused, often for well over a year. Some groups, like Core Landscapes in Hackney in London, are making gardens that they can shift when the builders step in – growing trees in pallet boxes, or making flower beds on wheels and a moveable pond – and are raising funds by renting raised beds and selling plants, some grown on site, others donated, including 'leftovers' from large landscaping companies. North of the border, this kind of project has taken more official form in 'Stalled Spaces Scotland'. This grew from

Legacy 2014, set up after the Glasgow Commonwealth Games to encourage local authorities to use empty land where development projects were delayed. Often these gardening schemes find matched-funding from groups for those with learning disabilities or addiction problems, or for pensioners and toddlers.

Cities always need more gardens, parks, green places. In London (allegedly 'Europe's greenest capital'), the scheme of the decade, of course, is the Garden Bridge, a 366-metre (1,200-foot) footbridge across the Thames, with paths weaving through copses and gardens, open from 6 a.m. to midnight, free to all. Whatever one's doubts, it's a romantic idea, its design inspired by history, crossing from the South Bank with its ancient marshes and willow-beds, where William Curtis of the Chelsea Physic Garden, author of *Flora Londinensis*, started his botanic garden at Lambeth in 1779, through the exposed central span, which will be treated as a scarp or a cliff top, to the gardens of the Temple, where the Knights Templar raised plants from the Holy Land – figs and lavender,

An impression of the Garden Bridge against the London skyline.

roses and iris. (Gertrude Jekyll's grandfather was in charge of these gardens in the early nineteenth century.) But there were heated debates about the granting of the design contract. And couldn't the millions be better spent on the many blighted places in London and other cities? Will it obscure rather than enhance the city's landmarks? Let's see. . . . Pieces of the bridge will be floated upriver on barges in 2018, and it should open later that year.

At the other end of the scale, the last ten years have seen a huge spike in the demand for allotments – good news for the nation's health, as well as its horticulture. The Allotment Society reckons that thirty minutes of allotment gardening burns around 150 calories, the same as low-impact aerobics, and in January 2016 new studies of the way allotments – and presumably any sort of gardening – can improve your health were published in the *Journal of Occupational Therapy* and the *Journal of Public Health*. The latter compared allotment-holders and non-gardeners around Manchester and discovered – surprise, surprise – that digging and weeding improve both mental and physical well-being. A flurry of books have appeared on therapeutic gardening, and now the Parks Alliance (which is also anxious about the cuts in government funding for parks) is asking for proper clinical trials to support 'green participation prescriptions'. I like the idea of going to the doctor and being told to garden more. Yet this may be out of reach for many: in 2015 it was estimated that 350,000 people in Britain had allotments, but more than 800,000 were on waiting lists. To meet the demand, some councils are cutting the size of the plot offered, making it too small to raise enough veg to feed a family, while many old plots are threatened by development. New fights lie ahead.

Gardeners have also become increasingly keen to lessen environmental damage, but the best intentions can easily fail. We may try not to use peat, but spokespeople for the Garden Organic's Peat Campaign believe that more than twenty-four million wheelbarrows of peat are still used every year by amateur gardeners, destroying the lowland raised-bogs that support rare and threatened species – merlin, curlew, lapwing, whimbrel, snipe, pipistrelle bats, hares and toads – and releasing thousands of tons of carbon dioxide from the exposed peat beds. In 2013 DEFRA (the Department for Environment, Food and Rural Affairs) worked out that the UK was gobbling up three million cubic metres of peat, and that most of it – 69 per cent – ends up with amateur gardeners, as multi-purpose compost and 'grow bags'. In response the Environment Ministry has called for peat to be completely eliminated from this particular market by 2020. Will this happen?

Another campaign. And more to come. We have new bugs too, and new blights. Formal gardeners lament the spread of box blight; woodland-lovers worry about ash dieback; and a new pest threatens in the eucalyptus leaf beetle – brilliant red with yellow streaks, like a luminous lily beetle. This arrived in Ireland in 2007 and is now widespread there: one was found in London in 2012 and more in Surrey and Sussex in 2015 . . . let's hope these are just odd strays. It's easy to turn to chemicals. The 1970s were awash with products that killed plant tissue and that damaged animals and humans too. Most have now gone. The RHS estimates that between 2002 and 2010 more than fifty products were taken off the market or restricted to professional growers. But there are still plenty around. And what about the plants grown on an industrial scale that we rush to buy? In the Netherlands, people are beginning to realise how dangerous their beautiful bulbs are to rivers, migratory birds, allotments and children's health. According to Dr Henk Tennekes, a Dutch toxicologist, tons of pesticides are dumped on the bulb fields each year, and the new insecticides, the neo-nicotinoids, work *inside* the plants and flowers. When bees collect pollen and nectar they are poisoned, while the fertilisers that drain off the fields are said to be leaving Holland's canals virtually devoid of life.

So gardening can be dangerous. But there are brighter sides too. British gardeners have become keener than ever on wildlife gardening, planting for the bees and butterflies and bugs. A new 'National Pollinator Strategy' for England tells me that 1,500 different insects are essential for pollinating food crops, so we should all plant wild flowers and allow grass to grow longer – a good excuse for reluctant mowers. And we are more aware of the disappearance of wild flowers on road verges, and of the danger to rare plants. To counteract the loss, there are cheering stories like the saving of the sea-stocks and water germander of the North Devon sand-dunes on Northam Burrows, where the sand has been exposed for them to flourish, and sheep and horses will graze to keep other foliage down.

That may be 'nature', not 'gardening', but the two go together in my mind. We don't have to have our own plot to love wild plants or to enjoy great gardens. I've added fifty gardens to my list of places to visit and that is just a beginning. It's heartening to see bold reconstructions, like the Roman Garden at the National Roman Museum in Caerleon in South Wales, which opened in 2008. It looks curiously modern, with its box hedges, bay trees and vines, and details like the Roman use of compost and the introduction of a version of the wild leek – later the Welsh national emblem. By contrast there are great schemes like the re-creation of the historical landscape at Trentham, where work has been continuing for fifteen years, beginning with the reconstruction of the formal Victorian Italian gardens and culminating in the restoration of the original Capability Brown landscape to celebrate the 300th anniversary of Brown's birth in 2016.

In a host of gardens, from north to south, east to west, we can walk through the past, from medieval herb plots and Elizabethan knot gardens, to the pergolas and terraces of Arts and Crafts designs and the austere vision of the modernists. Often, new techniques of archaeological investigation have shown evidence of grottoes and cascades, mazes and avenues and raised banks, or have confirmed earlier planting schemes of beds or parterres. In turn, such findings have prompted new layouts to restore the old schemes. Nothing stands still in a garden, and change is both a shock and a thrill. Some designs look back, others bring the past rushing into collision with the present. It's intriguing, for example, to see an old favourite like Sissinghurst being coaxed back from our modern love of constant flowering, to the original seasonal planting schemes of Vita Sackville-West and Harold Nicolson. Or, on the other hand, to find the old sunken garden at Packwood House turned into a brilliantly colourful dry garden, brimming with Mediterranean and South African plants, and to see huge herbaceous borders in many places transformed from the careful grading of the old Gertrude Jekyll style into something fresh, with swathes of perennials in repeat plantings like flowing, bursting and fading musical themes.

Sometimes the 'new' historic gardens are not reconstructions or rediscoveries so much as tributes or re-imaginings. Among the most stunning are the designs at Arundel Castle, where it feels as though the Duchess of Norfolk had embarked on a Tudor-style rivalry with the Duchess of Northumberland's fountains and cherry orchards and poison gardens at Alnwick. At Arundel in 2008, an old car park was turned into the Collector Earl's Garden, with rills, cascades and pergolas, a grass labyrinth and a folly, 'Oberon's Palace', where a gilt coronet balances on a jet of water. A mass of alliums is followed by great pots of agapanthus, and semi-tropical borders overflow with pillar-like blue echiums, banana fronds and swathes of persicaria and lilies. Beyond it the latest garden, the Stumpery, opened in 2012, is beginning to re-create a Victorian vision, full of ferns and hellebores.

Other new gardens are conceptual in a different way. At Througham Court in the Cotswolds, contemporary gardens inspired by science or mathematics – a Cosmic Evolution Garden, a Fibonacci Walk, a Pico mound – are woven into Norman Jewson's Arts and Crafts landscaping. 'Cosmic' features also fill the flower-filled terraces of Gresgarth in Lancashire, created over the last twenty-five years, with its sculptures, pebble mosaics and zodiacs. Old and new can mix well: at Boughton House, the Duke of Buccleuch has been restoring a landscape lost for 200 years – grand vistas, avenues, mounts and pools – but he has also added a twenty-first century landform, the Orpheus Project, a deep inverted pyramid, sunk into the earth. At Scampston in Yorkshire, where Piet Oudolf mingled modern, perennial meadow planting with old-fashioned formality, the stripes of grasses, box cubes and pleached limes have now reached a strange, timeless beauty. And recent years have shown that public gardens can also be thrilling. It's hard to resist the charm of the Sheffield School's Olympic Park, with its areas of planting from around the world, or the award-winning Angel Field at Liverpool Hope University, a Renaissance-style garden to evoke creativity, with quotations woven into its structure.

Grand gardens are wonderful in different ways, but some face tough times ahead. English Heritage used to look after 400 buildings and gardens, including Queen Victoria's Osborne and Kenilworth, where the Elizabethan garden was restored and reopened in 2009; but after a reorganisation, many of these gardens will have to pay their own way by the time the government grant runs out in 2022. So rally round and enjoy them now.

The history of gardening has been a boom field for books and television shows, and I am constantly learning something new. For example, I enjoy the eccentrics and the bizarre kind of garden history, so I was amused to discover one aspect of gardening in the 1960s that I missed first time around. Far from being only a middle-class, patio-and-decking pursuit, gardening had its place in the counterculture, a form of resistance to the military, mercantile business of the day. And it can be a 'virtual', mental escape too. The short-lived magazine *Gandalf's Garden*, born on the King's Road, Chelsea, in 1968, urged that we must 'stimulate our own inner gardens if we are to save our Earth and ourselves from engulfment'. Its letters page was called 'Seedbag'. Across the road from *GG* was a shop called 'Granny Takes a Trip' , while 'Grow Your Own' started out as a slogan directed at pot-smokers, and 'Headshops' sold special seeds and mushroom spores.

I'm not about to see fairies by the compost heap, but I am often amazed at the way gardening reflects, or helps to build, our changing culture. I hadn't expected, when writing about the last ten years, to make a list of campaigns, and I'm impressed by the new urgency and by the widely shared, passionate belief that gardening – both in our history and today – is a lasting joy, a tie to the natural world. We must make sure that our children and grandchildren, and the generations to come, will be able to revel in and enjoy this pleasure – as we do today.

Acknowledgements

My first thanks go to Eugenie Todd, whose enquiry sparked my quest, and to all who have offered suggestions, especially Malcolm Andrews, Debby Banham, Carol Biggam, Valerie Bott, Carmen Callil, Sarah Carter, Chris and Prue Cherry, Paul Dennett (Meadowgrange Nursery), Patricia Fara, David Kynaston, Shena Mason, Deborah Rogers, Jane Stephenson, Will Sulkin, Jane Turner, Marina Warner, Christopher Woodward and Ken Worpole.

I have really enjoyed being published by my own colleagues. For the first edition my thanks go to my ever-encouraging editor Penny Hoare and publisher Alison Samuel; the design team, Caz Hildebrand and Lily Richards (who is responsible for the colour plate sections); Suzanne Dean for the cover; Mary Gibson for production; Ilsa Yardley for copy-editing. For this new edition I am especially grateful to my old friend and new editor Poppy Hampson, Charlotte Humphery for her support, and to Stephen Parker for the cover.

Many writers and broadcasters have opened my eyes, as I hope my notes make clear. Among the libraries and archives, I would like especially to thank the RHS Lindley Library, the London Library, the British Library, the Museum of Garden History, the RIBA Library, and the University of Kent, and all those named on the list of illustrations.

John Barnard offered knowledgeable advice on early published books and Hermione Lee was, as always, the best of friends and readers. Steve Uglow trekked along with me to innumerable places, in rain and sun; Tom, Hannah and Jamie were amused and intrigued; and Luke delved into old magazines for articles. I thank you all. My greatest debt is to my late mother, Lorita Crowther, who created fine gardens in difficult places, and enjoyed her plants and landscapes to the last.

List of Illustrations

49 Ian Hamilton Finlay's Little Sparta. Andrew Lawson.
50 Derek Jarman's Garden, Dungeness. John Glover.

Illustrations in the text

Dedication: Thomas Mawson, *The Art and Craft of Garden Making* c. 1900
Foreword: Orchard, John Wright, *The Fruit Grower's Guide*, c. 1897–1905
Introduction: *Iris polakii*, watercolour by Paul Furse, 1965, RHS Lindley Library

PART I

5 Seeds and lupins, peas and honeysuckle, with snails and caterpillars, from John Parkinson, *Paradisi in Sole*, 1629.

7 Laurentinum, from the Earl of Orrery, *Letters of Pliny the Younger*, 1751.

11 Pompeian peristyle garden, from W. Gell, *Pompeiana*, 1832.

14 Reconstruction of Chedworth from the *Illustrated London News*.

16 A peasant digging, from the *Junius Psalter*, c 1000, Bodleian Library.

21 The St Gall plan for an ideal monastery, redrawn by the Revd R. Willis, in Ralph Dutton, *The English Garden*, 1937.

25 Medieval woodcut of a hermit in the garden by his cell.

31 Polypody fern, from the Bury St Edmunds herbal, c. 1120, Bodleian Library.

34 The garden of love, from a fifteenth-century Italian manuscript.

37 A game of bowls, c. 1280. British Library, in John Harvey, *Medieval Gardens*.

41 French tapestry, c. 1400, in Sylvia Landsberg, *Medieval Gardens*.

44 Woodcut of a medieval garden.

48 Plan of the village of Boarstall, Buckinghamshire, 1444.

52 Allotments at Kingston-upon-Hull.

54 Knot gardens, from William Lawson, *The Country Housewife's Garden*, 1638.

58 The mount at New College, David Loggan, *Oxonia Illustrata*, 1675, British Library.

62 Title page, Second Part of Thomas Hill's *The Gardener's Labyrinth*, 1577.

64 Leadenhall, from a copperplate map of London, c. 1559.

65 Garden plan, from William Lawson, *A New Orchard and Garden*, 1618.

67 Artichoke, from John Gerard's *Herball*, 1596.

71 Title page, William Lawson, *A New Orchard and Garden* 1618.

71 Instruments for grafting, Leonard Mascall, *Art of Planting and Grafting*, 1572.

76 Title page, John Parkinson, *Paradisi in Sole*, 1629.

Notes and further reading

Among the many books on garden history several offer an international perspective, notably Christopher Thacker, *The History of Gardens* (1979) and Penelope Hobhouse, *Plants in Garden History* (1992) and *Gardening: A History* (2002). On Britain, the early standard was set by Miles Hadfield, *A History of English Gardening* (1960, revised 1979). Useful later works include Richard Bisgrove's National Trust study, *The English Garden* (1990); Stephen Lacey, *Gardens of the National Trust* (1996); Mavis Batey and David Lambert, *The English Garden Tour* (1990); Christopher Thacker, *The Genius of Gardens* (1994); Jane Brown's elegant essays in *The Pursuit of Pleasure* (1999); Charles Quest-Ritson, *The English Garden* (2001); Jane Fearnley-Whittingstall's entertaining *The Garden, an English Love Affair* (2002) and Maggie Campbell-Culver, *The Origin of Plants* (2001). Another of my favourites is Susan Campbell, *Charleston Kedding: A History of Kitchen Gardening* (1996).

Laurence Fleming and Alan Gore, *The English Garden* (1979) has good original extracts, while Mary Keen, *The Glory of the English Garden* (1989) has appropriately glorious photographs by Clay Perry. Deborah Kellaway's anthology, *Virago Book of Women Gardeners* (1995), is inspiring and Martin Hoyles's two studies of gardening books, from 1560–1960, *Gardeners Delight* (1994) and *Bread and Roses* (1995), have a bracing political note. For 'native' plants I have turned often to Geoffrey Grigson, *The Englishman's Flora* (1955, rev. 1987) and Richard Mabey, *Flora Britannica* (1998). *The Oxford Companion to Gardens* (1986) by Geoffrey and Susan Jellicoe, Patrick Good and Michael Lancaster is still a great reference source. All these books are referred to below by the authors' names, or by short titles.

Among the many excellent garden-history books of the past decade, Ursula Buchan's *The English Garden* (2006) is a vivid study of historical trends, focusing on gardens open to the public. Other general histories include Helena Attlee and Alex Ramsay, *Great Gardens of Britain* (2011) and the more academic Tom Turner, *British Gardens: History, Philosophy and Design* (2013). Katie Campbell, in *British Gardens in Time: The Greatest Gardens and the People Who Shaped Them* (2014) considers four key gardens – Stowe, Biddulph, Nymans, Great Dixter – as explored in the BBC television programme, while many other well-known places are described in Stephen Lacey's *Gardens of the National Trust* (revised edition 2011) and *The Gardens of English Heritage* (2010) by Gilliam Mawrey and Linden Groves.

Many books have also appeared on regional gardens, including Tim Longville, *Gardens of the Lake District* (2007); Katherine Lambert, *The Gardens of Cornwall* (2012); and Victoria Summerley, Hugo Rittson Thomas and Marianne Majerus, *Great Gardens of London* (2015). More wide-ranging books include Jane Powers and Jonathan Hession, *The Irish Garden* (2015), Marilyn Brown, *Scotland's Lost Gardens: From the Garden of Eden to the Stewart Palaces* (2012) and three books on Wales: Helena Attlee, *The Gardens of Wales*, Stephen Anderton, *Discovering Welsh Gardens* (both 2009) and *The Finest Gardens in Wales* (2015) by Tony Russell, who has also written on gardens of the Cotswolds and the South-West.

There have been some quirky takes on garden history too, like Jackie Bennett's *The Writer's Garden: How Gardens Inspired our Best-loved Authors* (2014), which looks at the gardens of twenty authors, from Austen, Ruskin and Dickens to Henry James, Rudyard Kipling, Beatrix Potter, Virginia Woolf, Agatha Christie and Roald Dahl. My favourite book of recent years is Richard Mabey, *The Cabaret of Plants*: *Forty Thousand Years of Plant Life and the Human Imagination* (2015), a joy for gardeners, historians and lovers of the wild.

Introduction

Thoughts on national identity were prompted by Miles Ogborn's 'Identity parade', *Tate* (Winter 2001). Timothy Mowl's remarks appeared in an editorial in *Garden History Society News* (Spring 2003).

1 Did the Romans have rakes?

For prehistoric, Bronze Age and Iron Age cultivation, see Barry Cunliffe, *Iron Age Communities in Britain* (1991 edition), Brian K. Roberts, *Landscapes of Settlement* (1996) and Francis Pryor, *Farmers in Prehistoric Britain* (1998). Christopher Thacker and Penelope Hobhouse both eloquently describe ancient gardens in the Middle East. Linda Farrar, in *Ancient Roman Gardens* (1998), provides general information and for gardens in Roman Britain see Guy de la Bedoyere, *Roman Villas and the Countryside* (1993) and Barry Cunliffe's 'Roman Gardens in Britain: A Review of the Evidence' in *Ancient Roman Gardens* (1981) and his books on Fishbourne (1969, 1971). Tacitus on the weather is quoted by Campbell-Culver.

2 Aelfric's list

For information on Anglo-Saxon gardens – or the lack thereof – I am grateful to Debby Banham of Cambridge University and to Carol Biggam of the Anglo-Saxon Plant Name Survey (ASPNS) at Glasgow University: see their website.

Aelfric's Colloquies, edited by Scott Gwara and translated by David Porter, can be found in *Anglo-Saxon Conversations* (1997). See Richard Hodges, *The Anglo-Saxon Achievement* (1989) and Andrew Reynolds, *Later Anglo-Saxon England: Life and Landscape* (1999), which quotes the charm at the end of this chapter. John Harvey, *Medieval Gardens* (1981), discusses the Elmet survival, Charlemagne's *Capitulare* and St Gall (as does Campbell). Strabo's *Hortulus* is in a dual text edition, edited by R. Payne and W. Blunt (1966). The allusion to yarrow, from the *Lacugna*, is in J. H. G. Gratta and Charles Singer, *Anglo-Saxon Magic and Medicine* (1952). Sylvia Landsberg describes the cellarer's garden in *Medieval Gardens* (1995) and Edward Hyams quotes Neckam in *English Cottage Gardens* (1970).

Susan Oosthuizen provides new insights into land-use and gardening in this period in *Tradition and Transformation in Anglo-Saxon England: Archaeology, Common Rights and Landscape* (2013).

3 Monastic lore

John Harvey's *Medieval Gardens* is a principal source for this and the next two chapters. Sir Frank Crisp's two-volume *Medieval Gardens* (1924) is still invaluable for manuscript illustrations. The account books for Norwich and Ely were transcribed by Alicia Amherst for her *History of Gardening in England* (1895); she also tells the story of Matilda at Romsey. Beaulieu is described in A. B. Barlett, *Beaulieu Monks at Work, 1269-70* (1978) and Teresa Maclean in *Medieval Gardens* (1981). See also Sylvia Landsberg, *The Medieval Garden*. The description of 'dwale' comes from Carole Rawcliffe, 'Hospital Nurses and their Work', in ed. Richard Britnell, *Daily Life in the Late Middle Ages* (1998). Thacker, *Genius*, describes Becket's fig tree and quotes Neckam on tools.

4 Pleasure . . .

The definition of the pleasure garden from *De Vegetabilis et Plantis* by Albertus Magnus, Count of Bollstadt, c. 1260, is translated by John Harvey, who also gives the modern wording of Matthew Paris. Early bowling games are described in Joseph Strutt, *The Sports and Pastimes of the People of England* (1903). The version of 'The Flower and the Leaf' was quoted in 1905 by Alicia Amherst, who also translated Henry III's instructions about the queen's gardens.

Miranda Innes, in *Medieval Flowers*, describes rituals, herbals and flowers that we can still grow today, while for medical and other uses, see Peter Dendle and Alain Touwain, *Health and Healing from the Medieval Garden* (both 2008). For grand gardens, monastic and aristocratic, see Oliver H. Creighton, *Designs upon the Land: Elite Landscapes of the Middle Ages* (2013).

5 ... and Profit

For nursery gardens, see Harvey's *Early Nurserymen* (1974). Erdington's case is in Andrew Watkins, 'Peasants in Arden', in ed. Britnell, *Daily Life in the Middle Ages* (1998). For professional London gardeners see Mark Barnes, *Root and Branch: A History of the Worshipful Company of Gardeners of London* (1994). Sylvia Landsberg notes the Rotherhithe order in *Medieval Gardens*, Stephen Moorhouse explains watering pots in *Garden Archaeology* (1988) while the Hull allotments are described by F. E. Crackles in *Garden History* (Spring 1986).

6 Tudor conceits

The quoted account of Richmond is from the *Oxford Companion*, that of Thornbury is from Timothy Mowl, *Historic Gardens of Gloucestershire* (2002) and the description of Bindon from Mowl's *Historic Gardens of Dorset* (2003). John Stow's memories are from his *Survey of London* (1598).

Bisgrove and Quest-Ritson both discuss deer parks. For Kenilworth, and Robert Laneham's letter of 1575, see Thacker, *Genius*. Wollaton is described by Mark Girouard in *Robert Smythson and the English Country House* (1983), Aberglasney by Penny David with Penelope Hobhouse in *A Garden Lost in Time: The Mystery of the Ancient Gardens of Aberglasney* (1999) and Hales Place by Elisabeth Hall, *Garden of England: Evolution of Historic Gardens in Kent*. Henzner is quoted by Ralph Dutton, in *The English Garden* (1937); Henry VIII's heraldic gardens are explained by Roy Strong in *The Renaissance Garden in England* (1979), which also quotes Platter (1599). For mazes see Nigel Pennink, *Mazes and Labyrinths* (1990). The knot garden plans are in Thomas Hill, *The Gardener's Labyrinth* (1577, 1590), ed. Richard Mabey (1987). For the copperplate maps, see Felix Barker and Peter Jackson, *The History of London in Maps* (1990).

See Paula Henderson, *The Tudor House and Garden: Architecture and Landscape in the Sixteenth and Seventeenth Centuries* (2005). For the passions involved, read Trea Martyn, *Queen Elizabeth in the Garden: A Story of Love, Rivalry and Spectcular Gardens* (2009, 2013).

7 The plantsman cometh

The opening quotation is from William Harrison, *Description of England* (1587; first edition 1577), ed. Georges Edelen (1994). For nursery gardens see Harvey, *Early*

Nurserymen (1974); Tuggie was described as a 'painful planter' in *Gerard's Herbal* (1597). For grafting see Susan Campbell, although the story of Beddington is told in Thacker, *Genius*, quoting from Sir Hugh Platt (1608). Parkinson's *Paradisus* was reissued in facsimile by Dover Publications (1976); his later *Theatrum Botanicum – the Theatre of Plants; or an Universal and Complete Herbal* (1640) detailed 4000 plants and their medical qualities. For the Tradescants, see Prudence Leith Ross, *The John Tradescants* (1984).

Two very interesting books are Margaret Willes, *The Making of the English Gardener: Plants, Books and Inspiration, 1560–1660* (2011) and Timothy Mowl, *Gentlemen Gardeners: The Men Who Recreated the English Landscape Garden* (revised edition 2010).

8 Stuart fantasies

For relations between gentry and community, see Nicholas Cooper *The Houses of the Gentry, 1480–1680* (1999) and Malcolm Kelsall, *The Great Good Place: The Country House and English Literature* (1993). John James is quoted in Fleming and Gore; John Taylor's description of Adrian Gilbert at Wilton is in Roy Strong, *The Renaissance Garden*.

Salomon de Caus's book was *Les raisons des forces mouvantes* (1615). Evelyn's description of Bushnell, and John Worlidge, *Systema-Horti-culturae; or The Art of Gardening* (1677) are quoted in John Harris, *A Garden Alphabet* (1979). The Lennox family's shell work is described in Stella Tillyard, *Aristocrats: Caroline, Emily, Louisa and Sarah Lennox, 1740–1832* (1995). On grottoes, see Barbara Jones, *Follies and Grottoes* (1953, rev. 1974) and Naomi Miller, *Heavenly Caves: Reflections on the Garden Grotto* (1982).

9 'Wife, into thy garden'

Elinor Fettiplace is quoted by Quest-Ritson, from ed. Hilary Spurling, *Elinor Fettiplace's Receipt Book* (1986). For Thomas Hill see ed. Richard Mabey, *The Gardener's Labyrinth* (1997). Goodwife Cantrey's garden is from the Northamptonshire Archive Office, quoted in Mildred Campbell, *The English Yeoman* (1942). Tusser's *Good Points of Husbandry* (1557 and 1571 editions) edited by Dorothy Hartley (1931); the 1580 edition of *Five Hundred Points* (reprinted 1984) has an introduction by Geoffrey Grigson.

The mutton recipes are from Christina Hole, *The Seventeenth-Century Housewife*, quoting her manuscript of 'Household Book of Sarah Loveland'. Henri Misson's views are in *M. Misson's memoirs and observations in his travels over England,* translated by Mr Ozell (1719). Sir Hugh Platt's freckle cure is from *Delights for Ladies* (1609), the 'honey of roses' is from Richard Surflet, *The Country Ferme* (1600) and the instructions for seasonal picking from Gervase Markham, *The Country Huswife* (1615). For this period see also Antonia Fraser, *The Weaker Vessel: Women's Lot in Seventeenth-Century England* (1984).

Although the book's span is wider, these early housewife-gardeners are included in Catharine Horwood, *Gardening Women: Their Stories from 1600 to the Present* (2010).

10 Swords into pruning hooks

Jane Brown describes William III's garden and others in her chapter 'Military Gardens', and also cites *Tristram Shandy*. Hartlib's vision is in *A Designe for Plentie, by an Universall Planting of Fruit Trees* (1652). For Evelyn, see ed. John Bowle, *The Diary of John Evelyn* (1983); the story of Peter the Great comes from the *Oxford Companion to Gardens* (1986); Evelyn's translations included *The French Gardiner* (1658) and *The Compleat Gard'ner* (1693) and the plan of Sayes Court is in Roy Strong, *The Artist in the Garden* (2000). Worlidge's complaint is in *Systema-Horti-culturae* (1677).

For the Beauforts see Molly McCain, *Beaufort: The Duke and his Duchess, 1657–1715* (2001). *The Garden Book of Sir Thomas Hanmer* (1659) was discovered and published in 1933. Rea's verse is taken from *Flora, Ceres and Pomona* (1662); William Hughes's book on flowers is described by Quest-Ritson and Timothy Nourse is quoted by Mary Keen. Timothy Mowl writes on 'John Drapentier's views of the gentry gardens of Hertfordshire' in *Garden History*, (Winter 2001).

For Evelyn, see also Gillian Darley's biography, *John Evelyn: Living for Ingenuity* (2006).

11 Points of view

The research at Bramham was reported in *The Garden* (November 2002). For Celia Fiennes's remarks see ed. Christopher Morris Fiennes, *The Journeys of Celia Fiennes* (1947). On plashing see 'The Taming of the "Wilderness"', in Helen Leach, *Cultivating Myths: Fiction, Fact and Fashion in Garden History* (2000). Bisgrove writes of the destruction of Arden.

See Mavis Batey and Jan Woudstra, *The Story of the Privy Garden at Hampton Court* (1995), David Jaques and A. J. van der Horst, *The Gardens of William and Mary*, and Mark Griffiths on William and Mary's pots in 'Vessels of the Crown', *Garden* (May

1999). For 'Dutch style' see ed. John Dixon Hunt et al., *The Anglo-Dutch Garden in the Age of William and Mary*, but also David Jaques's essay in the special issue of *Garden History* (Winter 2002). Jane Brown describes the apples at Westbury Court in *Pursuit of Paradise*. On the Brompton nursery and Wise, see David Green, *Gardener to Queen Anne: Henry Wise and the Formal Garden* (1956).

12 Arcadia

On rollers, Batey and Woudstra, *The Privy Garden*, quote Evelyn's *Elysium Britannicum* (1659). Colonel Liddell is quoted in Edward Hughes, *North Country Life in the Eighteenth Century: the North East* (1952) and Pepys's disdain for cockney gardens (22 July 1666) is in eds Robert Latham and William Matthews, *The Diary of Samuel Pepys*, Vol. xx (1985). Stephen Switzer's book was *The Nobleman, Gentleman and Gardener's Recreation* (1715, enlarged as *Iconographia Rustica*, 1718) and Batty Langley's was *New Principles of Gardening* (1728). Addison writes in the *Spectator* (25 June 1712).

Among many books, see J. Dixon Hunt and P. Willis, *The Genius of the Place: the English Landscape Garden 1620–1820* (1975) David Jaques, *Georgian Gardens: The Reign of Nature* (1988), Douglas Chambers, *The Planters of the English Landscape Garden* (1993), Tom Williamson, *Polite Landscapes: Gardens and Society in Eighteenth-Century England* (1995). Horace Walpole's essay, 'Of Modern Gardening' (1771) is in *Anecdotes of Painting in England* (1780). For Hoare etc., see Kenneth Woodbridge, *Landscape and Antiquity* (1970) and for the garden circuit Mark Girouard, *Life in the English Country House* (1978). Shenstone's *Works* appeared in two volumes in 1764 and the Luxborough *Letters* in 1776.

An addition to these is George Plumptre, *The English Country House Garden: Traditional Retreats to Contemporary Masterpieces* (2014).

13 The citizen's box

For garden visiting see Adrian Tinniswood, *The Polite Tourist: A History of Country House Visiting* (1998) and Tom Williamson, *Polite Landscapes* (1995). The 1744 quotation comes from Vol. II of Mary Granville, Mrs Delany, *Autobiography and Correspondence*, ed. Lady Llanover (1861–62). Thomas Wright's books were *Universal Architecture I: Six Original Designs for Arbours* (1755) and *II: Six Original Designs for Grottos* (1758); John Harris includes three illustrations in his *Garden Alphabet*. For Defoe see his *Tour through the whole island of Great Britain* (1727). Thomas Fairchild is quoted by Joyce Ellis, 'Georgian Town Gardens', *History Today* (January 2000).

For small spas see W. Wroth *The London Pleasure Gardens* (1896). Todd Longstaffe-Gowan quotes Mrs Delany, Hannah More on hairstyles and tells the story of Eliza Robertson. The ideas for economic gardens are from Stephen Switzer, *Iconographia Rustica* (1718) and for classical vistas from Batty Langley, *New Principles* (1728). Hogarth attacks bad statues in *The Analysis of Beauty* (1753). The quotes are from Samuel Johnson, *The Idler* (July 1758), Robert Lloyd, 'The Cit's Country Box', *The Connoisseur* (1756); Francis Coventry from *The World* (April 1753); Garrick and Coleman, *The Clandestine Marriage*, Act II (1766).

For a detailed history of a pleasure garden, see David E. Coke, *Vauxhall Gardens: A History* (2011).

14 Miller & Co

Banister's walnut is in Charles Elliott, *Potting Shed Papers* (2002). For Collinson and Bartram see Douglas Chambers, *The Planters of the English Landscape Garden* (1993). *Catharanthus roseus*, source of the alkaloids vincristine and vinblastine, is described by Sue Minter in *The Apothecaries Garden* (2000), which also quotes the Chelsea gardeners' complaint of 1775. Edward Hughes includes the Ellison letters in *North Country Life* (1982). For Linnaeus see Lisbert Koerner, *Linnaeus: Nature and National* (2000) and Patricia Fara, *Sex, Botany and Empire* (2003). Banks on Cook is from Nigel Rigby, 'Seaborne Plant Transportation, 1769–1805' in ed. Margaret Rigby, *Science and Exploration in the Pacific* (1998).

White's garden calendar is quoted in Richard Mabey, *Gilbert White of Selborne* (1986). For Darwin's milometer letter to Edgeworth, see ed. Desmond King-Hele, *Letters of Erasmus Darwin* (1981).

Several books have treated early plantsmen and the history of Kew, notably Andrea Wulf, *The Brother Gardeners: Botany, Empire and the Birth of an Obsession* (2008); Mark Laird, *A Natural History of English Gardening, 1650–1800* (2015) on the role of amateur gardener-naturalists; and Vanessa Berridge, *The Princess's Garden: Royal Intrigue and the Untold Story of Kew* (2015).

15 Brown and his foes

See Roger Turner, *Capability Brown and the eighteenth-century English landscape* (1985) The account presented to the Earl of Egremont is in Fleming and Gore. On Repton see Stephen Daniels, *Humphry Repton: landscape gardening and the geography of Georgian England* (1999). Matthew Boulton's garden is described in an unpublished paper by

Shena Mason (Soho House, Handsworth, 1999). For gardens and sensibility, see Malcolm Andrews, *The Search for the Picturesque: Landscape, Aesthetics and Tourism in Britain, 1760–1800* (1989). The description of Mount Edgcumbe is from an 1821 guide, and Dr Johnson's reaction to Hawkestone is described in Thacker *Genius*.

For more details, see Jane Brown, *The Omnipotent Magician: Lancelot Capability Brown* (2011); Charles Watkins and Ben Cowell, *Uvedale Price (1747–1829): Decoding the Picturesque* (2012); and Michael Symes, *The Picturesque and the Later Georgian Garden* (2012).

16 Victoriana

Wordsworth's letters are in ed. Michael Charlesworth, *The English Garden: Literary Sources and Documents*, Vol. III (1993); Scott's views on gardening are in the introduction to *Quentin Durward* (1823) and 'On Ornamental Plantations and Landscape Gardening', *Quarterly Review* (1828).

On Loudon see Melanie Louise Simo, *Loudon and the Landscape, from country seat to metropolis* (1988). Brent Elliott describes Drummond Castle in *Victorian Gardens* (1986). Among countless rose books, see Graham Stuart Thomas, Peter Beales, *Roses* (2000) and Charles Quest-Ritson, *RHS Encyclopedia of Roses* (2003). The description of the rockery from the *Garden Book* is quoted in David Stuart, *The Garden Triumphant* (1988), while on gnomes, James Bartholomew in *Yew and Non-Yew* (1996) quotes the RHS article.

An invaluable, academic study is Sarah Dewis, *The Loudons and the Gardening Press: A Victorian Cultural Industry* (2014).

17 Brightness is all

The account in the *Gardener* (1867) is quoted by Hoyles. The RHS reports were found in the *RHS Diary* (1983). Mr Horner's outburst in 1836 is from Tom Carter, *The Victorian Garden* (1984); David Douglas's woe is in his *Journal During his Travels in North America, 1823–7*, while Sue Shephard describes the Veitch family and collectors in *Seeds of Fortune: A Gardening Dynasty* (2003). For flowers generally, see Brent Elliott and Andrew Clayton-Payne, *Victorian Flower Gardens* (1988).

The description of the Chatsworth stove is by Mrs S. C. Hall, 'A Day at Chatsworth', *The Art Journal* (1851); for Paxton see Kate Colquhoun, *A Thing in Disguise: The Visionary Life of Joseph Paxton* (2003). Thacker extols the Palm House in *Genius*. The Rothschild gardener, Ernest Field, is often quoted, but the source is 'Garden Memories at Hatton', *Country Life* (October 1973).

For a fascinating account of the Lobbs and the ethos of Victorian plant hunters, see Sue Shepherd and Toby Musgrave, *Blue Orchid and Big Tree: Plant Hunters William and Thomas Lobb and the Victorian Mania for the Exotic* (2014).

18 Cottagers, florists and shows

Cobbett's views are in *Rural Rides* (1822) and *The English Gardener* (1829). For the Revd Wilks see Piers Dudgeon, *The English Vicarage Garden* (1991). Flora Thompson's memories are from 'The Besieged Generation' in *Lark Rise to Candleford* (1939), while Mary Mitford's *Our Village* appeared in episodes in the *Lady's Magazine* from 1822: her delight in geraniums is quoted by Anne Scott James in the immensely enjoyable *The Language of the Garden* (1984), which also includes John Clare's journal entry for 1825. The prohibition against delphiniums is quoted in Tom Carter, *The Victorian Garden* (1984).

Solid histories include Jeremy Burchardt, *The Allotment Movement in England, 1793–1873* (2011) and Margaret Willes, *Gardens of the English Working Class* (2014), a people's history, from early records to florists and clubs and allotments today.

19 Town mouse

Loudon's mini-conservatories are in the *Villa and Suburban Gardener* (1838). Jean Lear of the Medway Gardens Research Group describes Dickens at Gadshill in *The Dickensian* (Spring 2002). George and Weedon Grossmith, *The Diary of a Nobody* (often quoted) was serialised in *Punch* and expanded into a book in 1892.

20 Don't sneer at Mrs Lawrence

For Jane Loudon, see Bea Howe, *Lady with Green Fingers* (1961); Jane welcomed the lawnmower in the *Lady's Companion* (1841). Louis Johnson's exhortation is in *Every Woman her Own Flower Gardener* (US edition, 1855), with thanks to Margaret Darby, who gave me the first quotation from Rosa; the instructions on clothes are from David Stuart, *The Garden Triumphant: A Victorian Legacy* (1988). For Mrs Gaskell see eds J. A. V. Chapple and A. Pollard, *The Letters of Elizabeth Gaskell* (1966).

The table arrangements are from *Mrs Beeton's Household Management* (1859–60) and Joan Morgan and Alison Richards, *A Paradise out of a Common Field: The Pleasures and Plenty of the Victorian Garden* (1990). On flower language see Brent Elliott, 'Floral Linguistics', *The Garden* (July 2002), also Beverly Seaton, *The Language of Flowers* (1998). Mrs Earle's advice is in ed. David Wheeler, *The Penguin Book of Garden*

Writing (1998). Jane Brown writes on several leading women gardeners in *Eminent Gardeners* (1990).

An extra delight, though not really on gardening, is Kathryn Hughes's *The Short Life and Long Times of Mrs Beeton* (2006).

21 Rebellion

The Gardener's Magazine is quoted by Fleming and Gore; Samuel Reynolds Hole, *Our Gardens* (1901) is quoted by Bisgrove, and Bowles by Keen. Elizabeth Gaskell's cottage garden description is in *Sylvia's Lovers* (1863–64) and George Eliot's from 'Janet's Repentance' in *Scenes of Clerical Life* (1858). Charles Elliot tells the story of Canon Ellacombe in the Alps in *The Potting Shed Papers* (2002).

Richard Bisgrove analyses the 'natural' style in *William Robinson: The Wild Gardener* (2008), while in *The Victorian Gardener* (2011) Anne Wilkinson offers a history of amateur gardeners from the 1860s, in country and town.

22 The big kitchen garden

For every aspect see Campbell, *Charleston Kedding*. On tools see Kay N. Sanecki, *Old Garden Tools* (1997). Ronald Blythe's interview with 'Christopher Falconer' is in *Akenfield* (1969). Virginia Woolf on Eleanor Ormerod is in *The Common Reader* (1984 edition): thanks to Hermione Lee. Mr Stewart on parsley, W. Taylor on 'Mushroom Growing' and the article on Rangemore Hall, all from *Journal of Horticulture* (1867, 1875, 1876 respectively) are in Morgan and Richards, *A Paradise out of a Common Field* (1990).

Normanby Hall is described by Simon Garbutt in *The Garden* (August 2002). Lost varieties are discussed by Bob Sherman in *The Garden* (March 2000) and by Carter in *The Victorian Garden*. On grape growing Campbell quotes from 'The Vinery' in John Abercrombie, *The Complete Forcing Gardener* (1781). The story of Lord Egremont's banana is in Hoyles, and William Cresswell's diary at Audley End was quoted by Stephanie Donaldson in *Country Living* (October 2002).

Susan Campbell's *A History of Kitchen Gardening* (2015) is a good revised version of her 1996 classic, *Charleston Kedding*.

23 *Country Life*

Quotations from Jekyll are from her *Wood and Garden* and *Home and Garden*. Lutyens on Flanders is quoted by Brown, from ed. Percy and Ridley, *The Letters of Edwin Lutyens* (1985). On Jekyll and Lutyens see Jane Brown, *Gardens of a Golden Afternoon*

(1982) and Sally Festing, *Gertrude Jekyll* (1991). Nathaniel Lloyd's book was *Garden Craftsmanship in Yew and Box* (1925).

On Farrer see Nicola Shulman, *A Rage for Rock-Gardening* (2002). Vita's snub to rhododendrons is quoted by Quest-Ritson. The problem with the moat walk is told in Harold Nicolson's *Diaries*, 3 vols, 1966–8, ed. Nigel Nicolson; the *Observer* article is in Vita Sackville-West, *In Your Garden* (1951), while the National Trust row is described in Jane Brown, *Sissinghurst: Portrait of a Garden* (1998); see also Brown's *Vita's Other World: A Gardening Biography of Vita Sackville-West* (1985).

See Vita Sackville-West and Sarah Raven, *Vita Sackville-West's Sissinghurst: The Creation of a Garden* (2014). In *First Ladies of Gardening* (2015) Heidi Howcroft and Marianne Majerus write about leading women gardeners and designers from the 1950s to today, and their influence on the English country garden.

24 From war to war

Quotations are from William Rowles, *The Food Garden* (1917); A. P. Herbert in ed. Miles Hadfield *The Gardener's Companion* (1938); Ethel Armitage, *Country Diary* (1936); for Armitage and Sackville-West see also Hoyles, *Bread and Roses*. The mock slogan 'Dig-for-Dear-Life' is in Peter Ender, *Up the Garden Path* (1940) and E. Graham's book is *Gardening in War-time* (1940), while Roy Hay wrote on the gardening spirit in the Blitz in *Gardener's Chance* (1946).

A useful overview is Twigs Way, *Digging for Victory: Gardens and gardening in Wartime Britain* (2010).

25 Modernists and artists

See Peter Shepheard, *Modern Gardens* (1953), Marjory Allen and Susan Jellicoe, *The New Small Garden* (1956), Sylvia Crowe, *Garden Design* (1958). On Jellicoe see Michael Spens, *Gardens of the Mind: The Genius of Geoffrey Jellicoe* (1992). For the artists see Jessie Sheeler, Andrew Lawson, *The Garden of Ian Hamilton Finlay* (2003); *Boyle Family* (catalogue from Scottish National Gallery of Modern Art, (2003), *Derek Jarman's Garden*, with photographs by Howard Sooley (1995) and Charles Jencks, *The Garden of Cosmic Speculation* (2003). John Brookes, *Room Outside* (1969) was updated in 1985 as *The Small Garden*.

John Dixon Hunt, *Nature Over Again: The Garden Art of Ian Hamilton Finlay* (2008).

26 Eat your greens

The best work is still David Crouch and Colin Ward, *The Allotment, Its Landscape and Culture* (1988). The Orwell quote is from *Coming Up for Air* (1939). Uplands was described by Alexandra Baulkwill, *The Garden* (September 2002). Ursula Buchan described several shows in *The Village Show* (1989) and in 2003 several allotments, including Uplands, and contemporary shows were subjects of programmes by Monty Don for *Gardener's World*, BBC TV.

Photographs of Barnsley appeared in Joy Larkom, *The Salad Garden* (1984) and in Rosemary Verey's own *Classic Garden Design* (1984). Anna Pavord wrote on Glenbervie in the *Independent Magazine* (6 September 2003). John Carey's articles appeared in the *Sunday Times* (1980). Sue Bennett on the Soil Association is in *Five Hundred Years of Women Gardeners*: the website for the Doubleday Association lists vegetables to be adopted.

There are many manuals and advice books on allotments, but for the history (in addition to books mentioned at Chapter 18), see Caroline Foley's *Of Cabbages and Kings: The History of Allotments* (2014), Lesley Acton, *Growing Space: A History of the Allotment Movement* (2015) and the enjoyable Bill Laws, *RHS Tales from the Tool Shed: The history and usage of fifty garden tools* (2008).

27 The flowers and the wild

See Elizabeth Coxhead, *Constance Spry* (1975). Graham Stuart Thomas, *Plants for Ground Cover* appeared in 1963 and *Perennial Garden Plants* in 1976; his three works on roses were collected as *The Graham Stuart Thomas Rose Book* (1994).

The survey was in the *Daily Express* (18 April 1970): with thanks to David Kynaston. Among Christopher Lloyd's many books see *Colour for Adventurous Gardeners* (2002) and the new edition of his classic *The Well-Tempered Garden* (2003). For colour, see also Sarah Raven's books, including *The Bold and Brilliant Garden* (1996), *The Cutting Garden* (2001) and *Grow Your Own Cut Flowers* (2002). James Fenton writes in *A Garden from a Hundred Packets of Seeds* (2001). As a parallel to Chris Baines, see also Jennifer Owen, *The Ecology of a Garden* (1991). Richard Mabey writes on 'Immigrant plants' in *Flora Britannica: the Concise Edition* (1998).

Several new guides have been published, including Adrian Thomas, *RSPB Gardening for Wildlife: A Complete Guide to Nature-friendly Gardening* (2010), Kate Bradbury's *The Wildlife Gardener* (2013) and John Lewis-Stempel, *The Wildlife Garden* (2014).

But see also Lewis-Stempel's *Meadowland: The Private Life of an English Field* (2015) and, for fun, Tania Pascoe, *Wild Garden Weekends: Explore the Secret Gardens, Wild Meadows and Kitchen Garden Cafés of Britain* (2015).

28 The cherry tree

I am indebted to Martin Hoyles on gardening books for children in 'From Cradle to Grave', *Gardener's Delight: Gardening Books from 1560–1960* (1994) and to 'The Formative Garden' in Jane Brown, *Pursuit of Pleasure*. The school competitions are run by the RHS and Encams (Environmental Campaigns), and the seed is distributed through the RHS Curricular Education Section.

Epilogue: All of us

The Register of Parks and Gardens of Special Historic Interest is produced by English Heritage; York University also has a database of 3500 entries. The National Council for the Preservation of Plants and Gardens (NCPPG) publishes a *National Plant Collections Directory*. Christopher Lloyd spoke out in 'Deadhead the past', *Guardian* (24 October 1998). In 2003: the magazine with 'period' schemes was *The English Garden* (July); the list of varied designers was in 'Choices, choices' by Mark Griffiths, *Times Weekend Review* (6 September); and Geraldine Bedell's article was in the *Observer* (29 June).

The government report is *Living Places – Cleaner, Safer, Greener* (2002). One of the most dynamic groups is the Black Environment Network (covering a wide ethnic range); others are the Institute for Earth Education, Common Ground and the BTCV Environment for All Project – all have websites. Global warming statistics are from the RHS Climate Change and Gardens Workshop, 2000.

Postscript, 2016

The figures on garden use come from the Horticultural Trades Association, Garden Retail Analysis 2015. Many of the campaigns can be followed on the Internet, which also gives links to their reports: see the websites for the RHS; Core Landscapes; Scottish Government 'Stalled Spaces'; National Society of Allotment and Leisure Gardeners; Parks Alliance; DEFRA (peat consultation). Henk Tennekes's work on pesticides is in his book *The Systemic Insecticides – A Disaster in the Making* (2010).

A sense of how design fashions have changed can be gleaned from John Brookes, *Great Garden Design: Contemporary Inspiration for Outdoor Spaces* (2015), which describes the best garden designs of the last ten years by Tom Stuart-Smith, Luciano Giubbilei, Charlotte Rowe, Ian Kitson, John Brookes, Cleve West, Dan Pearson. Another angle is given by Tim Richardson in *The New English Garden* (2013), which looks at twenty-five gardens made, or remade, since 2000.

Many books have come out on wildlife, organic gardening, allotments and guerrilla gardening, including Richard Reynolds, *On Guerrilla Gardening: Gardening without Boundaries* (2009). And I enjoyed the invigorating look at gardening history as counterculture in George McKay's *Radical Gardening: Politics, Idealism & Rebellion in the Garden* (2011), which gave me an insight into the 1960s, as well as taking a longer view into a different side of garden history.

Two hundred and fifty gardens

This is just a taste: the *RHS Garden Finder 2015* (online) lists nearly 1000 gardens, while *The Good Garden's Guide 2010–11* has 1200. The indispensable annual 'Yellow Book', *Gardens of England and Wales Open for Charity* (also online) includes over 2000. My selection is personal. Gardens are arranged by period, but no genuine early ones survive, so these are merely to give an impression. And since gardens go through many phases I have sometimes placed them according to particular features: thus reconstructions of knot gardens are under 'Tudor', while medieval sites, like Mottifont Abbey or Mannington Hall, are under 'Twentieth Century', for their rose collections. EH denotes English Heritage; NT National Trust; NTS National Trust Scotland. Opening times are seasons only: for days and times, check the above books or individual garden websites.

Celtic and Iron Age
Butser Ancient Farm, near Petersfield, Hampshire. Special events
Chysauster Iron Age Village, near Penzance, Cornwall. EH. Summer
Flag Fen Bronze Age Centre, Peterborough, Cambridge. All year

Roman
Chedworth Roman Villa, Yanworth, near Cheltenham, Gloucestershire. NT. March–November
Corinium Museum, Park Street, Cirencester, Gloucestershire.
Fishbourne Roman Palace, Fishbourne, Chichester, Sussex. All year
National Roman Legion Museum, Caerleon, South Wales. Open all year

Monastic and Medieval
Anglo-Saxon Herb Garden, Lucy Cavendish College, Cambridge. Open to college visitors, and by appointment.
Bede's World Herb Garden, Jarrow, Tyne and Wear. All year
Buckland Abbey, Devon. NT. February–November
Michelham Priory, Upper Dicker, near Hailsham, East Sussex. March–October

Mount Grace Priory, Northallerton, North Yorkshire. NT. All year

Queen Eleanor's Garden, The Great Hall, Winchester, Hampshire. All year

Weald and Downland Open Air Museum, Singleton, Chichester, Sussex. All year

West Stow Country Park and Anglo-Saxon Village, Bury St Edmunds, Suffolk. Open all year

Fourteenth and Fifteenth Century

Alfriston Clergy House, East Sussex. NT. March–November

Buckland Abbey, Yelverton, Devon. NT. All year

Elsing Hall, Elsing, Norfolk. Sundays, June–September

Ightham Mote, Ivy Hatch, Sevenoaks, Kent. NT. March–November

Lavenham Guildhall, Suffolk. NT. March–December

Medieval Pleasure Garden, Ypres Tower, Rye Castle, Kent. Open all year

Warwick Castle, Warwick. All year

Tudor

Aberglasney, Llangathen, Llandeilo, Carmarthenshire. All year

Canons Ashby, Daventry, Northampshire. NT. April–December

Chenies Manor House, Chenies, Rickmansworth, Buckinghamshire. April–October

Doddington Hall, Doddington, Lincoln. February–October

Falkland Place, Falkland, Cupar. NTS. Open all year

Godolphin, Cornwall. NT. Open all year

Haddon Hall, Bakewell, Derbyshire. April–September

Hardwick Hall, Chesterfield, Derbyshire. NT. March–October

Hatfield House, Hatfield, Hertfordshire. West garden, March–October

Helmingham Hall, Ipswich, Suffolk. May–September

Little Moreton Hall, Congleton, Cheshire. NT. March–December

Lyveden New Bield, near Oundle, Peterborough, Northamptonshire. NT. All year

Montacute House, Montacute, Somerset. NT. April–October

Mosely Old Hall, Wolverhampton, Staffordshire. NT. March–November

Packwood House, Lapworth, Solihull, Warwickshire. NT. March–November

Sudeley Castle, Winchcombe, Gloucestershire. March–October

Tudor Garden, Southampton University, Hampshire. All year

Tudor Pleasure Garden, Cressing Temple, Essex. Open all year

Wollaton Park, Nottingham. All year

Seventeenth Century

Antrim Castle Gardens, County Antrim, Northern Ireland. All year

Arbuthnot House, Laurencekirk, Kincardineshire. All year

Blickling Hall, Blickling, Norfolk. NT. All year

Boughton House, Kettering, Northants. August

Castle Bromwich Hall, Castle Bromwich, Birmingham. April–October

Chastleton House, near Moreton-in-Marsh, Oxfordshire. NT. April–November

Cranborne Manor, Cranborne, Dorset. March–September

Dalemain, Dacre, Penrith. March–October

Dunham Massey, Altrincham, Cheshire. NT. March–November

Edzell Castle, Brechin, Angus. April–September

Forde Abbey, Chard, Dorset. All year

Ham House, Richmond, Surrey. NT. Open all year

Kingston Lacy, Wimborne Minster, Dorset. NT. March–November

Knole, Sevenoaks, Kent. Irregular

Levens Hall, near Kendal, Cumbria. Easter–end September

Longleat, Warminster, Wilts. All year

Penshurst Place, Penshurst, Tonbridge, Kent. March–November

Powis Castle, Welshpool, Powys. NT. April–November

The Vyne, Hampshire. NT. Open all year

Woburn Abbey, Woburn, Bedfordshire. March–November

Eighteenth Century, Formal

Blair Castle, Blair Atholl, Pitlochry, Perthshire. April–October

Blenheim Palace, Woodstock, Oxfordshire. March–October

Bramham Park, Wetherby, West Yorkshire. April–September

Castle Howard, York, North Yorkshire. March–October

Castle Kennedy, Rephad, Stranraer, Dumfries and Galloway. Easter–September

Chatsworth, Bakewell, Derbyshire. March–October

Claremont, Esher, Surrey. NT. All year

Cliveden, Taplow, Maidenhead, Buckinghamshire. NT. March–December

Cottesbrooke Hall Gardens, Northampton. May–September

Dyrham Park, near Chippenham, Gloucestershire. NT. All year

Erddig, Wrexham, Clwyd. NT. March–December

Euston Hall, Thetford, Norfolk. June–September

Georgian Walled Garden, Norton Priory, Runcorn. Open all year

Grimsthorpe Castle, near Bourne, Lincolnshire. April–August

Hall Barn, Beaconsfield, Buckinghamshire. EH.

Ham House, Richmond-upon-Thames, Surrey. NT. All year

Hampton Court Palace, Hampton Court, Surrey. All year

Melbourne Hall, Melbourne, Derbyshire. April–September

St Paul's Walden Bury, Whitwell, near Hitchin, Hertfordshire. Occasionally

Stowe, Stowe College, Buckingham, Buckinghamshire. NT. March–December

Westbury Court, Westbury-on-Severn, Gloucestershire. NT. March–October

Wrest Park, Silsoe, Bedfordshire. EH. April–October

Arcadia

Chiswick House, Chiswick, London. All year

The Leasowes, Halesowen, Warwickshire. All Year

Painshill Park, Cobham, Surrey. April–October

Painswick Rococo Garden, Painswick, Gloucestershire. January–October

Rousham House, Steeple Ashton, Oxfordshire. All year

Shugborough, Milford, Stafford. NT. April–October

Stourhead, Stourton, near Mere, Wiltshire. NT. All year

Studley Royal, Fountains, near Ripon, North Yorkshire. NT. All year

West Wycombe Park, West Wycombe, Buckinghamshire. NT. April–August

Plantsmen

Chelsea Physic Garden, Royal Hospital Road, Chelsea, London. April–October

Gilbert White's Garden, The Wakes, Selborne, Alton, Hampshire. April–December

Museum of Garden History, Lambeth Palace Road, London. February–December

Oxford Botanic Garden, Oxford. All year

Royal Botanic Garden, Edinburgh. All year

Royal Botanic Garden, Kew, Richmond, Surrey. All year

Brown, Repton and Company

Audley End, Widdington, Saffron Walden, Essex. EH. April–September

Betchworth House, Surrey. By appointment

Blenheim Palace, Oxfordshire. Open all year

Bowood House, Calne, Wiltshire. April–November

Burghley House, Lincolnshire. March–October

Culzean Castle, Maybole, South Argyllshire. NTS. April–October

Endsleigh House, Milton Abbot, Devon. April–October

Harewood House, Harewood, Yorkshire. March–December

Ickworth House, Horringer, Bury St Edmunds, Suffolk. NT. All year

Kedleston Hall, Kedleston, Derbyshire. NT. March–November

Petworth House, Petworth, West Sussex. March–October

Plas Newydd, Llanfairpwyll, Anglesey. NT. March–November

Sezincote, Moreton-in-Marsh, Gloucestershire. January–November

Sheffield Park, East Sussex. NT. All year

Sheringham Park, Upper Sheringham, Norfolk. NT. All year

Syon Park, Brentford, Middlesex. All year

Picturesque

Downhill, Castlerock, County Londonderry. NT. All year

Hawkstone Park, Weston-under-Redcastle, Shrewsbury, Shropshire. EH. April–October

Killerton, Broadclyst, Exeter, Devon. NT. All year

Mount Edgcumbe, Cremyll, Torpoint, Cornwall. All year

Newstead Abbey, near Mansfield, Nottinghamshire. All year

Victorian and Grand Edwardian

Abbotsford, Melrose, Scottish Borders. June–October

Alton Towers, Alton, Staffordshire. April–November

Antony House and Garden, Torpoint, Devon. NT. March – end October

Ardtornish, Lochaline, Morvern, Highlands. March to November

Arley Hall, near Northwich, Cheshire. April–October

Ashridge Management College, Berkhamsted, Hertfordshire. April–September

Athelhampton, Dorchester. March–October, winter Sundays

Belsay Hall, Belsay, Northumberland. EH. April–September

Biddulph Grange, Biddulph, Stoke-on-Trent, Staffordshire. NT. April–December

Bodnant, Tal-y-Cafn, Colwyn Bay, Gwynedd. NT. March–October

Calke Abbery, Ticknall, Derbyshire. NT. March–November

Cragside House, Rothbury, Morpeth, Northumberland. NT. April–December

Drummond Castle, Crieff, Perthshire. May–October

Dunrobin Castle, Golspie, Sutherland. April–October

Dunster Castle, Dunster, Minehead, Somerset. NT. All year

Dyffryn Gardens, St Nicholas, Cardiff. All year

Elvaston Castle, Elvaston, Derbyshire. All year

Handspen House, Castle Cary, Somerset. March–October

Holkham Hall, Walls-next-the-Sea, Norfolk. May–September

Knebworth House, near Stevenage, Hertfordshire. April–September, sporadic

Knightshayes, Bolham, near Tiverton, Devon. NT. March–November

Lanhydrock, Bodmin, Cornwall. NT. All year

Lyme Park, Disley, Stockport, Cheshire. April–December

Manderston, Duns, Borders. May–September

Osborne House, East Cowes, Isle of Wight. EH. July–September

Pashley Manor Gardens, Ticehurst, East Sussex. April–September

Penryhn Castle, Bangor, Clwyd. NT. March–November

Rufford Old Hall, Ormskirk, Lancashire. NT. Mid. February–December

Scotney Castle, Lamberhurst, Tunbridge Wells, Kent. NT. March–September

Shrubland Park, Coddenham, near Ipswich, Suffolk. April–September

Somerleyton Hall, near Lowestoft, Suffolk. March–September

Standen, East Grinstead, Surrey. NT. Open all year

Stumpery, Arundel Castle, West Sussex. March–October

Tatton Park, Knutsford, Cheshire. NT. All year

Tyntesfield, Wraxall, Somerset. NT. March–October

Waddesdon Manor, near Aylesbury, Buckinghamshire. NT. March–December

Plant Collection Gardens

Abbotsbury Sub-Tropical Gardens, Abbotsbury, Weymouth, Dorset. All year

Arduaine Garden, Oban, Argyll and Bute. NTS. All year

Attadale Gardens, Strathcarron, Wester Ross. March–October

Benthall Hall, Broseley, Shropshire. NT. March–October

Bicton Park Botanical Gardens, Budleigh Salterton, Devon. All year

Caerhays Castle, Gorran, St Austell, Cornwall. March–June

Castelwellan National Arboretum, County Down, Northern Ireland. All year

Cotehele, St Dominick, near Saltash, Cornwall. NT. All year

Explorers Garden, Pitlochry, Perthshire. April–October

Glendurgan, Mawnan Smith, near Falmouth, Cornwall. NT. February–November

Inverewe, Poolewe, Ross-shire, Highland. All year

Leonardslee, near Horsham, West Sussex. April–September

Logan Botanic Gardens, Port Logan, Stranraer. March–October

Mount Stuart, Rothesay, Isle of Bute. May–September

Nymans, Handcross, near Haywards Heath, West Sussex. NT. March–November

Trebah, Mawnan Smith, Falmouth, Cornwall. All year

Trengwainton, Madron, near Penzance, Cornwall. NT February–October

Tresco Abbey, Isles of Scilly. All year

Trewithen, Truro, Cornwall. March–September

Westonbirt National Arboretum, near Tetbury, Gloucestershire. All year

Kitchen Gardens and Vegetables

(Many earlier sites, like Helmingham, and great Victorian gardens like Trengwainton
  and Mount Stuart, also have restored kitchen gardens)

Barnsley House, Barnsley, near Cirencester, Gloucestershire. Occasionally

Beningbrough Hall, Yorkshire. NT. Open all year

Clumber Park, Worksop, Nottinghamshire. April–October

Felbrigg Hall, Felbrigg, Norfolk. All year

Heligan, Pentewan, St Austell, Cornwall. All year

Llanerchaeron, Ceredigion, Mid-Wales. NT. Open all year

Mertoun Gardens, St Boswells, Melrose. Weekends April–September

Normanby Hall, Scunthorpe, Lincolnshire. Daily

Ryton Organic Gardens, Ryton-on-Dunsmore, Warwickshire. All year

Titsey Place, Oxted, Surrey. May–September

Trengwainton Garden, Cornwall. NT. Mid. February–October

Upton House, Banbury, Oxfordshire. April–November

Yalding Organic Gardens, Yalding, Kent. May–September

From the Arts and Crafts to the 1930s

Ammerdown, Radstock, Bath, Somerset. Occasionally

Anglesey Abbey, Lode, Cambridge. NT. April–November

Athelhampton, near Puddletown, Dorset. March–October

Batemans, Burwash, Sussex. NT. Open all year

Buscot Park. Faringdon, Oxfordshire. NT. April–September

Castle Drogo, Drewsteignton, near Exeter, Devon. NT. All year

Cawdor Castle, Nairn, Highland. May–October

Crarae Garden, Minard, Inveraray, Strathclyde. All year

Crathes Castle Garden, Banchory, Aberdeen. All year

Exbury Gardens, Exbury, Southampton. March–October

Godinton House, Ashford, Kent. March–October

Gravetye Manor, East Grinstead, West Sussex. Open to hotel guests

Graythwaite, Ulverston, Cumbria. April–June

Great Dixter, Northiam, East Sussex. April–October

Hestercombe, Cheddon Fitzpaine, Taunton, Somerset. All year

Hever Castle, Edenbridge, Kent. March–November

Hidcote, Hidcote Bartrim, Chipping Camden, Gloucestershire. NT. March–October

Iford Manor, Bradford-on-Avon, Wiltshire. April–October

Kelmscott Manor, Kelmscott, Lechlade, Oxfordshire. April–September

Kiftsgate Court, Chipping Camden, Gloucestershire. Occasionally

Kingston Maurward, Dorchester. Open all year

Lytes Cary Manor, Charlton Mackrell, Somerset. NT. March–October

Muncaster Castle, Ravenglass, Cumbria. April–October

Munstead Wood, Busbridge, Godalming, Surrey. Occasionally

Myddleton House, Enfield, London. All year

Newby Hall, Ripon, North Yorkshire. April–September

Parham House, Pulborough, West Sussex. April. October. Check times

Plas Brondanw, Llanfrothen, Gwynedd. Open all year

Polesden Lacey, Dorking, Surrey. NT. March–October

Port Lympne, Lympne, Hythe, Kent. All year

The Red House, Upton, Bexleyheath, Kent. NT. Times to be confirmed

Rodmarton Manor, Cirencester. April–September. Check times

Rowallane Garden, Saintfield, Ballynahinch. NT. All year

Sissinghurst Castle, Sissinghurst, near Cranbrook, Kent. NT. March–October

Winterbourne House and Garden, University of Birmingham. Open all year

Twentieth Century

Achamore Gardens, Isle of Gigha, Argyll and Bute. All year

Angel Field, Hope Park, Liverpool. Open all year

Anglesey Abbey, Cambridgeshire. NT. Open all year

Beth Chatto Gardens, Elmstead Market, Colchester, Essex. All year

Boughton House, Kettering, Northants. Selected days, check times

Denmans, Fontwell, Arundel, West Sussex. March–October

Derek Jarman's Garden, Dungeness, Kent. Open to road – be tactful

East Lambrook Manor, South Perton, Somerset. February–October

The Eden Project, Bodelva, St Austell, Cornwall. All year

The Garden House, Buckland Monachoruum, Yelverton, Devon. March–October

Gresgarth Hall, Caton, Lancaster. Selected days, check times

The Sir Harold Hillier Arboretum, Ampfield, Romsey, Hampshire. All year

Hinton Ampner, Hampshire. NT. Open all year

The Laskett, Herefordshire. NT. April–July, September

Little Sparta, Busyre, Lanark, South Lanarkshire. June–September

Middleton, National Botanic Garden of Wales, Llanarthney, Carmarthenshire. All year

Mottisfont Abbey, Mottisfont, near Romsey, Hampshire. NT. March–October

Mount Stewart, Newtownards, County Down. NT. March–December

Queen Elizabeth Olympic Park, London. Open all year

Scampston Walled Garden, North Yorkshire. March–October

Shute House, near Shaftesbury, Dorset. Occasionally

Sutton Place, Guildford, Surrey. Occasionally

Througham Court, Cotswolds, Gloucestershire. May–September, by appointment

Tintinhull, Farm Street, Tintinhull, Yeovil, Somerset. NT. March–September

Waltham Place Organic Gardens, White Waltham, Berkshire. May–September

Westwell Manor, Oxfordshire. Annual opening for National Gardens Scheme

Index